The Future of
Communist Power

The Future of Communist Power

BRIAN CROZIER

Eyre & Spottiswoode : London

First published 1970
© Brian Crozier 1970
Printed in Great Britain for
Eyre & Spottiswoode (Publishers) Ltd
11 New Fetter Lane, EC4
by Ebenezer Baylis and Son Ltd.
The Trinity Press, Worcester and London

SBN 0413 27550 7

Contents

Acknowledgements

My thanks are due, above all, to my tireless research assistant Miss Judith Miller. But I remember with gratitude the advice of the Kremlinologists and Pekinologists, too numerous to mention individually, who have helped, over the years, by putting me right when I strayed.

Author's Foreword

Faith is a gift. You either have it or you haven't: if you lack it, teaching won't give it to you; although, if you do have the capacity for faith, a teacher or a book may guide you towards acceptance of one faith rather than another.

For my part, I have no such capacity, and I think it fair to the reader to make this clear at the outset. How far this is due to nature and how far to nurture, is immaterial. Though not entirely irreligious, I am sceptical of revelation, whether religious, philosophical or political. By instinct as well as by intellectual self-training, I believe the deeper mysteries to be not merely unknown but probably unknowable. I concede value to idealism as a spur to action, but my interest in Utopias is academic: it would not occur to me to devote myself wholeheartedly to creating one. As regards political theories, I have a distaste for describing them as 'good' or 'bad'. In my eyes, they are either 'better' or 'worse' than alternative theories. Similarly, I might find a certain policy 'good' or 'bad' by the test of whether it will further a certain objective, which I may hold desirable or undesirable according to the circumstances prevailing at the time, and in comparison with other objectives that may have been politically possible.

The point of this preamble is simply to make it clear that unlike many other writers on communism, I do not write 'from the inside'. I am not a disillusioned ex-Communist, for I have never been a Communist at all. It is therefore necessary for me, as it is not for an ex-Communist, to make an effort of imagination to get inside the mind of a Communist and try to understand why he became one, remains one, or has decided to renounce his faith. (Not that it is always a question of faith: once a Communist Party is in power, many people who have no genuine faith in Marxism-Leninism may be tempted to join for reasons of

7

expediency, personal safety or the prospects of promotion open to members and denied to outsiders.) I do not, however, feel myself morally or intellectually superior to the many intellectuals who joined the Communist Party in the 1930s, at a time when there was much to be said for the view that Western society was irretrievably corrupt, inefficient and unjust. The furthest I got was to join the late Victor Gollancz's Left Book Club. Many others—such as Arthur Koestler, Ignazio Silone and Stephen Spender—took the final fateful step of joining the Party. These three, and others, later contributed to a remarkable book, published in 1950 with an introduction by Richard Crossman entitled *The God That Failed*, in which they described their journey into communism, their reasons for joining, the struggles within their conscience when they discovered the gap between their expectations and the reality of communist power, and in the end their final disillusionment and break with the Party. There have been other famous confessions: in Britain, for instance, that of Douglas Hyde; in America, that of Louis F. Budenz; and in Australia, that of Cecil Sharpley. It is interesting, I think, that each of the three I have just named turned to religion on leaving the Communist Party.* One religion thus yielded to another. This seems to argue a need as well as a capacity for faith; which I respect although I cannot share.

Too much should not perhaps be made of this. One of the most famous of Communist apostates, Milovan Djilas, once Vice-President of Yugoslavia, lost his faith in Marxism without turning to religion; though it would be fair to say that he retained the burning faith in the brotherhood of man which initially attracted him to Marxism, however mistakenly. The fact that communism has so often seemed to fill the need for a faith, by providing absolute answers to fundamental questions, is indeed a measure of its importance and an explanation of its persistent appeal.

My purpose in this short book is not, however, to explore in

* Budenz, a former editor of the American *Daily Worker*, left the party in 1945 and later returned to the Roman Catholic Church; Hyde, a former news editor of the British *Daily Worker*, left the party in 1949, and became a Catholic. Sharpley, a British-born trade union agitator in Victoria, also quit in 1949: the son of an Anglican vicar, he returned to the Church of his childhood. All three wrote books on their experiences.

depth the psychology of those to whom communism appeals, important though that is. My aim is wider, though not necessarily deeper. One doesn't have to be a specialist to have noticed that communism has changed profoundly and in many ways since Stalin died in 1953. My aim is to describe these changes, and to attempt to assess what effect they may have on communism as a political force in the world during the next two or three decades. I shall avoid precise prophecies. What I *shall* try to do is to discuss the possibilities of change in the various centres of communist power—including not only Moscow and Peking, for instance, but such powerful Communist Parties as the French and Italian—and to estimate how communism is likely to stand up to the competition now vigorously offered by the New Left.

For the most important thing to remember about communism is that it is a system of power and a means of acquiring it. The late R. N. Carew Hunt may well have been right when he argued —in his classic study, *The Theory and Practice of Communism* (Penguin, 1963)—that 'there is no doubt that communists do believe that they are applying to political situations a theory which they fervently accept and which they hold to be scientific'. But once a theory has become a State ideology, it can be bent and twisted in any direction to suit every expedient change of policy. Very likely, many of those who are attracted by the comforting certainties of Marxist ideology do not realize this at the time of their initiation. Ideology, in fact, 'hooks' some people, just as others are 'hooked' by hard drugs. And once they are hooked, it is hard to break the ideological stranglehold. From the standpoint of non-believers, however, ideology is above all a device for enforcing uniformity, conformity and obedience. This operates on a totalitarian scale in communist countries, and on a more restricted scale within each Communist Party.

The outsiders, those who have never been 'hooked' by ideology and remain unbound by party discipline, find it hard to understand the mental processes of those who have abandoned the 'normal' way of life and thought. Once you are hooked you are, as it were, through the looking-glass; and it is the world outside that looks reversed. It is for this reason that normal philosophical discussion with communists is useless, since on their side all the answers are

9

known in advance. Similarly, it is not enough to refute communist arguments (although whenever a forum is available, the attempt should be made, for the sake of those who might otherwise be hooked). In *The New Class*, Djilas showed where communism in practice had gone wrong. In his newer work, *The Unperfect Society** he goes much further: with intellectual brilliance, subdued by humility, calmly and without bitterness, he demolishes the whole philosophical edifice of Marxism. In a communist country, however, such refutations merely land the writer in gaol; where indeed Djilas has spent many years. In politics, power is more important than truth.

That is what totalitarianism is about. It would be the same, no doubt, if, say, a revolutionary government of flat-earthers were set up. In the flat-earth State, all who insisted that the earth was round would be forced to conform and retract, as Galileo had to in his day, whatever he may have muttered under his breath. The communist claim to scientific infallibility is only marginally less preposterous than the claims of the flat-earthers. But they have the good fortune to live in an age that has rejected pre-Copernican systems but is receptive to social theories. In time, I believe, it will become as difficult to find Marxists as it now is to find flat-earthers. But that time is still remote; and so long as it is, and so long as communism retains a power apparatus, it will continue to be a danger to those who reject its pretensions.

In Stalin's day, it was relatively easy for ordinary citizens to concede the fact that communism was a threat to their future way of life and to the peace of the world. Broadly speaking, what the late dictator said was law throughout the vast land mass stretching from East Germany's western border to Vladivostok. Communist governments took their policy instructions from him; even China was in line with the rest. And communist parties everywhere—in western Europe and as far from Moscow as Chile and Australia—took their cue from the Communist Party of the Soviet Union. In recent years, a confusion of dissident voices has blurred this monolithic picture. Many people in the West— conceivably the majority—have tended to dismiss communism from their minds in the sense of being aware that it is a problem.

* Methuen, 1970.

And then, in August 1968, the Soviet Army marched into Czechoslovakia; and people began to think again.

Even on the issue of the Soviet occupation of Czechoslovakia, however, there are differences of opinion. A distinguished authority on communism and Eastern Europe, Professor Hugh Seton-Watson, declared in a letter to *The Times* that the decision to invade had nothing to do with communism but was to be blamed on the Russian gang that happened to be in power in Moscow. Indeed, can one still talk of a 'world communist movement' at a time when Peking denounces Moscow and the Cubans so clearly pursue their own ambitions? Could General de Gaulle be right when he says, as he always has said, that ideologies are irrelevant, and that only nations, with their individual peoples and histories, mean anything in world affairs? Is there a connection between, say, a trade union election in England and the behaviour of the Viet Cong in South Vietnam? Have the Americans been containing 'communism' in Vietnam or merely hindering the legitimate aspirations of the Vietnamese people?

The questions could go on. Is there such a thing as 'Asian Communism', as various authorities have suggested? Isn't communism the best and possibly the only way out for the starving and deprived masses of Asia and Africa, as Mr Graham Greene apparently believes? Can one take seriously the proposition that there is a communist threat in Africa, when Russian and Chinese diplomats get themselves expelled from one newly independent capital after another? Turning to Europe and America, does not the New Left movement show that communism has lost its revolutionary appeal? Didn't the events of May and June 1968 in France, when the de Gaulle regime was very nearly overthrown, demonstrate that the French Communist Party has become a party of law and order? For that matter, does anybody on the political Right denounce the Communist Party and all its works with greater venom than Herr Cohn-Bendit?

There are, I believe, valid answers to such questions. They will emerge, explicitly or implicitly, in the course of this book.

Note on Communist Parties

A Communist Party is not always so called. To avoid confusing readers with too many names and initials, I have almost invariably referred to ruling parties in communist countries as 'communist' even when that term is not officially used. Here is a short list of ruling parties that style themselves differently (while remaining communist):

Albania: Albanian Workers' Party.
(East) Germany: Socialist Unity Party.
Hungary: Hungarian Socialist Workers' Party.
(North) Korea: Korean Workers' Party.
Poland: Polish United Workers' Party.
(North) Vietnam: Workers' Party of Vietnam.

Russia

China

WRMU
823-2414

Part 1: The Past

Part II: The Past

Part 1: The Past

1. *The Idol Toppled*

It was on 25 February 1956 that Nikita Khrushchev, the ebullient First Secretary of the Soviet Communist Party, began to deliver his sensational speech denouncing the Stalin cult. The occasion was one of some solemnity: the 20th Congress of the Soviet Party, to which observers from foreign communist parties had been invited. It was the first Congress since the death of Stalin. It was on such occasions that important interpretations of communist dogma and the sacred texts of Marxism-Leninism were made; although, since the 1920s, the Congresses had tended to be uniformly dull because the tenor of the speeches, documents and resolutions could be predicted in advance.

Khrushchev's speech was very long—it ran to some 26,000 words—yet it is safe to assume that nobody present could have been bored at any stage. For the unprecedented was happening. For nearly thirty years, ever since the expulsion of Trotsky from the Party in 1927, Communists everywhere had been conditioned to sing the praises of Stalin, to claim infallibility for him and see no evil in the empire he ruled—or if 'evil' were seen, to excuse it in the name of the higher purposes of socialism. And now, here was Khrushchev who, during those same decades, had served Stalin faithfully and by serving him had survived, denouncing the late dictator who had been his ultimate leader as well as theirs. Thousands of innocent persons, said Khrushchev, had been executed at Stalin's instigation. Confessions had been extracted from the innocent by extensive torture. During the Second World War, he said, ethnic minorities in the Soviet Union had been ruthlessly and unjustly deported. He referred to the 'Leningrad affair'—a term that was familiar to all those present. Their minds went back to 1948, when Zhdanov—Stalin's right hand man—died, and to 1949 when his most prominent followers in the Leningrad district, headed by the Politburo member Voznesensky, simply disappeared. Now Khrushchev revealed that they had been arrested and shot on charges trumped up by Stalin's secret police chief, Beria, and accepted by Stalin.

And there was much more in this vein, especially a reference to the so-called 'doctors' plot'. Here again, Khrushchev's audience knew what he meant. Towards the end of his life, Stalin had ordered the arrest of a group of eminent Soviet doctors, most of them Jewish. Once again, torture was used to extract confessions to charges that the doctors were plotting to poison a number of high-ranking personalities in the Party and Army. Before the doctors could be tried, however, Stalin died, and on his death the surviving doctors were released. And now Khrushchev gave details hitherto unpublished. It was Stalin personally who instructed the judge on the methods to be used to extract confessions. 'These methods were simple,' said Khrushchev—'beat, beat and beat again.'

It is impossible to overstate the impact of Khrushchev's speech, first on the delegates who heard it, and later on members of communist parties all over the world. It was not originally intended for publication, which is why it is generally referred to as Khrushchev's 'secret speech'. An edited version was circulated to communist parties outside the USSR. But the full version, universally accepted as authentic, was made available on 4 June 1956 by the American State Department—clearly one of the most successful coups of the Central Intelligence Agency. After that, it was scarcely possible for even the humblest probation member of the most insignificant communist party not to know that the First Secretary of the Soviet Party had denounced Stalin.

Strictly speaking, of course, there was little that was really new in Khrushchev's secret speech. For years, Stalin's crimes and other excesses of his regime had been denounced, by serious students of communism, by embittered exiles and by such defectors as Kravchenko (*I Chose Freedom*) and others. But for the faithful, such denunciations were invalid by definition, since they were uttered by 'traitors' or 'bourgeois intellectuals' or 'lackeys of capitalism'. But now the head of the ruling party in the original home of 'socialism', in the citadel of communism and in his capacity as repository of the ultimate truth, was saying what had been known all along by those outside the State: that Stalin's regime was a monstrous tyranny, based upon and sustained by tortures and other crimes. True, Khrushchev had stopped short of absolute candour. He had done nothing to rehabilitate Trotsky; nor had he complained about liquidations of men and women still considered 'enemies of the people'. But he had said enough to shake the faithful to the marrow of their convictions.

For, not content with smashing the idol of Stalin which he and they had worshipped, he called in question some of the most sacred of the Marxist-Leninist dogmas. One of these was the doctrine that wars were inevitable so long as 'imperialism' (that is, powerful Western countries) existed. At the 20th Soviet Party Congress, Khrushchev startled the delegates by declaring that war was no longer fatally inevitable. Another time-honoured precept—that violent revolution is necessary for the introduction of socialism—was also thrown overboard. Khrushchev went as far as to say that in certain circumstances, the transition to socialism might be achieved by parliamentary means.

All this was shattering to the communist parties of the world. It faced all party members, and individual parties, with a cruel dilemma. Khrushchev had told them that for three decades they had followed a false leader who was in fact a bloodthirsty tyrant. The doctrine of Moscow's infallibility was breached: could the faithful continue to regard the Soviet Communist Party as the fount of all ideological wisdom? What proof was there that Khrushchev was any more infallible than the idol he had shattered? Was it right, in any case, to make a clean sweep of Stalin and Stalinism?

Yet another dogma—a Stalinist one—was discarded by Khrushchev at the Party Congress of 1956: the notion that there was only one way to reach socialism and communism—Moscow's way. Khrushchev found words of praise for the way things were being done in the Chinese People's Republic and in Yugoslavia. And he quoted a saying of Lenin that: 'All nations will arrive at socialism, but not all will do so in exactly the same way.' This seemed tantamount to an invitation to all parties to go their own way. Was it to be taken literally?

One leading communist who was watching these developments from afar with anger as well as apprehension was Mao Tse-tung, Chairman of the Chinese Communist Party and President of the Chinese People's Republic (in that order of importance). With Tito of Yugoslavia, Mao shared the distinction of being one of the few communist leaders who had come to power mainly as the result of his own and his followers' exertions, and not on the points of Russian bayonets. True, Stalin's last minute declaration of war on Japan and the provision of vast quantities of war material in Manchuria had made an enormous difference to the Chinese Communists' chances in the civil war that followed the defeat of Japan.

But this does not affect the argument. Basically, China was simply too big to be a satellite in Stalin's empire. Not only had Mao achieved success virtually without Soviet aid, but he had also successfully seized power in defiance of the normal Marxist-Leninist precepts, by relying on the peasantry and not on the workers. In so doing, he had specifically defied Stalin's own advice to him. Moreover, as the supreme leader of the Chinese People's Republic, he was the heir to several millennia of Chinese history and civilization. Traditionally, in the eyes of the Chinese themselves, China was the centre of the world. It was inherently improbable therefore that Mao would consent for long to a position of inferiority relative to the Soviet Union.

Surprisingly, however, it seemed at first as though he would be willing to accept a relatively subservient position. Whatever private reservations Stalin may have had about the advent of this new and formidable communist power to the east, he lost no time in giving it full support. The Chinese People's Republic was proclaimed in Peking on 1 October 1949, and the following day it was recognized by the Soviet government. The Chinese, on their side, affirmed their devotion to Marxism-Leninism, and proclaimed their wish to learn from 'the Soviet experience'. From Mao's point of view, Russia's support was essential. Even during the Chinese civil war, he had declared antagonism for the United States and American 'imperialism'. In so doing, he had deprived China of the chance of massive aid from the United States, which might have been hers for the asking. If China, emerging from nearly forty years of revolution, war and civil war, was to have any chance of economic recovery and advancement, the only supplier in sight seemed to be the USSR. This presupposed a Moscow-Peking axis, with Peking as the junior partner.

It was in recognition of these international realities that Mao made his first journey outside China in December 1949. Inevitably, his destination was Moscow, where he spent two full months. The outcome was a thirty-year Treaty of friendship, alliance and mutual assistance, signed on 14 February 1950. Stalin was not a man who liked to be proved wrong, as Mao had proved him wrong by his victory in China; and his meeting with the Chinese leader is said to have been cool. Moreover, Mao is believed to have requested about ten times as much money as Stalin was prepared to lend China. The agreed amount was only $300 million at one per cent interest over five years—not a generous amount in the face of China's needs and aspirations.

Niggardly and aloof though Stalin had proved, the history of the next few years inevitably threw the two giants of the communist world closer together. There must be a strong presumption that Stalin incited the North Koreans to invade South Korea in 1950, and there is no evidence that Mao was consulted. But once the initial North Korean assault had been blunted by General MacArthur's United Nations forces, Stalin and Mao were united in resisting a counter-assault to the north that might obliterate the North Korean communist regime and threaten China and the Soviet Union alike. The Chinese then intervened with an army described as 'volunteers', and the Russians with arms and equipment and a promise to defend China if she were attacked. It was clear enough that Stalin was getting the best of this bargain too, since the Chinese and North Koreans were fighting in his cause. It is believed that Mao did, however, secure promises of considerably increased military and economic aid from Russia in return for China's contribution in blood and military valour in the Korean war. In later years, Russia repudiated this debt, and this was certainly a major cause of the Sino-Soviet split.

By the time of Stalin's death in 1953, little Soviet money had actually reached China, though Soviet military and civilian 'advisers' swarmed over the vast country. Not unnaturally, Mao Tse-tung declined to attend Stalin's funeral in Moscow. Instead, he sent his Prime Minister, Chou En-lai, and it was immediately apparent that Stalin's successors were determined to improve relations with the Chinese, for Chou was singled out in a number of ways for special honours that were denied to other foreign communist leaders. For instance he stood among members of the Soviet Party Praesidium when funeral orations were made on the balcony of Lenin's tomb; and he walked side by side with Malenkov, Beria and Khrushchev in the funeral procession. And indeed, the Russian leaders swiftly offered considerable increases in economic aid to China. Within three months of Stalin's death, they undertook to design and build ninety-one industrial plants, in addition to fifty they had promised to construct under the 1950 treaty. Further undertakings followed, and in October 1954 an additional long term loan of nearly half a million dollars was granted to China, together with other Soviet concessions to Chinese pride. In a sense, these additional Russian inducements were a reward for China's attitude during the Geneva Conference on Far Eastern problems earlier that year, when Chou En-lai generally supported the Soviet delegation headed by the then Foreign Minister, Molotov.

And yet—despite all that had happened during the past seven years—when it came to making major ideological changes, and to reversing the long-established cult of Stalin, as Khrushchev did in February 1956, the Chinese leaders were apparently not even consulted beforehand. This was evident from the fact that Mao Tse-tung's message of greeting to the 20th Party Congress included eulogious references to Stalin. (This may seem paradoxical to the non-believer, since Mao had no reason to eulogize Stalin on personal grounds. But to praise Stalin in this context had a ritual meaning; it meant a gesture of obeisance from one communist leader to the leader of the greatest party of them all, in the original home of socialism. It implied a recognition that the Soviet Communist Party had always been right, even though Mao had the best of reasons for knowing that it had not.) The whole-hearted demolition of the Stalin myth was therefore greeted in Peking with a sense of particular outrage. There was indeed another reason for this. With Stalin's death, Mao Tse-tung became the senior personage in the communist world—with the possible exception of Ho Chi Minh, whose revolutionary prowess was second to none but whose sphere of responsibility only extended over half Vietnam, which in the past had been a satellite of China's. Mao therefore felt himself entitled to the fullest consultation by a relative upstart such as Khrushchev, before a major change of policy affecting the future of the entire world communist movement. But Mao's outrage, although genuine and no doubt forcibly expressed in inter-party communications, did not alter the fact. The harm was already done.

Another senior foreign communist, the Italian party leader Palmiro Togliatti, watched the Moscow Congress with less apprehension, though no less interest, than Mao Tse-tung. Although, like all communists everywhere, Togliatti had mixed feelings about the destruction of the Stalin myth, he saw certain advantages in it from an Italian standpoint. His mixed feelings arose out of his own checkered personal history. The Italian Communist Party had been banned in Italy during Mussolini's fascist regime, and in common with the leaders of other foreign parties in a similar situation, Togliatti had spent many years in Moscow. He was there in 1927 when Trotsky was expelled from the Soviet Communist Party; and he was there throughout the great purges of the 1930s. All the foreign communist parties represented in the Comintern in Moscow were asked to condemn Trotsky—but the evidence, if any, against the defeated Russian leader was not laid before them. The Italians, Togliatti included, declined to subscribe to a condemnation the evidence for which they had not seen. It was then explained to them that this was a question of power, not of justice.

One of the best known Italian communists, the writer Ignazio Silone, could not stomach such high-handedness and resigned from the party and the Comintern. Togliatti, however, decided that the best hope for his own and his party's future lay in collaborating with Stalin, right or wrong. Thereafter, he supinely supported everything Stalin did, including the most monstrous of his iniquities. For instance, during the Spanish Civil War, Togliatti transmitted Stalin's orders for the arrest and torture of Andrés Nin, the leader of the Trotskyist section in Catalonia. As one of Togliatti's closest collaborators said years later, Togliatti had lost his faith but not his zeal.

Togliatti was therefore in the fullest sense of the word a Stalinist; but for that matter, so was Khrushchev, if acquiescence in Stalin's crimes was the criterion. In the context of Italian politics in the mid-1950s, however, it rather suited Togliatti that Stalin should be dethroned. Unlike Mao, Togliatti was not in power. On the other hand, he was the leader of what was at that time the largest communist party outside the Soviet bloc—with a claimed membership of 2,145,317. Whatever Italy's difficulties, such as the persistence of deep peasant poverty in the south, the country was hardly ripe for revolution on any Marxist analysis. For one thing, modest affluence was beginning to reach the workers, for another, Italy was still overwhelmingly a Catholic country. Togliatti reasoned that as industrialization proceeded, the peasants would move into the towns and the hold of the Church on the people would weaken. Simultaneously, the townspeople would become more inquisitive, less bound by superstition and more refractory to the authority of the priests. The prospect of some kind of understanding with the Communist Party looked brighter than in the past. Some Catholics might be tempted by the prospect of seeing their views in print in communist publications; others might be attracted by the chance of a visit to Moscow. For all these reasons, it suited Togliatti that Khrushchev had in effect given his blessing to the notion of autonomy for foreign communist parties.

Khrushchev's secret speech was debated in a national assembly of the Italian Communist Party before the municipal elections of April 1956, and it was decided that the speech would be studied immediately after polling. Accordingly, in an interview published in the Italian Communist Party paper *L'Unità* on 17 June, Togliatti declared that 'the Soviet model cannot and should not any longer be obligatory' as far as communist parties outside the Soviet Union were concerned. 'The whole system,' said Togliatti, 'is becoming polycentric'; and the term 'polycentrism'

thereupon passed into the international vocabulary to describe
the idea of 'different roads to socialism'.

There have been conflicting interpretations of what Togliatti
meant by 'polycentrism'. The French Communist Party which,
under Thorez, was far more rigid than the Italian Party, was
determined to preserve the old Stalinist structure, and Thorez
accused Togliatti of wanting to set up a number of independent
centres of direction and inspiration in the international communist
movement. This was certainly not what Togliatti had in mind:
all he meant when he used the word 'polycentric' was that henceforth, as Khrushchev had suggested, each individual party should
find its own way to power according to the conditions prevailing
in its own country. But Togliatti continued to acknowledge
Moscow's authority, while claiming for the first time the right to
criticize the Soviet leadership in public.

If Khrushchev's secret speech and his doctrinal pronounce-
ments at the 20th Party Congress caused outrage, alarm or
excitement in communist parties outside Russia, anguish is a
more appropriate word to describe the reaction among the
satellite communist parties in power in Eastern Europe. Owing
their authority to Soviet power, and without popular support,
they had long derived comfort from a slavish imitation of the
Stalinist model: in effect, each party and each regime was a carbon
copy of the Soviet original. And now, the Soviet party boss was
denouncing the author of the whole system, and inviting individual parties to go it alone. The satellite leaders understood, of
course, that this invitation did not extend to foreign policy, but it
was bad enough that they should be required to show initiative
in home policy.

In each of the parties were many men with a taste for independence, good communists no doubt but who had never seen why
the Soviet model should be so minutely imitated. Emotions were
particularly strong in Poland and Hungary. The original Polish
Communist Party had been almost literally wiped out under
Stalin. Between 1937 and 1939 the twelve members of the Polish
Central Committee present in Moscow—at Stalin's invitation—
were executed, along with hundreds of minor Polish communists.
One of the Polish leaders, however, escaped death because he

happened to be in a Polish gaol at the time. This was Wladyslaw Gomulka. During the Second World War, Gomulka had played a leading part in organizing the new Polish Workers' Party—which succeeded the old party purged into extinction by Stalin. Always a strong nationalist as well as a Marxist, Gomulka incurred the Russian dictator's displeasure in 1947 for advocating a distinctive 'Polish road to socialism'. As a result, he was expelled from the government early in 1949 and towards the end of that year, ousted from the party. Accused of Titoism and subversion, he was gaoled in 1951 and tortured under interrogation, but never brought to trial. In 1954, after Stalin's death, he was released but isolated. Not unnaturally, he had acquired considerable popularity, even among non-communists. After the 20th Soviet Party Congress, it was no longer possible to keep him out. His rights as a party member were restored and he was elected First Secretary of the Central Committee.

Below the surface, popular discontent had been building up, and in June 1956, it erupted in serious rioting in Poznan, when thousands of factory workers attacked the headquarters of the security police and of the local Communist Party. In October, there was a crisis of a more fundamental kind. The Central Committee of the Polish Party, meeting from 19 to 21 October, decided to drop all Stalinists from the Politburo—including the Soviet Marshal Rokossovsky, the Minister of Defence. In a major speech on 20 October, Gomulka denounced Stalinism and the personality cult and called for a Polish road to socialism. He spoke, in effect, with a sword hanging over his head, for the previous day Khrushchev, Molotov and other Soviet leaders had flown to Warsaw without prior notice to warn the Polish leaders not to go too far in their liberal policy. As they arrived, Soviet tanks closed in on Warsaw and Soviet warships steamed to within sight of the Polish port of Gdynia. Gomulka, however, got away with it. The Soviet leaders stayed only twenty-four hours, having failed to browbeat Gomulka into retreat.

In contrast, when a very similar crisis broke out in Hungary a few days later, the Russians decided to intervene with force. There is no need to retell this story here—except to recall that the Hungarian uprising swept away one of the most odious of the

Stalinist regimes, but that Russia's brutal repression removed its short-lived successor, the government of Imre Nagy. His place was taken by Janos Kadar, like Gomulka a victim of a Stalinist purge in 1951, and—again like Gomulka—released in 1954. Kadar's first concern on reaching power was to crush the remnants of the Hungarian revolution.

It is now known that the Chinese leaders played an important part behind the scenes in both the Polish and the Hungarian crises.* For instance, they advised the Russians against intervening in Poland, but insisted that they should intervene in Hungary (though at the outset of the Hungarian crisis, they fleetingly denounced Russia's 'great nation chauvinism'). This conflicting advice was only superficially contradictory. Mao Tse-tung and his colleagues were less concerned about doctrinal purity than about the threat to the cohesion of the communist bloc. As regards Poland, they had no qualms. Only Soviet power stood between the Poles and a Germany intent on regaining the lands occupied by Poland during the Second World War. Whatever Gomulka might do inside Poland, his regime was bound to follow Moscow's lead in foreign policy. But the Nagy government in Hungary had gone much further: it was promising party democracy, and even threatening to break away from the Moscow-controlled Warsaw Pact. This was intolerable, and Mao insisted that Khrushchev should not tolerate it.

This was the first time the Chinese communists had intervened directly in Europe, and especially in affairs that concerned their Russian comrades. Not only had they forced their advice on Khrushchev, but in terms of communist power, they had been proved right. Gomulka stayed in power, and went considerably farther along the road to liberalism than Khrushchev would have liked; but Poland stayed firmly in the Soviet camp. Similarly, it was clear that if the Russians had not intervened militarily in Hungary, that country would have left the Soviet camp. Admittedly, an enormous price had been paid in blood and the esteem of the world at large. But the Kadar regime also stayed firmly within the communist bloc.

* See Edward Crankshaw, *The New Cold War* (Penguin, 1963), Chapter 6.

From that point forward, it was idle for the Russian leadership to suppose that they could treat China as a satellite in the way Stalin had. At this stage, however, Mao was still not denouncing Moscow's position as the leader of the communist world. Indeed, he was the first to condemn any European satellite that wanted to break away from Moscow's domination. He showed this beyond doubt in November 1957, when Khrushchev summoned a conference of the ruling communist parties. With full Chinese backing, the conference adopted a formal declaration re-emphasizing the leading role of the Soviet Union and warning parties not to carry polycentrism too far.

In return for this support, Mao expected certain things of the Soviet Union. He expected full support in his own policy of total hostility towards the capitalist world, and in particular its major citadel, the United States. He expected a major share of Soviet economic aid, by which he meant specifically that the Russians should give only minimal assistance to such non-communist countries as Egypt and India. Above all, perhaps, he expected Soviet technological know-how in the manufacture of nuclear weapons—or failing that, the provision of Soviet nuclear weapons. In addition, Mao expected Khrushchev to consult him before launching any major policy in the world, as the Soviet leader had failed to consult him at the time of the 20th Party Congress. In all these respects, Khrushchev's policy was a bitter disappointment to Mao. He had embarked on massive aid programmes to Egypt, India and other underdeveloped countries, and had increased these programmes to the detriment of China's economic prospects. He had initiated a policy of *détente* with Washington. He had failed to consult China during the Middle East crisis of 1958, when the British and Americans intervened in Jordan and Lebanon respectively. Worse still, he had visited President Eisenhower and toured the United States; and, adding insult to offence, he had struck a neutral attitude between India and China in their dispute over Himalayan frontiers. Finally—and this may have been the decisive point—not only had Khrushchev declined to give nuclear weapons to China, he had even refused to teach the Chinese how to make them for themselves. The incipient crisis in Sino-Soviet relations broke into

the open in 1960, and the Soviet technicians who had been helping the Chinese in their economic projects were withdrawn.

The major points at issue between Moscow and Peking related
to matters concerning China's interests as a great power. Because
the two countries were communist, however, the dispute largely
took the form of statements concerning ideology. In my view,
there has been too much emphasis on the ideological side of the
dispute, important though this is. One should remember that,
fundamentally, this is a clash between two great powers, the
expression of which takes an ideological form. In the next chapter
I shall briefly consider some of the ideological arguments used
on either side. The main lesson of this chapter, in the meantime,
is that Khrushchev, by tampering with established dogmas and
myths, started a process of disintegration which he was powerless
to arrest, except in Russia's immediate neighbours and satellites,
Poland and Hungary. All over the communist world, polycentrism proliferated. The Soviet intervention in Hungary—itself
the direct consequence of Khrushchev's speeches at the 20th
Party Congress in February 1956—shattered the faith of many
whose loyalty had survived the destruction of the Stalin myth.
In many countries, thousands or tens of thousands quit the
communist party, in most cases for good. Stalin, the absolute
dictator of the communist world, had understood the value of
ideology as an instrument of his power. Perhaps Khrushchev
understood this too; but he was no Stalin. In the end, Stalin's
reign of terror had held the Soviet Union back. As *primus inter
pares* in a collective leadership, Khrushchev was in no position
to maintain integral terror. The road to the future seemed barred
so long as the Stalin myth remained intact. A scapegoat for the
frightful injustices of the past had to be found, and that scapegoat
could only be Stalin himself. Khrushchev may have hoped that
the long tradition of discipline would keep the world communist
movement together once the shock of his secret speech had died
down. If so, he gravely miscalculated the consequences of his
words.

2. 'National Democracy'

So much has been written about the ideological and national division within the communist world that many people tend to forget the important points of doctrine that are still held in common in Moscow, Peking and Havana. One of the most important of these, as far as the rest of the world is concerned, is the relationship between 'peaceful co-existence' and 'the international class struggle'. The use of jargon is unfortunately inevitable when writing about communism, since all communist texts, without exception, are couched in jargon and a knowledge of the semantics of communist terminology is essential to any attempt to understand communist power politics. Take 'peaceful co-existence'. This reassuring term means one thing to communists and another to non-communists. To non-communists, it means living one's own life in one's own way and allowing others to live as they please. To communists, however, it means the absence of a shooting war; it is, in fact, virtually synonymous with what Westerners understand by 'cold war'. It means specifically, that non-communists must on no account interfere in communist countries, whereas communist parties have a duty to continue to try and overthrow non-communist systems by any means at their disposal.

This may seem an exaggeration or an over-simplification; but it is neither. The point becomes plainer, perhaps, if one defines the term 'international class struggle'. One does not have to be a Marxist-Leninist to know what the class struggle means to those who use the term as a fighting slogan. At its very simplest, the implication is that the capitalists exploit the workers, and that the workers will arise and overthrow their exploiters. Marx called this 'the expropriation of the expropriators'. But present-day Marxist-Leninists extend this concept to the world as a whole. The peoples of the world, according to the doctrine, are oppressed by the 'imperialists'. In time, they will arise and overthrow their imperialist oppressors. That is what Communists mean by the 'international class struggle'. Here again, the precise connotations of jargon terms must be remembered. 'The people', or 'the peoples', often means simply 'the communist party' or 'the communist parties'. In certain cases, where a local communist party is weak, the term 'people' will be conferred upon such local revolutionaries as seem most likely to overthrow capitalist enterprises, or in other ways adopt policies acceptable to Moscow or Peking, as the case may be.

Such interpretations and definitions are more important than they may seem. Without them, much that happened in Moscow in November 1960 would be meaningless to outsiders. The date is important, for this was the last time that the communist parties of Russia and China both felt able to sign an important document of international communist policy. They were not, of course, alone for with them were the representatives of seventy-nine other communist parties throughout the world, gathered together to celebrate the forty-third anniversary of the so-called 'October' revolution of 1917, when Lenin and his Bolsheviks overthrew the moderate democratic government of Kerensky. Already, the differences between Moscow and Peking were becoming too patent to disguise, and much wrangling attended the speeches and debates, which dragged on for several weeks. Finally, a massive and important 'statement' — now generally known as the World Communist Declaration of 1960—was published on 6 December. In this lengthy document two passages stand out as ominously important for non-communist countries. Each deals with 'peaceful co-existence'. The first read:

... by upholding the principle of peaceful co-existence, Communists fight for the complete cessation of the cold war, disbandment of military blocs and dismantling of military bases, for general and complete disarmament under international control, the settlement of international disputes through negotiation, respect for the equality of States and their territorial integrity, independence and sovereignty, non-interference in each other's internal affairs, extensive development of trade, cultural and scientific ties between nations.

Could anything have been more reassuring to non-communist readers or listeners? Peace, freedom, the end of the cold war — such ideas were clearly designed to strike responsive chords in ordinary human beings everywhere. The passage, however, was heavily qualified by another, which read:

> ... peaceful co-existence of countries with different social systems does not mean conciliation of the socialist and bourgeois ideologies. On the contrary, it means *intensification of the struggle* of the working class, of all the communist parties, for the triumph of socialist ideas. But ideological and political disputes between States must not be settled through war. (*My italics.*)

To communists everywhere, the message of this key passage was clear. To them, the cold war meant anti-communist words and deeds, ascribed to imperialists and reactionaries. No communist anywhere could fail to approve the end of *this* cold war; but non-communists everywhere could also be expected to applaud, since for them the cold war meant the state of tension and incipient conflict between the communist and non-communist powers. To non-communists, peaceful co-existence meant what it said, but in the passage I have just quoted, it was clearly stipulated that it meant the intensification of the struggle to overthrow non-communist governments, by all means short of war. Strictly speaking, the implication was not that *all* wars should be avoided, but only wars between the great powers.

The World Communist Declaration of 1960 did not spell out communist doctrinal differences on war and revolution. Indeed, the whole idea of the conference was to paper over such differences as had already appeared in private gatherings of communists. For communists, the differences were important enough to merit a mounting scale of mutual vituperation. But for non-communists, once again the areas of agreement may be more important than those of disagreement. Let us look at the differences first.

The main difference is about nuclear war. Even in 1960, and for several years later, before they themselves had developed nuclear weapons, the Chinese did not go so far as to *advocate* nuclear war. But, in comparison with the Russians, they did minimize its destructive capacity. By the time of the 1956 Soviet Party Congress, Khrushchev and the other Soviet leaders had already realized that nuclear war was a mutually suicidal way of settling accounts with the 'capitalist' countries. All talk of the 'inevitability' of a socialist victory in a war between the great powers had become meaningless since it was evident that the Soviet Union itself might be destroyed in the process. Hence Khrushchev declared that war was no longer fatally inevitable.

The Chinese, lacking nuclear weapons and deriving confidence from their overwhelming numbers, let it be known that they did not fear nuclear war, since even if half China's 650 million people were wiped out in a nuclear holocaust, the other half would survive to build afresh and consummate the victory of socialism. This was obviously dangerous talk, and Khrushchev would have nothing of it—though in 1962, he was to risk nuclear war with the United States by installing Soviet rockets on Cuban soil. His defeat in the ensuing confrontation with President Kennedy was, however, a decisive lesson. Thereafter, Soviet strategy, on the whole, was based upon the premise that nuclear war must be avoided. The Chinese knew no such restraints, and bitterly attacked Khrushchev for having backed down.

As regards other kinds of war, however, the Chinese and Russians are in basic agreement. In a speech on 6 January 1961, Khrushchev distinguished between 'just' and 'unjust' wars. Among the 'unjust' wars were 'local' wars, which Khrushchev defined as wars launched by 'imperialists' for their own ends. One example was the Suez Expedition of 1956. Local wars were unjust on two counts, both because they were imperialist and because of the danger that they might escalate into nuclear wars. Some wars, on the other hand, were always just. These were 'national liberation' wars, whose seal of justice was the fact that they were anti-imperialist. In this speech, Khrushchev went on to say:

> There will be wars of liberation as long as imperialism exists, as long as colonialism exists. They are revolutionary wars. Such wars are not only permissible but inevitable . . . what should our attitude be to such uprisings? It should be most favourable.

Khrushchev's natural ebullience did of course lead him from

C

time to time into making ill-considered statements. But this was not a case in point. On 6 December 1963, *Pravda*, the official daily newspaper of the Soviet Communist Party, declared that it was the Party's duty to give all political and economic support to national liberation movements—*and if necessary, support by arms*. On 11 May 1964, Khrushchev publicly declared that weapons should be given to nationalists struggling against imperialism. He was speaking before an audience that was not likely to disagree with such sentiments: the Egyptian National Assembly. Some months later, Khrushchev was overthrown in a 'palace revolt' in Moscow. But his successors did not repudiate him on this issue. On 6 November 1964, Brezhnev, the new leader of the Soviet Communist Party, reiterated his country's support, if necessary with arms, for the national liberation movements.

It is important to realize that the Chinese agree whole-heartedly with the Russians on the question of assistance to the national liberation movements. Indeed, in common with the other parties who attended the 1960 meeting in Moscow, they recognized

> ... their duty to render the fullest moral and material assistance to the people fighting to free themselves from imperialist and colonial tyranny.

Once again, Marxist-Leninist jargon clouds communication. What is a 'national liberation movement'? The answer to this apparently simple question is less simple than might be expected. One should always remember than in any discussion of communist theory, one is not dealing with objective studies of the real world, but with political dogma. When, as inevitably happens, dogma conflicts with reality, it may be necessary to modify dogma by the creation of suitable new terminology. In this instance the dogma goes back to Lenin's early days in power. Lenin expounded his views on the subject in a number of publications, but especially in *Imperialism: The Highest Stage of Capitalism*, and in his *Theses on the National and Colonial Questions* which were adopted by the Second Congress of the Comintern in July 1920. In defiance of the facts of history, Lenin considered imperialism to be the ultimate stage of capitalism. He argued that the survival of capitalism depended on the maintenance of imperialist control over the raw materials and cheap labour of the colonies. It followed that if the imperialists could be deprived of their colonies, the expected collapse of capitalism would be hastened. The Comintern, or Communist International, was formed in 1919, under strict Soviet control, with this object in mind. As part of the exercise, communist parties were set up in Indonesia (1920), China (1921), India (1925) and Indo-China (1930). Lenin's 1920 *Theses* referred to 'revolutionary liberation movements'. Communist parties were ordered to support such movements, forming a common front with non-communist nationalists and linking the anti-colonial movement with 'the proletarian movements of the advanced countries'. The ultimate aim was to set up local Soviet dictatorships; but the first objective was to defeat and expel the imperialist authorities. After Lenin's death, Stalin took over his policy and the Comintern, the chosen instrument for its fulfilment.

In this field as in others, however, the expectations of Marxist-Leninist dogma remained unfulfilled. Lenin and Trotsky had expected the Russian Revolution to be followed by revolutions in the advanced capitalist countries; but such revolts as did occur—in Hungary, Germany and Britain (in the shape of the General Strike of 1926 which, though not of communist inspiration, aroused communist hopes) came to nothing; and Stalin, abandoning Trotsky's doctrine of 'world revolution', set about establishing 'socialism in one country'. Attempts to set up Soviet States in Indonesia, Singapore and the Philippines in the 1920s failed dismally, though the Comintern remained extremely active in what is now known as the Third World. The Second World War revived communist expectations of anti-imperialist revolutions. In 1943, Stalin decided, now that the Russians had become the 'gallant allies' of the Western powers, that the Comintern should be dissolved as a reassuring gesture. There were strong grounds for hope that what communist agitation and subversion had failed to achieve during the 1920s and 1930s the wartime plight of the imperial powers would achieve unaided from outside.

This hope was particularly high in South-East Asia, where the Western powers had been defeated and humiliated by the conquering Japanese Army, and where local resistance groups, in most cases under communist control, had sprung up in the hills and jungles. It seemed unlikely that the colonial powers could ever fully restore their authority, and the expectation in Moscow was that the local communist revolutionaries, helped by the prestige of their wartime resistance, would swiftly take over after the defeat of Japan, thus accomplishing in one stage the socialist revolution which — according to dogma — was inevitable anyway. And once the Western powers had been deprived of their colonies the demise of capitalism would draw measurably closer.

History did not, however, live up to communist expectations. The imperial powers did indeed find it necessary or desirable to transfer sovereignty to their dependent territories. In some cases, such as Burma, India and Pakistan, the transfer was, if not peaceful, at least orderly. In others, most notably in the Netherlands East Indies and French Indo-China, the transfer was protracted and bloody. In the Philippines, the Americans set the pace of change by granting independence in 1946. But neither of the major expectations of the communists was fulfilled: power went not to the expectant local communists, but to 'bourgeois nationalists'; and the imperialist countries, far from being weakened by the loss of their colonies, actually seemed to thrive on their deprivation. Everywhere, indeed, nationalism had proved stronger than communism.

If communist theorists were simply students of history and society, the failure of their predictions could be borne with equanimity by the rest of mankind. But Karl Marx had launched the explosive doctrine of *Praxis*, which meant that it was the duty of communists to make sure that history did what was expected of it, by fulfilling the master's prophecies. Since history had let the communists down in South-East Asia, the communists would have to guide it in the right direction.

Not very long after the end of the Second World War — in 1947 — Stalin had in effect revived the Comintern, but in a more restricted form and under the name of Cominform (Communist Information Bureau), one of whose major purposes was to transmit Moscow's policy directives to the communist parties of the world. In September 1947, the Cominform met to hear a major speech by Stalin's then right-hand man, Zhdanov. What the delegates heard was momentous indeed. The world, Zhdanov told them, was now split into two hostile blocs; the time had come for the colonial peoples 'to expel their oppressors'. Within the next year, with a natural time gap to allow for the transmission of orders and the organization of guerrilla forces, communist-controlled insurrections began in Burma, India, Indonesia, Malaya and the Philippines.

The plan was a vast one, but it misfired. In one degree or another, but unmistakably, all these insurrections failed. In one country only, and in only a part of that country—North Vietnam —was a communist insurrection successful; and it is hardly by coincidence that the Vietnam uprising was not launched in response to Moscow's orders, but in fulfilment of the long-standing plans and ambitions of the local leader, Ho Chi Minh, who was undoubtedly a communist, but who managed success-fully to harness communist techniques to nationalist aims. (The same was true, of course, and on a much vaster scale, of China, where Mao Tse-tung successfully carried through a peasant revolution; but Mao also acted independently of Stalin, and he too combined communism and nationalism.)

The collapse of dogmatic expectations and practical hopes alike caused much *post facto* theorizing in Moscow and other communist centres. The failure of the capitalist economies to collapse when deprived of the human and natural resources of the colonies was explained by the new theory of 'neo-colonialism', the substance of which was that imperialist exploitation did not cease with the advent of independence in the former dependencies. The difference, according to the theory, was that economic domination of one kind or another continued, so preserving capitalism a little longer. Thus was the term 'neo-colonialism' added to the already rich communist vocabulary of anathema. The failure of the nationalist revolutions to be followed, as the texts demanded, by 'socialist' revolutions was perhaps more tricky. And the World Communist Declaration of 1960 came up with an ingenious explanation. This was the new concept of 'States of National Democracy'.

What was a State of National Democracy? By communist

37

revolutionary criteria it was a State that had overthrown its imperialist oppressors but had not yet become a 'socialist' State, although apparently well on the way to the socialist solution. The World Communist Declaration of 1960 defined it in the following words:

> A State consistently defending its political and economic independence, fighting against imperialism and its military blocs, and against military bases on its territory, a State fighting against new forms of colonialism and the penetration of imperialist capital, a State rejecting dictatorial and despotic methods of government, a State in which the people are guaranteed broad democratic rights and freedoms (freedom of speech, press, association and assembly and freedom to create political parties and social organizations), the opportunity to achieve agrarian reform and the realization of other aspirations in the field of democratic and social reorganization and the opportunity of participating in the determination of State policy.

The reference to 'democratic rights and freedoms' should be seen in the light of communist definitions. The context makes it plain that what is understood is the freedom to form a united front of 'all patriotic forces' — a formula which has always meant an alliance between the Communists and those willing to work with them and weak enough to be discarded when their usefulness has ceased. A further passage in the Declaration reminded communist revolutionaries of their ultimate aims:

> Knowing that the brunt of the struggle for the liberation of its people from capitalist oppression rests upon it, the working class and its revolutionary vanguard will with increasing energy press forward its defences against the domination of oppressors and exploiters in every field of political, economic and ideological activity in each country. In the process of the struggle, the people are prepared and conditions arise for decisive battles for the overthrow of capitalism, for the victory of the socialist revolution.

The launching of this new theory was a classic case of the revision of ideology to fit doctrinally difficult circumstances. A number of independent and militantly anti-Western regimes had emerged in the world. This was, on the surface, encouraging to communist believers—but for one fact: anti-Western though they were, they seemed in no hurry to entrust their destinies to the communists. A case in point was Nasser's United Arab Republic, which was both anti-capitalist and anti-Western, but in which the Communist Party was illegal and its leaders were in gaol. Another was Algeria—still at that time in the throes of a 'liberation war'. The trouble was that the revolutionary Algerian National Liberation Front (FLN), though likely to break with imperialism and overthrow capitalism, had good reasons to fear and distrust the local communists. In 1945, for instance, the communists had helped repress an uprising at Sétif, for no better reason than that the French Communist Party was at that time represented in General de Gaulle's government. There were other promising cases, such as Ghana, Guinea and Mali; but these militantly anti-Western nations of independent Africa did not have a communist party between them. In South-East Asia, President Sukarno's very anti-Western republic did have a large and powerful Communist Party, but in 1960 it had still not managed to join the government. (Success in this respect did not come until 1964.)

Perhaps the most tantalizing case of all was that of Cuba where, at the beginning of the year 1959, a flamboyant and anti-American revolutionary, Fidel Castro, had come to power after an insurrection in which the local communists had played no part at all. But the Castro regime's fast deteriorating relations with the United States and increasing dependence on Russian economic and financial aid encouraged Khrushchev and his colleagues to hope that it might be brought under communist control. It is now generally accepted that the theory of 'national democracy' was created to fit the special case of Cuba, with similar cases also in mind. In Cuba's case, the doctrinal gamble seemed to have paid off, for a year after the World Communist Declaration, Castro obligingly declared himself a Marxist, and went on (in 1965) to create a Cuban Communist Party. We shall see later, however, that even when Cuba had become a communist State, it continued to escape Moscow's control.

It is clear that 'national democracy' was a Russian idea, if only because the World Communist Conference was followed by a spate of Russian commentaries on it, while Peking maintained complete silence. In theory at least, however, the Chinese were doctrinally bound by it since they had signed the World Declaration. It should be remembered, moreover, that the Russians did make an important concession to Chinese views by including a reference to the need for a 'united front' in the Declaration. That this was indeed a concession may be inferred from what is known of the Chinese and Russian theories of revolution. The Russians, theorizing from their experience in 1917, favoured a two-stage revolution. First the feudal, reactionary or imperialist government could be overthrown and a bourgeois democracy introduced; then the communists could initiate the second stage by overthrowing the bourgeois democrats. This was what happened in Russia in 1917, when the democratic government of Kerensky was overthrown by Lenin's Bolsheviks. The Chinese, however, distrusted the idea of a two-stage revolution. Mao's doctrine, based upon his own experiences in fighting both the Japanese and the Chinese Nationalists, was the victory of the 'united front'. He had first stated it in 1940 in his tract, *New Democracy*, which had proposed a dictatorship of several social classes in alliance. Nine years later, when victory in the Chinese civil war loomed ahead, he issued a statement *On the People's Democratic Dictatorship*, which firmly laid down that the communist party was to be in control of its allies throughout the revolution. The passages on 'national democracy' in the World Communist Declaration were thus a compromise, though weighted in Russia's favour. The Russians thought of national democracy as the first stage of a two-stage revolution; but the tactics of the united front were advocated for the second stage.

It will be seen, then, that at all stages divergences go hand in hand with similarities. After the World Communist Conference of 1960, the respective positions were roughly as follows:

ON WAR
The Russians: Liberation wars are just, local wars involving imperialists are unjust; nuclear wars are also unjust because they may destroy a socialist homeland.

The Chinese: All wars against imperialism are just. Socialism will survive even a nuclear war.

ON REVOLUTION

The Russians: A two-stage revolution favoured; first stage is bourgeois, second stage is socialist (communist). Revolution may in certain cases be achieved by constitutional and non-violent means. It may be expedient for a local communist party to be on good terms with a bourgeois government.

The Chinese: Communism or socialism can be introduced *only* by means of a violent revolution. The communist party is to form an army of workers and peasants, to wage war against the government. When certain areas are liberated, the bourgeoisie and 'middle peasants' (but not the 'rich peasants') are to join the workers and poor peasants in a united front. National liberation is achieved by means of a final offensive against the demoralized government forces. Throughout the revolutionary process, the communist party must be firmly in control of the united front, and at all times must be implacably hostile to the government.

Perhaps the most important things to remember, however, are these: the Russians and Chinese (in common with communist parties of all shades everywhere) are permanently committed to the destruction of all non-communist regimes, differing only as to the means of the envisaged revolution. And both are committed to helping national liberation movements by all available means, including weapons. This fact, which is spelt out in the World Communist Declaration of 1960 and subsequent commentaries in Moscow and Peking, is fundamental to any assessment of the future of communist power. It should not be forgotten in the welter and confusion of doctrinal clashes between the rival centres of power in the communist world.

Part 11: The Present

Part 11: The Present

1. Russia tightens the Screw

November 1967 was a good time to look at and assess the position of the Union of Soviet Socialist Republics, for that month it was fifty years old. This was not, of course, the fiftieth anniversary of the Russian Revolution; and the fact needs to be restated, since it has been obscured by Soviet historians and repeated by the ignorant or the faithful. In fact, the old Russian regime of the Tsars was overthrown in March 1917 by moderate socialists with mass support from the populace. Lenin was brought back to Russia in a sealed train provided by the Germans who rightly believed he would conclude a peace of defeat with them. On 7 November, he and his Bolshevik Red Guards overthrew the provisional government of Alexander Kerensky, this time without the benefit of mass support, and installed the totalitarian regime that still rules over the Empire of the Tsars. Since 7 November was 25 October in the old Russian calendar, Lenin's *coup d'état* is known in the history books as the October Revolution.

In November 1967, then, the communist regime had been in power for half a century. Since this small group of men professed to have the only scientifically valid theory of society and with it the key to all social, economic and political problems, and since their monopoly of power was total, this was a good time to ask what they had done during their fifty years. The achievements are undeniable, and so is the profound transformation of society. In 1917, Tsarist Russia was an overwhelmingly peasant society. Even in 1928, nine years after the Bolshevik Revolution, nearly 78 per cent of the population were peasants. Now, however, workers and other urban employees constitute more than half (55 per cent) of the Soviet population.

With this social transformation has gone a tremendous increase

45

and improvement in education. Between 1926 and 1939, the percentage of the population able to read and write rose from 56.6 per cent to 87.4 per cent and by 1959 illiteracy had been virtually eradicated, with 98.5 per cent of literates. Today it is widely conceded that, at any rate in the physical sciences and in mathematics, the level of education in the Soviet Union compares favourably with the best available in other countries. The numbers of engineers and other technicians produced by the system is impressively high.

In technology, indeed, the system has remarkable successes to its credit. In space technology, from satellites to moon probes, the Soviet Union rivals the United States. And at the end of 1968, the Russians were the first to test a supersonic jet airliner, the Tupolev Tu-144, ahead of the Anglo-French Concorde and of similar American experiments.

In heavy industry, which has always dominated Soviet economic thinking since the days of Stalin's five-year plans, the backward country taken over by Lenin has soared ahead of Britain, Germany and France. To recognize such achievements, however, is not enough. One must also ask what their cost was in human terms, and to what extent they may be attributed to the system created by Lenin and his successors. One is also entitled to ask what benefits the system has brought ordinary citizens in the Soviet Union, as compared with the citizens of other industrial countries.

In making comparisons, the observer is of course hampered by fifty years of Soviet propaganda. Served by the Communist Party's monopoly of communications, the Soviet propaganda machine has built an elaborate myth of miraculous economic growth and transformation directly attributable to 'socialist' planning. In a few decades, it is argued, Russia's under-developed economy transformed itself into an advanced industrial one. This is partly true, but misleading. Between 1917 and 1967, the Japanese economy underwent a similar transformation, without the benefit of socialist planning. For that matter, the United States transformed itself from under-development in the mid-nineteenth century to the status of a rising great power in the early twentieth century. In the American case, this rapid transformation, which pre-dated Russia's by about thirty to fifty years, was achieved under a liberal economic system, and paid for by exports of agricultural produce and raw materials. Nor should one overlook an important fact which Soviet historians try to conceal: that economic history in Russia did not begin in 1917. Russia's industrial development began under the Tsars, and was already advancing rapidly when the Great War began in 1914. By then, as Professor W. W. Rostow notes,* Russia was producing about five million tons of pig iron, four million tons of iron and steel, forty million tons of coal, ten million tons of petroleum and a food-grain export surplus of about twelve million tons.

Russia, of course, was devastated by war, revolution and civil war. This may account for the fact that it took the Bolsheviks ten years in power (that is, until 1927) to reach the level of economic production Tsarist Russia had attained in 1914. The following year—1928—Stalin launched the first of his five-year plans. It is customary to date the Soviet Union's economic growth from this period. Even today, however, it is not sufficiently realized that this economic growth was remarkable for heavy industry, and only for that. In other sectors, the growth was either relatively small or non-existent. In agriculture, Stalin's policies were disastrous. Communist dogma required the collectivization of the land, and in pursuit of it, Stalin wrecked Soviet agriculture. The harvest in 1932 was lower than in 1927, although the State commandeered more than twice as much. Half the livestock in the whole country had died or been slaughtered by 1933. As late as 1953, when Stalin died, Soviet farming had not progressed further than where the Tsars had left it during the Great War. The Russians were eating less, and their diet was less nutritious than it had been twenty-five years earlier.† For this too, the Russian peasants had paid an exorbitant price: five million so-called kulaks had been liquidated, and millions more deported.‡

It may be objected that Stalin was a monstrous tyrant, an

---

* *The Stages of Economic Growth* (Cambridge United Press, 1960), p. 66.
† W. Klatt in *Survey*, October 1967.
‡ In education, too, it should be remembered that literacy was gaining rapidly in the last few years of the Tsarist regime, and that it regressed in the early years of the Revolution. See Solomon M. Schwarz in *Survey*, October 1967.

aberration, an exception to normal rules of behaviour even in a totalitarian system. This may be granted. But Khrushchev, in his ten years of power, performed relatively little better than Stalin had. Yet Khrushchev was personally obsessed by the need to do something about agriculture. He made nearly two hundred speeches exclusively on this theme. He backed his verbal exhortations with not inconsiderable reforms. He reclaimed virgin lands lying fallow in Central Asia; he introduced maize as a feed grain; and he ploughed up the grass lands. On the administrative side, he abolished the machine tractor stations which Stalin had set up as the basis of his collective system. Instead, the tractors and other machines were distributed to the collective farms themselves. He removed the controlling responsibility for agriculture from the special ministries and allocated it directly to new departments within the Communist Party.

All this yielded satisfactory returns for about five years. But his remedies were essentially short-term ones. The virgin lands refused to perform as consistently as Khrushchev had hoped. Unpredictable rainfall and wind erosion, with the natural poverty of the soil, took their toll. The ploughed up grass lands needed more fertilizer than was available. Disaster struck in 1963 with a crop so short of expectations that over the next three years the Soviet Union had to import twenty million tons of grain from Canada, Australia and the United States. At the summit of his optimism, in 1959, Khrushchev had boasted that, by 1961, the Russians were going to produce more meat, butter and milk than the Americans. But when the two years had elapsed, nothing more was heard of this boast. By the end of Khrushchev's decade, the American farmer still produced seven or eight times as much as his Soviet counterpart. In milk and livestock, Soviet yields were only half the American.

Khrushchev's agricultural failures were undoubtedly one of the main causes of his downfall in 1964. His successor as General Secretary of the Party, Leonid Brezhnev, wisely decided in a new agricultural programme launched in March 1965 to provide better prices for producers and to increase supplies of equipment to the farms. With these reforms and the luck of better weather, the Soviet Union achieved a record grain crop of 171 million tons in 1966, and a satisfactory one of 165 million tons in 1968. In effect, what the Party leaders had decided to do was to spend large sums on incentives to the farmers, in the hope of saving the equally large sums that had gone abroad to pay for grain imports during Khrushchev's last years in power. As a result, the USSR found itself in 1968 with a comfortable surplus.

It is indeed relevant to this study to note that the performance of Soviet agriculture is invariably at its worst at times of doctrinal orthodoxy; and that it thrives to the extent that doctrine yields to pragmatism. Nowhere is this truer than in the private sector of agriculture. In the Soviet Union, as in other communist countries, small plots of land, privately farmed, make an altogether disproportionate contribution to the agricultural total. Officially, private farming is considered a transitional phenomenon, due to disappear when the collectivized agriculture can feed the entire population.* (The trouble is that this day never seems to dawn.) For clearly doctrinal reasons, Khrushchev interfered with private agriculture, thus aggravating his own difficulties. His successors have made fresh concessions to the private farmer; but without abandoning the fundamental doctrine that collective agriculture must go on. It is probable that so long as it does, Soviet performance will fall far short, in relative terms, of that of private farms in the advanced western countries and Japan. Whatever the yardstick, it cannot be shown that communist methods are successful in agriculture.

The same is true, broadly speaking, of Soviet light industry, that is, of the products that affect the everyday life of the Soviet citizen. The Soviet system has always given priority to heavy industry over the consumer industries, and to industry as a whole over agriculture. The reasons for this choice of priorities is to be found in what is possibly the most curious ideological aberration of all. Karl Marx had envisaged revolution only in the advanced industrial States, with an overwhelming population of oppressed proletarians. This was not the case in Russia, as Lenin was well aware. This did not worry him too much, because he and his friends expected a wave of revolutions in other and more advanced countries. When these failed to materialize, the

* Karl-Eugene Wadekin in *Problems of Communism*, January-February 1968.

Bolsheviks set about creating the conditions *ex post facto* that should have been in existence in the first place to justify the taking of power—by forced industrialization.*

Preference was given to heavy industry for two reasons in particular. One was so that the future generation for whose benefit socialism was being built could gather the fruits of the new productive capacity that was being created. But the main reason was probably the fact that it is easier, in a State-controlled economy, to plan for heavy industry than for the consumer industries. Consumers have needs of their own, which are normally met in a market economy through the law of supply and demand. But the market economy, by definition, had been abolished, and the consumer did not need to be consulted about the planned production of pig iron and steel.

Against this rigid doctrinal background, it is hardly surprising that living standards in the Soviet Union remained static for many years, if they did not actually decline; and that in recent years they have risen much more slowly than those of comparably industrialized areas of the world. On 15 September 1967, the Communist Party organ *Pravda*, anticipating the fiftieth anniversary of the October Revolution, published percentage claims that illustrated the point. Between 1913 and 1967, said *Pravda*, total industrial production increased 71 times; in the same period, the output of light industry rose 17 times, and of food production 14 times. These figures are, however, suspect, as are many Soviet statistics. In 1913, the real wages of the average Russian—that is, what he could buy for his money—were about 40 per cent of the American average real wage. In 1967, the average American could buy five times as much with his money than his predecessor of 1913. If the average Russian in 1967 had 14 to 17 times as much food and consumer goods at his disposal as his father or grandfather in 1913, then one might conclude that in 1967 real wages had caught up with the American level. This, however, is untrue; and the fallacy probably lies in the fact that in 1913 the bulk of the consumer goods produced in Tsarist Russia came from the cottage industries. But these are ignored

* See Robert Conquest, introduction to Milovan Djilas, *The New Class* (Allen & Unwin, 1966).

by Soviet statisticians, who base their calculations on the output of Tsarist industry before the Great War.

In fact, living standards remain low. After twenty-five years of forced industrialization under Stalin, they were no higher when he died than in 1928. Although rents are low, adequate housing space has not yet been provided. The Soviet élite has large flats and modern comforts. But most workers live in overcrowded conditions, and often in dilapidated properties. At the time of the fiftieth anniversary celebrations, the average Soviet working class family spent about 60 per cent of its income on food, compared with about 30-35 per cent in Western Europe. The shoddiness of many of the goods available in the shops was notorious.

There was a time when this shoddiness and insufficiency didn't matter very much to the average shopper. The ruling élite had its own shops, and the people, kept down by an omnipresent police system, were not consulted about their needs or wishes. But in this respect as in others, Khrushchev was the victim of his own logic. He himself had denounced Stalin's police terror. But the alleviation of the terror meant that people could begin, however modestly, to express their views. Moreover, the economy itself was becoming more sophisticated. Even before Stalin's death, it was apparent that forced labour was producing diminishing returns. Similarly, the over-production of capital goods had its natural limits. The needs of the consumer could not be ignored indefinitely. Malenkov, who had briefly succeeded Stalin, had realized this, and Khrushchev—although he had ritually denounced Malenkov for his 'heresy' in calling for more consumer goods—took over the policy, when he himself was in supreme power.

Over the years, however, it became apparent that a system that had deliberately avoided paying attention to the consumer could not suddenly produce goods that would meet the need for choice and discrimination. Though Soviet citizens still lacked so many of the things taken for granted in non-communist industrial society, goods began to accumulate in the shops and warehouses unsold and unwanted because their quality fell short of the standard now required by consumers whose need for the relatively shoddy or unsophisticated goods on offer was fast diminishing. By 1965, the situation was becoming desperate. Vast unsold inventories had accumulated. The economy was still growing but the rate of growth had declined. Between 1956 and 1960 the rate of growth had been 8.2 per cent, between 1961 and 1965 it was no more than 6 per cent.* Before 1958, the Soviet Union had tied with capitalist West Germany in producing the highest return on investments of all industrial nations. Since then, the USSR has tied with another Western nation, Britain, for a more dubious honour—that of having the lowest investment return of all. True, the average Soviet worker continued to produce more per hour each year, but there again the rate of increase had dropped surprisingly, to 6.4 per cent from 1961 to 1964, as compared with 8.2 per cent in 1951–1955.

The main cause of this disappointing performance lay in the fact that prices were fixed arbitrarily by the army of planners in Moscow who were unaware of, and uninterested in, the needs of the consumer. Everything was centrally directed and controlled. Factories were told what to produce and how much of it. Raw materials were allocated in relation to centrally determined targets. If the planners decided that the production of men's shoes was to rise by five per cent, then that was what had to happen, regardless of whether the additional number could be sold or not. There being no free market mechanism, the 'norm' was all. There were penalties for failing to produce the 'norm', and bonuses for exceeding it. In many cases, however, since the planners had been wrong in their initial calculation, the norm could not be reached, let alone exceeded, because insufficient raw materials had been allocated to particular factories. Hence a very rapid growth of illegal, private enterprise delivery systems. These worked, but woe betide the smart operator who was caught, even though his initiative might have contributed to the good functioning of the State's economy. In May 1961, Khrushchev extended the death penalty to a number of economic 'crimes': death awaited the free-lance supplier.

It may well have occurred to some Soviet economists that what was wrong was the system itself; but if so, they kept their

* Theodore Frankel in *Problems of Communism*, May-June 1967.

thoughts to themselves. Central planning was basic to the system and private enterprise was out. One man did speak out however: Professor Yevsei Liberman, who wrote articles in the early 1960s advocating views that sounded dangerously heretical. Profits, said Liberman, should be the indication of the efficiency of an enterprise. The very word 'profits' was enough to send a shudder through the offices of Gosplan, the Soviet centralized planning organization, and indeed through the entire hierarchy of the Communist Party. Liberman, however, was very careful to express his views within the recognized modes, with frequent ritual references to Lenin, and drawing a sharp contrast between socialist profits and capitalist ones. This was not particularly difficult in Marxist terms. Capitalist profits were said to go straight into the pockets of the exploiting capitalist. Socialist profits could be ploughed back into people's enterprises, or into the pockets of deserving workers and managers.

What Liberman complained about was that under the old system a manager's bonus depended upon the volume of his production. This encouraged quantity as against quality. Instead, he proposed to determine bonuses by the amount of each factory's production that could actually be sold and by the size of the profit. In the highly conservative Russia of the 1960s, this was a very revolutionary thing to preach. Professor Liberman got his way, however, and in September 1965, the Soviet Premier, Kosygin, made proposals to a plenary meeting of the Party's Central Committee, incorporating some of the Professor's reforms.

The following January, a pilot scheme was launched. Forty-three enterprises in seventeen industries, employing 300,000 people, were brought under the new scheme. Apart from the new criterion of profitability, this meant that each of the forty-three enterprises was given greater autonomy over its own production, for instance in making direct contracts with one another.* The pilot scheme was in fact on a very modest scale, since it affected less than one in a thousand of the Soviet Union's 45,000 industrial enterprises. Allowing for teething troubles, the scheme was on the

* See Professor Liberman's own explanation of the reform in *Foreign Affairs*, October 1967.

whole a success. By the end of 1968, more than 25,000 enterprises had switched to the reformed system. Together, they accounted for seventy per cent of Soviet industrial output and eighty per cent of industrial profits. The results of this partial adoption of capitalist principles were immediate and satisfying. In 1966–67, industrial output rose by twenty per cent, and labour productivity by nearly thirteen per cent.

On 1 October 1968, the Chairman of Gosplan, Nikolai Baibakov, declared his pleasure in an article in *Pravda*, and talked of giving more independence to Ministries and enterprises, while restricting central planning. There were even signs of a new deal for the consumer. True, when Baibakov presented the Budget on 10 December 1968, before the Supreme Soviet, he announced an increase in military expenditure in 1969 of six per cent over the 1968 figure.* The allocation to science, including the space programme, also rose, and the economy remained strongly weighted in favour of heavy industry. Nevertheless, for the second year in succession, the growth rate for consumer goods was to exceed that of producer goods. Small though the difference was (7·5 per cent increase for consumer goods, compared with 7·2 per cent for producer goods) the new Budget must have pleased the ordinary Soviet citizen.

In the past, the benefits the citizen derived from 'socialism' had lain almost entirely in the field of social welfare. Free medical attention; old age benefits payable to men at 60 years of age and women at 55 (with qualification at 50 for those who have worked at least ten years in arduous jobs); disablement pensions; 112 days' fully paid leave for employed mothers; special recreational, sports and holiday facilities for Trade Unionists—these are collectively a source of pride to the Soviet regime. Even in welfare, however, there is an omission that is directly attributable to a doctrinal inability to admit the existence of a problem. Since 1930 no unemployment relief at all has been payable, on the ground that there cannot be unemployment in a 'socialist' State. Unjust dismissal of a worker is compensated by a payment

---

* Actually, the defence allocation dropped slightly as a percentage of the total Budget (13·2 per cent compared with 13·5 per cent in 1968), but allocations for science include an unknown proportion for defence.

of wages for up to twenty days; and a worker acquitted of a criminal charge may receive up to two months' pay—but that is all. Indeed, in 1966 there were only two labour exchanges in the whole of the Soviet Union—one in Gorky, and the other in Armenia. Since then, a network of exchanges has gradually been established, for it has no longer been possible to disguise the fact of unemployment. In fact, there has always been disguised unemployment in the Soviet Union. In Stalin's day, it was concealed by the existence of a vast unpaid labour force in the concentration camps. Apart from that, there has always been seasonal unemployment, and considerable under-employment—in factories rendered idle, for instance, by the non-delivery of raw materials. Latterly, the Liberman economic reforms have produced redundancies, since managers are now able to dismiss surplus workers and redistribute their wages to those still needed.

While giving all possible credit to the Soviet Union for its social services, one is entitled to recall the high price paid for such achievements, and to ask whether comparable results could not have been achieved without the forced starvation of the peasants, the liquidation of the 'kulaks', the great purges, the officially decreed deprivation, and the denial of elementary justice under a police system. Franco's Spain offers holiday homes and vast recreation parks for its workers. Britain, too, has its National Health Service, though whether or not charges are made for medicines is a matter of fluctuating political calculation; in Russia, incidentally, citizens have always had to pay for their medicines. Sweden pays lavish old age pensions, and twelve per cent of its gross national product goes on welfare expenditures. The list could go on. The point is not to denigrate Soviet welfare services, but to show that they are neither unique, nor even outstanding in comparison with other examples. One is bound to ask: if this is the best the regime can show, was the Russian communist system really necessary?

The question is interesting not only on moral grounds but for its relevance to the problem that concerns us: the survival of communist power, and the continuing appeal of its philosophy. It is easy, of course, to blame the unnecessary sufferings of the Soviet people under communism on Stalin's aberrations. One may indeed concede that things would not have been as bad if he had not been in power. But the explanation is insufficient. It was Lenin who re-created the secret police, and started the reign of terror. Moreover, in scattered communist regimes without a Stalin, and out of reach of Soviet power, such as North Korea, North Vietnam and Cuba, the oppressive features of the communist State are reproduced. In the Soviet Union itself, of course, conditions have improved since Stalin's death. But the arbitrary character of the State has, if anything, been reinforced since Khrushchev's removal in 1964.

The manner of this removal was in itself symptomatic of totalitarian methods. Nearly fifty years after Lenin's Revolution it was still not possible to change a head of government by peaceful and constitutional means. True, there was no bloodshed, but Khrushchev was removed by a conspiracy with the help of the secret police. The last touches to the plot appear to have been made when he was on holiday on the Black Sea. He was summoned back to attend a meeting of the Praesidium, which in effect turned into a trial of his policies. The secret police had co-operated by making sure he could not reach anybody by telephone or physical contact. When he asked to put his case before the Central Committee, he found it had been prepared for his removal. The following day, 15 October 1964, the Praesidium of the Supreme Soviet granted Khrushchev's 'request' to resign as Chairman of the Council of Ministers (Prime Minister) on grounds of advanced age and deteriorating health.*

One of the many reproaches against Khrushchev was that he had liberalized too fast; although his liberalization was in fact a spasmodic process with one step back for every two forward. Under his successors, Kosygin and Brezhnev, there has been no wholesale return to Stalinist terror. On the other hand a number of show trials have been staged, recalling earlier abuses of justice. The ones that attracted most international attention were those of Sinyavsky and Daniel in 1966, and of Ginsburg and others in 1968. The former were writers accused of having published abroad, under the pen names of Abram Tertz (Sinyavsky) and Nicolai Arzhak (Daniel), works alleged to be slanderous of the

* Mark Frankland, *Khrushchev* (Penguin, 1966), pp. 205, 206.

Soviet Union and subversive of its system. The former was sentenced to seven years severe detention in a corrective labour colony, and the latter to five years. The Ginsburg case was in a sense a continuation of the Sinyavsky one, for Ginsburg and another defendant, Galanskov, were accused of compiling a 'white book' on the Sinyavsky-Daniel Trial. Ginsburg and Galanskov were sentenced to seven years and five years respectively.

Nor were these isolated cases. In October 1968, Yuli Daniel's wife and others, including Dr Pavel Litvinov, a physicist and grandson of Maxim Litvinov, a Foreign Commissar of the 1930s, were sentenced to terms of exile. It was no help to the accused that the Soviet Constitution 'guarantees' freedom of association and of speech. The defendants had shouted their views in Red Square, and no doubt this was reprehensible. But Mrs Daniel's principal crime may have been the fact that she was her husband's wife; and Litvinov's that he had earlier denounced the conduct of the Ginsburg trial, with Mrs Daniel's support.

Another man who had contested Soviet justice in the Ginsburg trial was General Peter Grigorenko (retd.), and it was only a matter of time before he, too, found himself in trouble. He was arrested in May 1969, in the central Asian city of Tashkent, for championing the cause of the oppressed Crimean Tartars, and confined to a lunatic asylum. More recently, Alexander Solzhenitsyn, Andrei Amalrik, and other writers have been persecuted in various ways, while Anatoli Kuznetsov has taken refuge in England.

Russia, then, is still a police State, and perhaps the most significant aspect of the celebrations of the fiftieth anniversary of Soviet communism was the fact that the secret police was given a special celebration of its own on 20 December 1967. Fifty years earlier on that date, Lenin's government had set up the *Cheka*, named after the first two initial letters of its full title, 'The Extraordinary Commission for the struggle against Counter-Revolution and Sabotage'. To any Russian old enough to have memories, there was something chillingly surrealistic about the official praise now heaped upon the 'glorious deeds' of the *Cheka* and its grim successors, the OGPU, NKVD, MVD, and the present KGB. Not a word about the millions of victims of trials, deportations and executions; indeed, the present head of the KGB, Yuri Andropov, described the record of the security services over the past half-century as 'in keeping with the whole spirit of Soviet rule'.

True, several speakers in the commemoration ceremonies emphasized the need for 'strict observance of socialist laws'. But what was the socialist law (in the singular)? For in practice the KGB continued to be a law unto itself. As the trials of Daniel and Sinyavsky and other intellectuals had shown, the KGB still had the power to arrest at will, to try before tribunals of its own judges, in courtrooms packed with its own personnel, in defiance of the Constitution. In this kind of situation, it mattered little to the ordinary Soviet citizen whether the Party or the secret police was on top in an internal struggle the outcome of which left him still unprotected.

Once again one faces the obsessive question: was communism really necessary? In the name of a Messianic mission, presented in pseudo-scientific terms, a small band of fanatics had seized power in Russia fifty years earlier. In that half-century they had achieved great things, but no more than other nations had achieved without their system. They had not abolished unemployment; they had merely not paid unemployment benefit. They had not abolished crime or hooliganism; they had merely proclaimed that such things were impossible in a socialist society.* Whenever the economy had run into difficulties, bourgeois or capitalist devices – reluctantly adopted, or merely tolerated – had rescued it. This was true of both private land ownership and of Professor Liberman's reforms. Even in technology, the high point of Soviet achievement, the Soviet Union continues to lean heavily on Western technological developments. To get the supersonic jet airliner, Tupolev TU-144, off the ground at the end of 1968 was undoubtedly an outstanding achievement. But many of the TU-144 components – including electronic and navigational instruments, valves and generators – were British, and indeed identical with those in the

---

* In a speech on 8 June 1966 before his Moscow constituents, Kosygin called for harsher methods in 'an intensification of the struggle against criminal elements' – without attempting to explain the prevalence of crime in a society in which, theoretically, it could not exist.

Anglo-French Concorde. Since 1957, the Russians have bought complete plants from Western countries and purchased manufacturing rights to a whole range of processes, especially in the chemical industry, but also in automobile production: the deals with Imperial Chemical Industries, Fiat and Renault are major examples. Nor is there anything wrong with this. But the Soviet claims for supremacy in this field, as in others, must be measured against the facts of international interdependence. In any event, Soviet achievements in space and defence technology serve only to point the contrast with the everyday lives of Soviet citizens. As so many foreign visitors to Moscow have noted, the Russians may be reaching for the moon, but they are not comparably advanced when it comes to designing and maintaining toilet flushing systems that actually work, and providing plugs for hand basins in luxury hotels.

Such points need not, however, be laboured. The real point is of deeper importance. It is surely this: that all the Soviet achievements are paralleled elsewhere, and not one is directly attributable to Marxism-Leninism. It is, moreover, grotesque to suggest that such achievements as there have been can ever justify the sufferings imposed on the Soviet peoples over more than half a century. Marxists are fond of pointing to the sufferings of England during the industrial revolution, and saying, or implying, that in comparison even Stalin's forced industrialization was not all that bad. But neither the event nor its consequences were deliberately willed as an act of State policy. In Russia, the purges, the deportations, the executions and the forced labour camps were imposed from above in the name of an ideology. Can it be seriously argued, however, that Stalin's excesses, in themselves, contributed to the modernization of the USSR?*

These arguments seem to me to remain valid, even if comparisons less remote in time from the Russian experience than the English industrial revolution are made. It could be argued, for instance, that violence of one kind or another, including a civil war, accompanied the first industrial revolution in America; and that the current second industrial revolution (in technology)

* For a fuller discussion of such arguments, see Sidney Hook, 'The Human Costs of Revolution', in *Survey*, January 1968.

in that country has produced a migration of Negroes from the South and led to social tensions marked by violence. It could also be argued that there was a link between Japan's accelerated industrialization in the 1930s and the rise of militarist ultra-nationalism. But these examples do not, by themselves, prove the view that violence is inseparable from industrialization. (In Sweden, strikes were endemic until the Saltsjöbaden agreement of 1938 created lasting industrial peace; but the creation of an industrial society, though rapid, was by and large non-violent.)

Still less do such examples support the view that there was any special merit in communist methods or that what Stalin achieved could not have been achieved in any other way. It is not my wish to defend the American system against the charge that it has failed to prevent domestic violence; and even further from my mind to condone the brutalities and plunders of Japanese militarism. But it seems to me fair comment to note that it has never been American State policy to liquidate Negroes and poor whites; nor Japanese State policy to keep the people poor. It *was*, however, Soviet State policy to liquidate the 'kulaks', and keep living standards low. But it is only fair to add that Stalin did create a magnificent heavy industry that enabled a brave people to stand up to Hitler's fearsome military machine. And this, indeed, is the point: what Stalin created, and his successors have improved, was essentially a war economy, that remains operative in peace time.

All nations have their myths, but nowhere else is the gap between myth and reality wider than in the Soviet Union. In 1961, Khrushchev presented the Programme of the 22nd Soviet Party Congress, which claimed that 'the threshold of communism' would be substantially reached by 1980. Full communism (that is, the age of plenty, under the slogan 'From each according to his ability, to each according to his needs') was to be completed in a 'subsequent period', the length of which remained undefined. The dogma that the Soviet State was destined to wither away was repeated, but the means left unstated. This Utopian and unprovable vision of the future was supported by an economic section making concrete claims. One was that by 1970 Soviet industrial production would surpass the American figure for 1961. Another claim, vastly more ambitious, was that by 1970 the Soviet Union would surpass the American figure for the same year (1970) of industrial production *per head of the population.*

One should perhaps not do such propaganda claims the honour of taking them seriously, but since so many people did at the time, it is worth recalling them. One difficulty in verifying Soviet statistical projections is that they are based on unspecified criteria. What, for instance, does 'industry' include – extractive processes, manufacture, semi-manufacture? Is value, weight or number of units the basis of comparison? If value, does one accept the Soviet valuation of the rouble? It should be remembered, moreover, that Western economists attach great importance to the concept of GNP – the sum of the value of all goods and services – whereas Soviet economists (mindful perhaps of their country's paucity of services) discount it entirely.

Whatever the yardstick, however, the 1961 claim was optimistic. On 7 June, addressing the assembled Communists of the world, Mr Brezhnev, head of the Soviet Communist Party, declared: 'In 1960, our industrial output was 55 per cent of that of the United States; in 1968 it was about 70 per cent.' By the Soviet government's own reckoning, therefore, industrial output still fell considerably below that of the United States in global figures. On a *per capita* basis, of course, the disparity would be even greater, since the population of the USSR exceeds that of the US by 25–30 million.

Using Soviet figures, one may calculate that in 1968 Soviet industry was producing about 90 per cent as much as American industry was in 1961. The more modest of the two major claims made at the time of the 22nd Party Congress was therefore attainable by 1970. Short of the kind of miracle that 'scientific' Marxists are supposed to decry, there is no chance whatever that the other claim will be fulfilled. What is often forgotten is that a relatively small percentage growth rate on an economic base as huge as the American one requires a proportionately much higher rate on a smaller base if the lesser economy is to catch up appreciably. Assuming an American industrial production of 160, increasing by 4 per cent annually and a Soviet output of 70 (borrowing

Brezhnev's percentages) it would take a Soviet growth rate of about 8 per cent to improve on US actual growth by about 1½ per cent of the American starting figure. Thus:

Base year, US output — 100   Soviet output — 70
Second year (US)   — 104   USSR   — 75·6

In other words, if the US output grows by 4 per cent and Soviet output by 8 per cent, the Soviet Union will catch up only at the rate of 1·6 per cent per year. Such percentages, however, slightly understate recent American performance, and overstate current Soviet growth. In any case, such comparisons, conducted by Soviet criteria, take no account of quality or variety, the omission of which flatters Soviet performance. The gap between the 1961 promise and current achievement is very wide, and for understandable reasons Soviet propagandists have quietly dropped Khrushchev's claims.

The literary intellectuals are not the only group in the Soviet Union to have become aware of such discrepancies. In recent months, one of the most secure, affluent and previously un-troubled groups — the scientific intelligentsia — have begun to question the philosophical assumptions of the regime. The most striking evidence of this was the critical essay by a leading Soviet physicist, A. D. Sakharov, *Progress Co-existence and Intellectual Freedom.** With astonishing boldness Sakharov compared Stalin's tyranny with Hitler's and pointed to the gap between claims and realities in the Soviet Union. Sakharov was one of the scientists who, in June 1970, questioned the KGB's right to hold the well-known biologist, Dr Jaures Medvedev, in a mental home. (Medvedev was released later.)

The problem of ideological disaffection among the scientific élite has become a major concern of the Communist Party; and as usual, the remedy proposed is still more propaganda and agitation among young scientists. When the myth is questioned because the reality belies it, the remedy proposed by the ruling party is always a reaffirmation of the myth. In economics, Marxist theory has become a hindrance rather than a help, but anti-

* André Deutsch, London, 1968.

Marxist reforms are presented in the name of Marxism. In international affairs, Russia's nationalistic and imperialist invasion of Czechoslovakia is justified in the name of socialist internationalism. The same slogan presides over Moscow's attempts to regain control over the international communist parties. The ideology is bankrupt, but it is constantly restated.

Nor indeed could it be otherwise. The ruling party justifies its monopoly of power on ideological grounds. If it abandoned the claims to ideological purity, it would be discarding the philosophical and indeed moral justification for that monopoly. This is to me the most depressing aspect of recent Soviet history. There is a definite, though not precisely measurable, connection between economic and political freedom. It would not have been possible for Liberman to propose his reforms in the darkest days of Stalin's tyranny. The modest changes he initiated were possible in the relatively freer atmosphere of the 1960s. Conversely, the advent of real consumer choice, though implicit in the Liberman reforms, would imply a much more sweeping liberalization of the Soviet system as a whole than seems at all probable. All experience so far suggests that the ruling group sees all liberalization as a threat to its tenure of power, and is therefore unlikely to create the political climate that would enable economic liberalization to develop and flourish.

The erosion of belief is, however, bound to go on, as the gap between myth and reality widens. The next phase in the Soviet Union is likely to be increasingly dominated by the struggle between the sceptical intellectuals who wish to escape from the straitjacket of ideology and the ruling élite who reaffirm ideology because they have no justification, in terms of efficiency and achievements, for their continued and absolute power. Possible outcomes of this struggle are examined in Part III of this book.

2. *China on the Rampage*

In April 1966, China entered a prolonged period of revolutionary chaos and violence. This is not a new phenomenon in China's long history. What makes it different from anything that has gone

before—and indeed unique in the history of communist regimes—
is that this chaos was *decreed from above*. It was an astonishing
attempt by one man, Mao Tse-tung, to impose his revolutionary
will on this gigantic nation of more than 700 million people. It was
also a struggle for power, between Mao, the creator of the
Chinese People's Republic and the apostle of 'permanent revolution' on the one hand, and on the other, the apparatus of the
Chinese Communist Party, controlled by President Liu Shao-ch'i.
For three years, Mao plunged China into turmoil, disrupting
education and the economy; he also removed Liu from all his
posts, including the Presidency of the Republic. More surprisingly,
he smashed the apparatus of the Communist Party which had
imposed its will on the world's most populous nation, and
rebuilt it in his own image. To some extent, this is what Stalin did
during the years of the great terror; but Mao's objects and
methods were totally different.

To outsiders, and perhaps initially to the Chinese themselves,
the most confusing thing about this period was the fact that what
took place was called 'the great proletarian cultural revolution'.
For if 'revolution' was a fair description, the connection with
culture and the proletariat seemed remote. Indeed, it seems
probable that Mao, who has so often demonstrated his awareness
of the value of subterfuge, did not want people to know what the
cultural revolution was about.

It began, undisturbingly in a communist context, with the kind
of cultural purge familiar to students of communist regimes
everywhere. The initial scapegoat was the playwright, Wu
Han, who had written a play of which Mao Tse-tung disapproved.
The reasons for his disapproval give a clue to the underlying
reasons for the cultural revolution. Its title was *The Dismissal of
Hai Jui*, and the central character, though drawn from Chinese
history, bore a marked resemblance to an important figure in
China's communist revolution, Marshal Peng Teh-huai. Many
ordinary Chinese seeing Wu Han's play might have regarded it
simply as an evocation of the historical past. But the more acute
ones might construe it as a defence of Marshal Peng, who had
been in disgrace for several years. It was this that Mao could not
tolerate. Through Wu Han, he was hitting at the disgraced

Marshal, and at all those prominent members of the Communist Party who supported Peng.

The clash between Mao and Peng had come to a head in 1959, when the Party's Central Committee met at Lushan. Peng, who at that time was the Defence Minister, had rashly attacked Mao's policies of the past few years. Mao's trouble, in Peng's eyes, was 'petty bourgeois mania'. He had tried to go too fast, by attempting to achieve communism in one exhilarating bound through the creation of agricultural communes, and above all by his famous 'great leap forward', launched in 1958, which had flopped because the economic objectives were too ambitious. But there was more to it than Peng disclosed at the time. Peng headed the party group that thought China needed economic aid from somewhere; and since American aid was not, for obvious reasons, available he advocated accepting aid from Russia and being grateful for it, instead of engaging the Russians —as Mao had—in a profitless ideological battle.

By any criterion of commonsense, Peng was right and Mao wrong. But Mao got his way: Peng was disgraced and removed from the Defence Ministry (though not executed). As Peng had foreseen, the Russians withdrew all their technicians and left China to her own economic devices. This was in 1960. Though Mao Tse-tung had defeated Peng Teh-huai, he had not emerged unscathed from the events for which Peng had criticized him, for in April 1960 he was forced to retire from the Chairmanship (Presidency) of the Chinese People's Republic. True, this was a largely honorific post, and Mao remained Chairman of the Communist Party: his retirement was, however, a loss of face in Chinese terms. Moreover, his formidable rival, Liu Shao-ch'i, Vice-Chairman of the Communist Party's Central Committee, stepped into his shoes as Head of State. The net outcome seemed to be that Mao had stepped down and Liu had stepped up.

Typically, as might be expected of the man who had invented protracted peasant's war, Mao chose an indirect strategy. There was no question of a frontal assault on Liu, who was too powerful at the centre. Not only did he control the apparatus of the Chinese Communist Party, which he had largely built up himself, but all that went with it and with the Presidency of the Republic.

Peking was *his* capital, and the *People's Daily* his mouthpiece. Moreover, the Mayor of Peking, Peng Chen, was on his side; so, indeed, was the playwright Wu Han, who was Peng Chen's deputy. Moreover, Liu had other formidable allies, most notably the Secretary-General of the Party's Central Committee, Teng Hsiao-ping, and the Chief of the General Staff of the People's Liberation Army, General Lo Jui-ching. Of these, possibly the most formidable was General Lo, who had been Minister of Public Security until September 1959, and therefore retained links with China's highly organized repressive apparatus.

On paper, at least, Mao's own allies looked somehow less impressive. One was his fourth wife, the former actress Chiang Ching. Another was the man who had replaced Peng Teh-huai as Defence Minister, Marshal Lin-piao; and yet another was the most famous man in China next to Mao himself, Chou En-lai. Not that these personalities were ineffectual. Chiang Ching, once unleashed by her husband, proved a vituperative and fanatical spearhead of the cultural revolution. Chou En-lai was never a man to be underestimated. Though worsted in past clashes with Liu Shao-ch'i, he had revealed a facility, recalling that of Talleyrand, for staying at or near the top. China observers who decided that Mao Tse-tung was bound to win because Chou En-lai supported him were not wrong: political judgement was Chou's strong point. He weakness at the outset was that, unlike Lin and Teng, he had no independent power base.

Marshal Lin was important to Mao because he alone could ensure the support of the majority of the armed forces, which in the end might be decisive. Slightly built and a consumptive, he had a great and deserved reputation as a military tactician, for his prowess both in the revolutionary civil war and in the Korean war. Significantly, Mao had picked him in October 1965 to launch a dramatic call to the peoples of the world to rise up against their imperialist oppressors. The point of this militant appeal lay in the form it took: as in China's own revolutionary war, the 'countryside' of the world was to encircle and overcome the 'cities' of the world. In other words, the under-developed countries of the Third World were to encircle the capitalist countries, headed by the United States. Geographically, this made no sense; but ideologically, it did. It meant that Mao's own doctrine of peasant revolutionary war was to be of world-wide validity. Looking back, one might say that Marshal Lin's call to the peoples of the world was the first shot in the cultural revolution.

Since Peking seemed impregnable as a base, Mao launched his first attack on Liu Shao-ch'i from Shanghai. It was in Lin-piao's mouthpiece, the *Liberation Army Daily*, published in Shanghai, that Wu Han's historical play was first criticized. Had Liu been able to see several moves ahead in the complicated game that was now beginning, he might have saved his career and his power. Instead, he cautiously allowed the *People's Daily* to join in the criticism of Wu. This played into Mao's hands, for the attack soon switched from Wu himself to other supporters of Liu.

To the world at large, the cultural revolution means the hooliganism of the Red Guards. Who were the Red Guards? They were young people of both sexes, many of them teenagers, formed into groups with lightning speed between May and August 1966, as Mao's answer to the twenty million members of the Young Communist League, whose organization was firmly controlled by Liu Shao-ch'i and Teng Hsiao-ping. Already, in the late 1920s, when the Chinese Communist Party was going through its most dismal phase, there had been Red Guards in China, under a slightly different name. The idea of reviving them may have been Mao's, but is more likely to have been suggested to him by an important but relatively little-known figure, who came into the news about this time. This was Mao Tse-tung's former political secretary, Chen Po-ta who, with Mao's wife, was given control of the Central Cultural Revolutionary Group, which in turn controlled the Red Guards. It was a bold and dangerous weapon. In effect, Mao turned the youth of the country into young hooligans, then turned them loose on the country.

From this point forward, everything was fair game and nothing was sacred. 'Old' and 'bad' were equated. Everything old was bad: the thoughts and customs of old China, her traditions and habits. Equally, everything Western, bourgeois, capitalist was a target for the wantonness of the Red Guards. This indeed was revolution. There was no question of preserving anything that was good, wise or civilized in China's age-old past, before the modern contaminations of the Western intruders. For the best part of a year, the youth of China was on the rampage. Old people were molested, historic buildings defaced or pillaged, government officials humiliated and Party leaders frog-marched through the streets.

Among those ill-used in this way were Peng Chen and Teng Hsiao-ping, both of whom lost their jobs. Liu Shao-ch'i himself was placed under house arrest, repeatedly denounced for revisionism and given the pejorative label of 'China's Khrushchev'. In time, the epithets became more lurid. When the Central Committee met in October 1968, he was called a 'renegade, traitor and scab' and for good measure, 'a lackey of imperialism ... who has committed innumerable crimes'. It was resolved to expel him from the Party and remove him from all his posts, both in the Party and the government. By this time, Marshal Lin Piao had clearly emerged as Mao's successor, followed in the Party hierarchy by the adaptable Chou En-lai. The new power structure was confirmed in April 1969, when the Chinese Communist Party held its ninth Congress and Lin-piao was formally designated as Mao's successor.

Mao, then, had won. The fact that he had, bearing in mind the initial weakness of his position and the apparently irrational methods he used, is perhaps the most puzzling aspect of a generally incomprehensible affair. Both his methods and his victory are, however, intelligible in a Chinese context and in the special circumstances that faced Mao Tse-tung in the mid-1960s. Between 1959 and 1966, control of the Communist Party and its bureaucracy had gradually slipped out of Mao's hands. At the same time, the revolution—Mao's revolution—was settling down into a mould familiar to students of Marxist revolutions: a bureaucratic, self-contented mould, with a privileged élite (Djilas's 'new class') controlling affairs and forgetting the fervour that had inspired the revolutionaries during their years of struggle. The 'mass line' — a peculiarly Chinese contribution to Marxism, whereby the ruling party tries to understand the aspirations of the inarticulate masses, interpret them in Marxist-Maoist terms and impose them in the form of policies upon the whole population—was being forgotten.

Since Mao could no longer rely on the Party, he opted for direct and demagogic action from outside, imposing his own mass line on the Party through the Red Guards, with the support of such prominent Party leaders as were willing to associate their own future with his success. Such was the force of his prestige and personality that he was able not only to plunge the whole country into turmoil but also to shake the Party from top to bottom, purging his opponents and reconstructing the apparatus. In the process, he reasserted his own absolute power and reimposed 'permanent revolution' as a way of life and a continuing policy. By his own terms of reference, the cultural revolution was logically consistent.

From our standpoint, however, the questions of interest are these. Where did the cultural revolution leave China? How much of the original revolution was left? What kind of a revolutionary regime was it, twenty years after Mao's victory in the Chinese civil war? To answer these questions, it is necessary to glance briefly at the recent past, under appropriate headings.

Power
Having come to power virtually unaided Mao Tse-tung rapidly set up a totalitarian regime that differed from Stalin's in several respects, both in the form and in the techniques of imposition. The 'national united front' which Mao had created during the civil war to help defeat Chiang Kai-shek's Kuomintang survived the creation of the People's Republic, in the sense that several minor political parties are tolerated. But they have no power independent of the will of the Communist Party. Mao was less concerned to liquidate people physically than Stalin was, although capable of doing it when it seemed necessary. About 830,000 Chinese were executed after the civil war. They were described as landlords, reactionaries, irreconcilable members of the Kuomintang or simply bandits and war lords. This was a high figure, but relatively to China's population a fraction of the millions put to death at Stalin's orders. Mao relied less on the

secret police and more on his technique of mass persuasion. The Communist Party, which eventually numbered about seventeen million members, had its branches all over China, including every village however remote, and nearly every street of every town. *It became impossible to opt out of politics in China.* Whether one was interested or not, one *had* to take part in political indoctrination courses, and be prepared to stand up and confess deviant thoughts. For those who resisted such treatment, often extended into weeks of pressure, including night sessions designed to break the will by deprivation of sleep, there were always the labour reform camps, where the indoctrination continued.

Apart from the categories I have mentioned, and such individuals as naturally rebelled against the Party's authority, class enemies as such were not eliminated as they had been in Russia. Lenin had murdered or exiled Russia's capitalists; Mao turned them into factory managers and even paid them interest on their confiscated assets. Everything was harnessed to politics, and this included religion. All church property was taken over by the State, and the Party set up parallel religious organizations, in competition with the existing ones. For instance, no Christian might join the Party; but a National Christian Council was set up, which of course supported 'socialism'. There was also a Chinese Catholic Patriotic Association, but it had no truck with the Vatican. The Buddhist temples were carefully preserved, together with a small priesthood; but only as quaint museum pieces of China's feudal past. There were fifty million Moslems in China, and they could, if they so desired, join the Party; but only if they declared themselves atheists.

This all-embracing system, more totalitarian than any other for all its apparent tolerance, accomplished many things and transformed the face of the vast country, so that those who had known it in earlier times found it unrecognizable. Cleanliness became universal. Beggars and prostitutes vanished. Even flies were eliminated. No longer were girl babies abandoned in the streets to die of exposure and hunger. No longer did people starve: the rations might be slender, but each had his share. The complicated Chinese ideographic system was simplified and literacy bounded forward.

As in other communist countries, but more so, ideology became the handmaiden of political power. Mao Tse-tung's own advent to power had, as he preached during the revolutionary civil war, grown 'out of the barrel of the gun'. But once he had achieved it, guns were out of sight and in reserve. Ideology was the device to enforce conformity, and the only question that dominated the struggle for power at different stages was: whose ideology? Officially, of course, the Party's power rested on the dogmas of Marxism-Leninism. But the true State ideology was Maoism, and Maoism was essentially whatever Mao decided to say or write at any time. His doctrines of protracted war and peasant revolution were Maoism. But so was his view that the creation of gigantic agricultural communes could usher the communist millennium almost overnight. For many years, before he was deposed, Liu Shao-ch'i had been regarded as the official ideologist, and his short work, *How to be a Good Communist*, written in 1939, was held up as a classic. But when Mao decreed that Liu was a revisionist and reactionary, *How to be a Good Communist* became an essay in 'self-cultivation'. There was, indeed, only one ideologist who counted, and that was Mao Tse-tung. The little red book containing his Thoughts became the repository of all Chinese communist wisdom, and was waved ecstatically by Chinese of all ages wherever they might be.

To an outside observer, however, the greatest revisionist of them all was Mao himself. Marx and Lenin had preached urban revolution. It was an ideological impudence on Mao's part to come to power through peasant revolt. The Russians knew that communism could no more be built in a day than Rome was. Yet Mao said it could come almost immediately through the creation of agricultural communes. The Russians were not alone in finding this instant communism distasteful or Utopian. But Mao, and Mao alone, could bend or break the ideological rules and get away with it. In 1957, he astonished the world and his own people by announcing that henceforth he would let 'a hundred flowers bloom, a hundred schools of thought contend'. Many intellectuals rushed to take advantage of this new freedom of speech and writing. Mao Tse-tung was probably taken aback by the volume and vehemence of the opposition revealed during this turbulent period. But one advantage it had brought was undeniable: the opposition had been forced into the open. Predictably, a massive purge ensued. Once again, ideology had been harnessed in the service of power. And so it was in the still more turbulent period of the great proletarian cultural revolution. In ideological terms, no greater heresy could be conceived than the technique of turning the youthful mobsters loose and smashing the elaborate structure of the Communist Party. But in the end, it paid off on Mao's terms.

By 1969, the Red Guards themselves had been disciplined and brought under control. Power resided, as always, in Mao's own hands. Beneath him, a reconstituted Communist Party stood for 'permanent revolution'. And the guns whose barrels held the final sanction of power were in the grip of soldiers and officers of the People's Liberation Army, themselves conditioned to the new Maoism. At times, during the early stages of the cultural revolution, the Army's loyalty was, however, doubtful. The attitude of many Army commanders was to stand on the sidelines and restore order when it was threatened. But there were some local military revolts and clashes, especially in the central, southern and western provinces. The Western press, by and large, had fallaciously labelled the Army factions pro-Mao and anti-Mao; but by 1968, it was plain that every local commander, however dissident in appearance, was a Maoist. Some, however, were more Maoist than others. At the end of the cultural revolution, the Army was politically more powerful than it had been. But its politics were those of the cultural revolution, as enunciated by Mao and interpreted by Lin-piao. The new Party, in fact, permeated the armed forces.

There was of course a great gulf between these political realities and the formal provisions of the Constitution. The National People's Congress, or parliament, is supposed to be the highest organ of State authority (Article 21) and the sole legislative authority in the country (Artical 22). It is supposed to meet at least once a year and to have the power to amend the Constitution with a two-thirds majority vote of all the deputies. In reality, however, the National People's Congress does what it is told to do by the Communist Party; which in turn, as events have shown, takes its orders from Chairman Mao. In fact, the National People's Congress has not met since September 1964. For that matter, the Communist Party is supposed to meet in Congress very year. But it did not meet between the second session of the Eighth Congress in 1958 and the Ninth in April 1969—a gap of eleven years. This prolonged failure to convene was a measure of the intensity of the power struggle within China.

Economics
People's China conformed to the normal communist model in that the Communist Party opted for centralized planning and a concentration on the development of heavy industry, to the relative detriment of agriculture. The first five-year plan was launched in January 1953. By then, the State had expropriated both the landlords and the capitalists. Between 1955 and 1956, the land that had been taken away from the landlords and re-distributed to the peasants was taken back and collective farms were set up. Collectivization was completed in 1957. By the time the first plan was completed, at the end of 1957, considerable successes had been achieved. New light industries had been set up and overall production was said to have risen by about sixty per cent. Steel production had risen fast, to reach 5·2 million tons during the last year of the first plan.

For the second plan, which began in January 1958, however, the Chinese leaders set their sights considerably higher. Mao Tse-tung himself intervened to declare that a 'great leap forward' was to be launched. By this time, China's population exceeded 600 million people, and this vast mass was to be mobilized in a tremendous effort which, at one bound, was to carry the People's Republic forward over the threshold of 'communism'. People's Communes were to be set up all over China; and indeed, almost overnight, the 750,000 collective farms were merged into vast communes—26,000 of them—in which the individual was virtually to lose his identity. From that point forward, meals were served in communal messes, and the peasants had to sleep in communal dormitories, with one room reserved for husbands and wives to be together at predetermined times for their matrimonial duties. Urban communes, too, were set up in the towns and cities

73

based upon the factories; though these were a failure virtually from the start.

Looking back on this curious episode, it may well be that the great leap forward was not entirely without benefit. But its achievements fell far short of expectations to the extent that it might be fair to call it the 'great fall downward'. It is an open question whether future historians will decide to date Mao's madness from 1958 — the year of the great leap forward, and the Communes — or 1957 — the year of the 'hundred flowers'. Certainly the year of the great leap forward was punctuated by an ever-rising crescendo of mass hysteria inspired from above. Almost lyrical exhortations to the people were supplemented by new and ever more extravagant production targets. The Chinese were enjoined to produce steel in their back yards — and the landscape was dotted with the so-called 'backyard furnaces' that were to give China a yearly output of eleven million tons of steel. Faced with these extraordinary demands, the local Party leaders falsified the figures wholesale. That falsification had indeed taken place was officially admitted in Peking in August 1959, when it was announced that the 1958 grain harvest did not exceed 250 million tons, whereas a fantastic crop of 375 million tons had been claimed earlier. As for steel, eleven million tons had been claimed, but now only eight million tons was said to be 'usable in industry'. This was, of course, considerably higher than the actual 1957 figure of 5·2 millions, but terrible damage had been done to the economy in attempting to reach impossible targets.

China is vast and mineral deposits are far from the centres of industry. Transport is therefore vital, and the whole transport system was clogged and brought to a standstill by official directives to carry scrap iron and home-made 'steel' from place to place. Cancellations of orders for China's traditional exports flowed in from Western Europe as more and more goods failed to get shipped by stated times. And now nature intervened with three years of freak weather and low harvests. Industrial production may have dropped to little more than one-third of the 1957 figure in that period. Food was short, and in some provinces — notably Kwangtung — famine was barely avoided. No more was heard of the second five-year plan, which apparently petered out in a maze of unsatisfactory statistics. Indeed, from 1960 the Chinese stopped issuing meaningful statistics at all. That is, they stopped issuing figures of actual production; instead, they gave meaningless figures of claimed percentage increases—as happened in the Soviet Union during the early five-year plans.

Undoubtedly, however, there was some measure of recovery between 1962 and 1966. But in January 1967, Mao ordered the cultural revolution to be extended to the agricultural and industrial sectors, which until then had been shielded from the excesses of the Red Guards—who had already done much to disrupt the transport system. Mao and his followers had been calling on them to travel round the country, emulate the Long March and exchange revolutionary experience with their contemporaries. When the cultural revolution was extended to the farms and factories, disruption turned to total chaos. Rural workers drafted to the countryside seized their chance of returning to the towns. The workers took the opportunity to travel to Peking and other main centres to press revolutionary demands for better wages and working conditions. In the prevailing state of the economy, such demands could not be met. Thereupon, some workers struck or went slow—both because their revolutionary aspirations had been frustrated and to indicate their disapproval of the Red Guards, who were busy smashing up the factories.

On 1 September 1967, Chou En-lai was reported to have said that China was six months behind in production. Violent clashes took place in the great industrial centres, such as Changchun, Shanghai, Lanchow, Shenyang and Chengtu. Coal, steel and iron output dropped catastrophically—perhaps by half in the case of coal. Strike and riots disrupted turn-around in the ports. Some cargoes were held up for three months. Exports fell to Britain, West Germany and France, and even more to Japan and Hong Kong.

By its very nature, there was no plan in the cultural revolution. It lurched this way and that, and there were periods of calm. Fortunately, the planting of summer and autumn crops took place during such periods. The harvest was therefore adequate, but there was great difficulty in collecting and distributing supplies because the transport system had been disrupted. Not surprisingly, all central planning seems to have come to an end during this violent year.

By 1968 even Mao Tse-tung appears to have decided that the cultural revolution had gone too far, or at any rate far enough. Lawlessness in various parts of the great republic had become a major problem. The Shanghai paper *Wen Hui Pao* commenting on three readers' letters published on 4 August 1968, declared war on 'a small band of hooligans and teddy boys, a reactionary partisan force of the class enemy'. From Mao's point of view, the cultural revolution, although it had inflicted great damage on China's economy and administrations, had served its purpose. It had removed his opponents; it had created a nation-wide revolutionary mood; and it had made it possible for him to smash the existing Communist Party and replace it with one of his own choosing. Accordingly, in 1968, new Revolutionary Committees were set up in all China's twenty-nine major administrative areas, to replace the old Party and government structures. It was these committees that dominated the Ninth Congress of the Party, which was at last convened in April 1969.

Technology

There is some evidence that the nuclear and guided missiles industries were originally to be protected from the attentions of the Red Guards. At any rate, on 8 August 1966, the Party's Central Committee announced that scientists and technicians had nothing to fear if they were 'patriotic', did their work properly without opposing the Party, and had 'no improper association with foreign countries'. But the Red Guards, once unleashed, were hard to restrain. It was difficult to tell the young hooligans: 'Thou shalt make revolution here, but not there'. For years, Mao had talked and written about the collective genius of the people. Innumerable speeches and Party documents had made it clear that it was more important to be 'red' than expert. Teachers and even university professors had been sent into the fields to plough and collect refuse and clean latrines. The people's genius was supposed to enable it to produce steel in 1958, though failure was later recognized. In these circumstances it was unrealistic to expect the Red Guards to refrain from molesting the small band of men, some of them authentic geniuses and all highly trained, whose job was to give China a modern weapons system.

To give one instance, Nieh Jung-chen, chairman of the State Council's Scientific and Technological Commission and probably the man in charge of nuclear development, was attacked in the Red Guard press in January and May 1967, although he had been defended by no less a person than Chen Po-ta, the main organizer of the Cultural Revolution. In May 1968, leading nuclear scientists were attacked for revisionism (and in one case for being a secret enemy agent). Indeed, if Mao's supporters had hoped to make an exception of the scientific community, they had reckoned without Mao himself, whose instructions on technical training, issued on 21 July 1968, stressed the importance of practical labour, as opposed to theoretical research, and called for resistance to foreign and revisionist views, such as those of Liu Shao-ch'i ('China's Khrushchev'). These instructions were interpreted as a sanction to molest scientists and technicians. As a result, work was brought to a standstill in the Seventh Ministry of Machine Building, probably the controlling body for the production of atomic weapons and missiles.

Once again, then, Mao Tse-tung's personal intervention had slowed down progress that previously had been faster than outside experts had expected. China's first atomic bomb was exploded on 16 October 1964; and on 17 June 1967, her first hydrogen bomb was dropped from the air. Some months earlier, on 27 October 1966, the Chinese press had announced a 'guided missile-nuclear weapon test'. These dates were all indicative of rapid progress. But when Mao's Cultural Revolution caught up with the scientists, intervals between tests began to lengthen, and in mid-September, the authoritative publication of the Institute for Strategic Studies in London— *The Military Balance* — reported a slowing down in the production of fissile material and in missile development, which it tentatively attributed to 'political harassment of the small scientific community engaged on the programme'.

How, then, is one to summarize China's experience of Communism? For the first nine years from 1949, progress was undoubtedly rapid; though it might have been equally rapid if the Kuomintang had vanquished in the Chinese civil war, for the Chinese are an industrious and able people, whose progress had been held up by seventeen years of civil and international strife. Once again, as in Russia, however, the communist system had fostered the emergence of an absolute dictator with megalomaniac tendencies. Mao was the new emperor of China. He had reconquered Tibet and fought the United States to a standstill in Korea. He had given China nuclear weapons. But he had also disrupted the educational system, damaged the economy and erected hooliganism into a State policy. After twenty years of Maoism, China was still—in all sectors except the nuclear one—a backward and over-populated country. Under a system of free economy, her nearest rival, Japan, had soared ahead to become the third industrial power in the world. In comparison, China—with its 700 million people or more—still lagged well behind Britain, with less than one-thirteenth of her population. In 1958, Mao had proclaimed that China would overtake Britain's gross national product in fifteen years. Like so many communist prophecies, this one was shattered by the unpleasant realities of actual performance. And the price paid for this inadequate achievement was distressingly high, both in human lives and in mental torture. The best estimate in 1969 was that China's concentration camps still held between 10 million and 15 million people. For the people, at least, unemployment might seem a preferable condition.

3. *The Satellites*

Many things have changed in Russia's East European Empire since Stalin's death. It could scarcely be otherwise, once Stalin's iron grip had been removed and Khrushchev had denounced his misdeeds. But the interesting thing is not that Moscow's control has weakened but that it has remained so strong. Today there is greater diversity between the satellites*, both individually and in

---

* After 1956 it became fashionable to call them ex-satellites, but after the occupation of Czechoslovakia in 1968, the earlier term again seemed appropriate.

relation to the Soviet Union, than in Stalin's day. But two things have not changed. One is that all the original satellites remain communist. This goes for Yugoslavia, which successfully defied Stalin in 1947, and Albania, which opted for China in the Sino-Soviet dispute. Different from each other though they may be, however, they resemble each other more closely than any of them resembles, say, Britain or France. The other unchanging factor is that Russia claims—and indeed has solemnly reasserted—the right to intervene by force in the affairs of her neighbours to the west. It is even possible that this claim extends to Yugoslavia; though the matter has yet to be put to the test.

To what, it may be asked, must this astonishing persistence be attributed? To the unshakeable nature of a communist dictatorship, or to the physical proximity of Russia? The experience of recent history in Eastern Europe suggests that the two causes are inextricably mixed. In Rumania, for instance, the adoption of a nationalist foreign policy did not affect the Stalinist character of the regime at home, and the Party's hold on power remained unshaken through the dangerous 1950s and 1960s. In Czechoslovakia, the Party wavered; and the Russians intervened in an attempt to restore the original tyranny in the name of 'socialism'. In conjunction, the Rumanian and Czechoslovak experiences suggest that for the people of Eastern Europe, it is Heads the Communists win, Tails the people lose. Either the home-grown tyrants would stay in power, or the Russians would see that the tyranny went on.

The hopes that flared passionately in eastern Europe in the autumn of 1956 were dashed, but not immediately or entirely. For several years, Gomulka's Poland was inspiringly free. Polish journalists could write more or less what they pleased—though they always had to be careful of what they said about the Russians—and took full advantage of their liberty. Artists could paint with a new freedom, and dramatists stage the plays of their dreams. The Poles began to travel to Western Europe, and came back full of what they had seen. For those who stayed behind, Western newspapers were available. The Poles talked of their 'October Revolution', and it really meant something. They still do, but by now a wistful or cynical note has crept in. For somewhere between 1956 and 1960, the clock had stopped, and Gomulka was afraid or reluctant to wind it again.

There was a tragic paradox in Gomulka's position. In effect, he had been the first 'revisionist' in Eastern Europe, taking his cue from Khrushchev's speeches of February 1956. Apart from Yugoslavia, which no longer fully belonged to the Soviet bloc, his government had been the first in communist Europe to in-augurate economic reform. The land was virtually decollectivized. But in 1959, strict control from the centre was reimposed on several branches of the economy. Three years earlier, workers' councils had been set up; but in 1958 they were replaced by 'Self-Government Conferences', with reduced powers. True, four Polish factories were given the right, in July 1964, to export and import without Party control. And in July 1965, industrial enterprises were told that they must show a profit or suffer the consequences. None of this, however, led to any improvement in the standard of living. And in 1964, the Plan and Budget drearily prescribed increased investment in industry; depriving schools and housing, welfare and consumer goods of available resources.

The Polish people were told by their leaders in 1959 that there were no political prisoners left. This was an exaggeration, though many had indeed been released; for in July 1964, some 33,000 people were released under a new amnesty. True, their 'offences' were described as 'administrative' or 'economic'. But this deceived nobody; for in most non-communist countries, the admini-strative and economic offences listed would not have been punishable. A year earlier, Gomulka had declared revisionism to be still the greatest danger to the ruling party. From the original satellite revisionists, these were strong words. As early as November 1961, he had boasted that 'revisionist tendencies' had been overcome, along with 'dogmatism and sectarianism'. In plain English, this was a claim of absolute doctrinal purity and unity. Neither Stalin's teachings nor Khrushchev's, nor yet Mao Tse-tung's prevailed; or so Gomulka said. But here he was, in 1961, calling for an intensification of ideological training.

Meanwhile, Gomulka's running fight with the church, in the person of Cardinal Wyszynski, continued and continues to this day. On the cultural front, the Poles remain freer than some of their neighbours, but the rate of decline in this respect has been gathering speed. They may still read Western newspapers. The writers have repeatedly clashed with authority, as symbolized by the Party-controlled Polish Writers' Union. Inexorably, supporters of the orthodox communist line, irrespective of literary merit, have excluded the dissidents and maintained themselves in office. In January 1969, two Warsaw university lecturers were gaoled for three and a half years each, for 'anti-State activity' and alleged contacts with the (Trotskyist) Fourth International. The students, too, were regimented in a way that would be intolerable to New Left agitators in the West. In February 1969, the Congress of the Polish Students' Union, meeting in Warsaw, declared patriotism to be inseparable from acceptance of the system as it stood. This was the price the students paid for widespread rioting in March 1968.

By now, little indeed is left of Poland's 'October Revolution'. Things have changed, since 1956, but not always for the better. By the late 1960s, Poland was beginning to resemble not so much the Soviet Union as a dead and dreadful enemy, Nazi Germany. For under the ruthless direction of the Minister of the Interior, General Moczar, the regime had launched a vicious anti-Semitic campaign, which affected many prominent Polish Jews in influential positions. Perhaps 8,000 Jews (of 30,000 who survived Nazi persecution) left Poland for good during the campaign, which began with the Six-Day War in the Middle East and reached fresh peaks with the student riots of March 1968 and the invasion of Czechoslovakia.

Hungary's experience after 1956 was in a sense the converse of Poland's. The Hungarians had no 'October Revolution' to look back on; only the traumatic memory of a mass uprising ruthlessly repressed by Soviet arms. Within three months of taking over from Imre Nagy on 4 November 1956, Kadar had restored many of the repressive features of the regime the Hungarian people had tried to overthrow. Summary jurisdiction was established against 'counter-revolutionary elements, professional criminals, irresponsible trouble-makers, and other persons not entitled to possess arms'. Here again, as in Gomulka's case, there was a

F

paradox. Kadar himself had suffered torture in the cells of Hungary's notorious secret police, the AVH. Now, however, he set up a new security police, turning to former AVH members for his recruits. Strikes were outlawed, and many students and professors arrested. Strict supervision of the press was re-established and unauthorized public meetings and demonstrations were banned.

Then, in 1961, Kadar announced a policy of national unity and reconciliation. Already, on 1 April 1960, he had declared a partial amnesty, suspending jail sentences of six years or less for political offences committed before 1 May 1957, and abolishing detention without trial. Many prominent prisoners were indeed released. In March 1963, a further amnesty extended freedom to those held for political offences committed since 1945. In July that year, Kadar claimed that no Hungarian remained in jail for political beliefs. In harmony with this more 'liberal' policy, the privileges of the secret police had gradually been reduced.

In the second half of the decade, therefore, the average Hungarian could breathe more easily and sleep more soundly at night. Moreover, he could buy more for his money. In earlier years, exorbitant taxes had been imposed, which stifled any attempt at private enterprise. Under Kadar's new policy, taxes were reduced and more private craftsmen were given permits to practise their trade. As in other communist countries, there was official recognition that private plots cultivated by collective farm workers in their spare time made a disproportionate contribution to the nation's food resources. Previously attempts at private cultivation had been frowned upon or actively repressed; now it was officially encouraged.

Hungary remained—and remains—a communist country. As in other such countries, two steps forward were invariably followed by one step back, if not more. As Kadar himself said on 11 May 1963, in a comment on the recent amnesty: 'The cells are there . . . and those who want to get there . . . shall get there.' In July that year he had claimed that there were no political prisoners left, but there is strong evidence that several hundred of them still languished in State gaols. Besides, the amnesties for past offences did not imply political freedom for the present or future. On 11 December 1964, for instance, five people were jailed for long terms for attempting to set up a political party — an illegal one by definition, since the Communist Party retained a monopoly of power. In August 1965, three other Hungarians were gaoled for setting up a 'hostile anti-State organization'.

Instructive though the Polish and Hungarian examples are, it is to Rumania and Czechoslovakia that one must turn to grasp the limits of change in communist Europe. Here again is a study in contrast. When Stalin died, there was little to choose, politically speaking, between the two countries, which in common with the satellite regimes had been fashioned in a mould made in Moscow; at home, a police State under a monopolistic party; abroad, a gramophone echoing Moscow's words and executing Soviet policy. In the 1960s, the Rumanian communists challenged Moscow's assumption that the foreign policy of a European 'Socialist' country must invariably obey Soviet dictates. And the Czechs briefly experimented with 'liberal communism' at home. Abroad, however, the Czechs continued to follow Moscow's line; while at home, the Rumanians maintained Party orthodoxy, varied only by appeals to Rumanian nationalism.

What happened in both countries can perhaps be best explained in terms of the personalities of four men; the Rumanians, Gheorghiu-Dej and Ceausescu; and the Czechoslovaks, Novotny and Dubcek. Gheorghiu-Dej and Novotny represented the old Stalinist order, and Ceausescu and Dubcek were the new men. Gheorghiu-Dej, who died in 1965, was the perfect Stalinist autocrat. As Secretary-General of the Rumanian Workers' Party (PMR),* his power was absolute. In the government, until Stalin's death, he was merely the first Deputy Prime Minister, but he had complete charge of economic affairs. In his eyes, Stalin and the Soviet Union provided the example, to be imitated and obeyed. While he ran Rumania's economic affairs, mixed Soviet-Rumanian companies were milking the country for Russia's benefit. After Stalin's death, his deeply-engrained habit of slavish imitation persisted. In Russia, Stalin's heir-apparent Malenkov had resigned his Party post in favour of the premiership, in the interests of what was called 'collective' leadership.

* Renamed the Rumanian Communist Party in 1965.

In Rumania, Gheorghiu-Dej did the same. Later, when Malenkov was replaced by Khrushchev, Gheorghiu-Dej gave up the premiership and returned to the Party's official leadership. This was in October 1955. He duly attended the 20th and 21st Congresses of the Soviet Communist Party and the 1960 World Communist Conference. In each case, he dutifully came home and advocated imitation of the Soviet example.

In every way, he was prepared to serve Soviet interests. For instance, he offered to detain Imre Nagy, the deposed Hungarian Premier, after the 1956 uprising. And the following year, he provided a secret Rumanian meeting-place for Tito of Yugoslavia and Khrushchev when the two leaders met to patch the differences that had arisen after the Soviet suppression of the Hungarians. For years, however, he resisted all suggestions that Rumania should follow Khrushchev's example and 'de-Stalinize'. One of his difficulties was that Rumania had a large Hungarian minority, which demonstrated its sympathy with the Hungarians in 1956. In December that year, Gheorghiu-Dej attended the regional Party congress in the so-called Hungarian autonomous region, and delivered the following warning: 'We cannot and never will agree to that liberalization which would give the enemies of the people a free hand to strike at the socialist conquests of the people or to impede the dictatorship of the Proletariat.'

As time went on, however, Gheorghiu-Dej faced the penalty of unpopularity, inherent in the unchanging repressiveness of his regime and in his country's stagnant economy. Something had to be done. To liberalize was unthinkable, an impossibility to one of Gheorghiu-Dej's character and training. But if he could resist such calls as reached him for a measure of liberalization, there was no need for him to turn an equally deaf ear to those who appealed for a show of Rumanian nationalism. Since he was no more a patriot than he was a liberal, flag-waving did not come naturally to him. But economic independence seemed a safe way of complying with the demand for self-assertion, and one which, moreover, was consistent with the consolidation of the communist regime. Accordingly, it was in the realm of economic relations within the Soviet bloc that Gheorghiu-Dej took action.

The body that supervises these international economic relations is usually known as Comecon, though its real name is the Council for Mutual Economic Aid or CMEA. In Stalin's day, the key word was autarky: each satellite economy was to be a carbon copy of the Soviet original, with the emphasis on heavy industry, to the relative detriment of agriculture and consumer goods. In effect, however, Comecon had been a clearing-house for the Soviet Union's colonial exploitation of the satellites. Khrushchev and his associates had different ideas for Comecon. Instead of autarky, the motto became 'international division of labour'. In other words, each component of the Soviet bloc was to concentrate on the things it could do best, to the benefit of the bloc as a whole, and of the Soviet Union in particular. In the new Comecon, Rumania had been cast in an agricultural role. But this did not suit Gheorghiu-Dej at all: Stalinist autarky had given Rumania the beginnings of industrialization, and having acquired the taste, the Rumanians wanted more of the same. In 1962, the Rumanian delegates to Comecon stated their views. As far as they were concerned, there was to be no supra-national planning. Some co-ordination of national development plans was possible, of course, but national interests must be respected. In mid-1963, the Russians summoned the economic leaders of all member-States to Moscow to discuss the Rumanian hostility to supra-national planning. But the Rumanians stood their ground: and got their own way.

At the next full meeting, held in Prague at the end of January 1965, Comecon announced that economic co-operation between member-States had progressed 'in full conformity with the principles of equality, respect for sovereignty and national interests, mutual advantage, and comradely mutual assistance'. Since 1963, said the communiqué, the East European power grid had been extended to Rumania, a joint oil pipeline had been completed and a common pool of railway wagons set up.

Having asserted his country's right to independence in economic affairs, Gheorghiu-Dej began, belatedly, to free his political prisoners. The penal code, already severe, had been made harsher still after the Polish and Hungarian events of 1956. For instance, a new capital offence was created: that of having dealings with foreigners in an attempt to persuade Rumania to declare her neutrality. The dread *Securitate* was ever-present and unfailingly ruthless. There were more than 10,000 political prisoners, many of them starved or tortured. Between 1963 and 1964, however, all of them were released, often in pitiful physical condition.

Shortly after the economic confrontation in Moscow, Gheorghiu-Dej died. Into his shoes stepped Nicolae Ceausescu, who was elected First Party Secretary on 22 March 1965. He was forty-seven: that is, he belonged to the generation born after the Russian Revolution. His whole adult life had been spent in the ruthless political manoeuvring of Rumanian communism. Unlike the generation of East European leaders who had grown up to venerate Russia as the 'home of socialism', Ceausescu was an impassioned nationalist. As early as the 1960 Party Congress in Rumania, he had come out as an aggressive advocate of greater economic independence for his country. It was largely because of his determined eloquence within the Party that Rumania had opted for neutrality in the Sino-Soviet dispute — the first ruling Communist Party to take this stand. He and the Prime Minister, Maurer, had led a mission to Peking in March 1964 in an unsuccessful attempt to mediate between the Chinese and Russians. Characteristically, Ceausescu had an important part in the drafting of a resounding Rumanian 'declaration of independence' issued by the ruling party on 26 April 1964. That was not, of course, what it was called; but the message that the Rumanians would find their own way to communism without Russian interference came through loud and clear.

Soon, Ceausescu was making the kind of ringing nationalistic speeches which his predecessor would never have dared to make. Especially by communist standards, there was a certain flamboyant daring about his speeches, which went down very well with Rumanian audiences. In June 1966, for instance, on a speaking tour in the provinces, he lavished praise on the nineteenth-century Rumanian revolutionary and historian, Nicolae Balcescu. This was the second time he had referred to this hero of the past. On 7 May, in a major speech on the forty-fifth anniversary of the Rumanian party, he had quoted passages from Balcescu's work denouncing Russia's treatment of the Rumanian principalities in 1848 as 'satellites, forever destined to move within her sphere and her pleasure'. The full flavour of this reference did not, however, become apparent until the printed text of Ceausescu's speech was published. It contained a footnote explaining that the quotation from Balcescu had been taken, not from the expurgated communist edition of 1953 but from the banned 'bourgeois' edition of 1940. In the same speech, incidentally, he had praised the 'bourgeois' politician Titulescu, who had often championed Rumania's claim to Bessarabia. The point of this reference to a once denounced politician of Rumania's past was not lost on his audience, for twenty-six years earlier the Soviet Union had annexed Bessarabia.

The interesting point about such nationalist assertions was that Ceausescu could get away with it. No threatening Soviet army massed upon Rumania's border. No Soviet-manufactured crisis broke about his head. Indeed, the Russians showed every sign of wanting to treat him with kid gloves. In his speech of 7 May 1966, Ceausescu had gone so far as to refer to the ana-chronism of military pacts—a reference that could apply to the Warsaw Pact as well as to Nato. This time, it is true, the Russians did react, by sending their Party boss, Brezhnev, to Bucharest on an unheralded visit. The result was interesting. On 11 June, during his provincial tour, Ceausescu again called for the disbanding of all military blocs in Europe; but he did add, in obvious deference to Soviet views, that so long as Nato continued to 'threaten' Eastern Europe, the Warsaw Pact members, including Rumania, would need to continue to build up their military strength. Five days later, he was host to the Chinese Premier, Chou En-lai, who stayed a whole week. Little was accomplished, but Ceausescu had again demonstrated his independence of the Soviet Union.

On the economic side, he continued to resist any attempt by Comecon to impose its rules upon Rumania. The Rumanians, in fact, were discovering that their programme of industrialization could be furthered only if Rumania improved her economic links with Western countries. If Comecon found this disagreeable, then as far as Ceausescu was concerned, it was too bad for Comecon. It was part of the logic of this situation that Rumania should encourage Western tourists to visit their country, and contribute to Rumania's economic development with their

87

expenditure of hard foreign currencies. And this in turn implied a few further measures of visible 'liberalization'. Already, in Gheorghiu-Dej's latter years, the French daily *Le Monde* had been on sale in small numbers in Bucharest. Now the Rumanians went further still, in such curious ways as staging exhibitions of abstract art, thought to be pleasing to Western visitors, and previously condemned as bourgeois and decadent. For good measure, the internationally famous Rumanian sculptor, Brancusi, was rehabilitated.

One thing was plain, however; there was never the slightest intention on the part of Ceausescu or other Rumanian communist leaders to extend political freedom to those who might disapprove of a communist regime. The party maintained its iron grip on all aspects of life in Rumania. Indeed, Ceausescu's underlying political motive in laying such bold emphasis on Rumanian patriotism was to make his regime more popular by identifying communism and nationalism. In his speech of 11 June 1966, he had more or less said so, by claiming that the Communists were 'the continuers of the best traditions of the Rumanian people'. To say this is not, of course, to question the sincerity of Ceausescu's nationalism; but it cannot be doubted that his sincerity served the legitimate political objective of consolidating his hold on power.

The acid test of his assertion of Rumanian independence came with the Czechoslovak crisis in 1968. Alone among member States of the Warsaw Treaty, Rumania refused to contribute troops to the Soviet-commanded army that occupied Czechoslovakia on 21 August. Again, Rumania was alone within the Warsaw Treaty in denouncing the occupation. On the day of the invasion, Ceausescu announced the formation of 'armed patriotic detachments' to defend Rumania against possible aggressions. These were fighting words. But despite weeks of tension and threatening Soviet Army manoeuvres, Rumania herself remained uninvaded; and despite signs of Soviet displeasure, a twenty-year friendship treaty between the two countries was concluded in July 1970.

Rumania, then, had got away with 'independence'. Czechoslovakia, in contrast, failed to get away with the apparently more modest desire to run her own affairs in her own way inside her own country. In Czechoslovakia's case, as in Rumania's, the experiment bridged the transition between the older generation leadership and the new men. In Antonin Novotny, Czechoslovakia had her own equivalent of Gheorghiu-Dej—the petty, local Stalinist tyrant who had moved upward in the Party hierarchy over the graves of purged rivals—in Czechoslovakia's case, Slansky. Novotny was first secretary of the Czechoslovak Communist Party from September 1953 until January 1968; and from November 1957 until March 1968 he combined formal control of the State as President of the Republic with his more important office of Communist Party boss. Thus if any one man could be held responsible for the condition of Czechoslovakia, it was Novotny. And there can be no doubt that in the last two or three years of Novotny's reign, conditions went from bad to worse.

True, there was some liberalization. Political prisoners were freed under amnesties in 1962 and 1965, and in 1963 a number of men executed for 'bourgeois nationalism' and other alleged crimes in the 1950s at the height of the Stalinist period were rehabilitated. In various ways, the regime's hostility towards religion was softened. For instance, the Primate, Archbishop Beran, who had been released in October 1963 after four years in gaol, but not allowed to officiate, was made a cardinal after negotiations with the Vatican; and allowed to settle in Rome on February 1965. On the cultural side, controversial writers such as Kafka and Čapek, banned during the Stalinist phase, were allowed to appear again, though the regime maintained a continuing fight with independent-minded authors. Finally, a number of restrictions on foreign tourists were lifted and Czechoslovak citizens were able to write to foreigners without personal risk.

In Czechoslovakia, as elsewhere, these slight relaxations after years of totalitarian darkness merely stimulated demands for still more freedom. Moreover, there was plenty to grumble about on the economic side. Between 1960 and 1963, Czechoslovakia's economic growth declined steadily and in August 1962, the authorities were forced to abandon the third five-year plan, which had another three years to run. The point of interest is that the system, in furtherance of which terrible sacrifices had been imposed on the Czechoslovak people, did not seem to be working, and the slightly greater freedom they now enjoyed emboldened the critics to speak their minds.

This is exactly what some of them did in June 1967 at the congress of the Czechoslovak writers union. Loud voices were raised in protest both against economic and political stagnation. For their pains, three of the most outspoken writers were expelled from the union. *Literarni Noviny*, the union's journal, was brought under the direct control of the Ministry of Culture.

About the time the Czechoslovak writers were meeting, Israel was fighting her six-day war against the Arab States. Because the Czechoslovak Communist Party, taking its cue from Moscow, supported the Arabs, the Six-Day War became a major issue among the intellectuals, who seized upon it as a channel for their grievances against the regime. The most outspoken figure in this controversy was the Czechoslovak author Ladislav Mnacko, whose case became a news sensation. Mnacko had already visited North Vietnam as a correspondent, and – as expected – had filed home strongly anti-American despatches that had met with official approval. He was, however, unable to stomach his government's Middle East policy, and he went to Israel leaving behind him a personal statement in which he declared that the object of his trip was to protest against 'a policy designed to lead to the extermination of a whole people and the liquidation of a whole State'. But he went further, and said that his country was facing a moral crisis, the roots of which he found in her imperfectly liquidated Stalinist past. Only radical changes in the system, he added, could cure the crisis. The Party's reaction to this challenge was predictably harsh. Mnacko was expelled from the Party, deprived of his citizenship and stripped of his State decorations.

In the autumn, the intellectual unrest spread to the students, who on 31 October staged a demonstration at Charles University. Ostensibly, they were protesting against nightly power cuts, which deprived them of illumination for their studies. But as in the many student protests in the West, they seem to have been aiming at something deeper – at the machinery of the State itself. At all events, the police clashed with the students and used 'excessive violence' — an unprecedented admission made later as a result of an official inquiry.

Czechoslovakia's brooding crisis came to a head in October 1967, when the Central Committee met. It was then that the outside world first heard of Alexander Dubcek. Since April 1963, Dubcek had been first secretary of the Slovak Communist Party. He was, of course, a Communist, and the seal of orthodoxy had been conferred upon him when he graduated with honours from the Soviet Communist Party High Political School in Moscow. In his Slovakian Party job, however, he had given some indication of the kind of communism he favoured. He had presided over the rehabilitation of Slovaks executed or imprisoned for 'bourgeois nationalism' and encouraged Slovak intellectuals to work for greater cultural freedom. Now, on 31 October 1967, Dubcek (who was forty-six at the time) accused Novotny of 'behaving like a dictator' and attempting to sabotage the programme of economic reforms proposed by the able and controversial Dr Ota Sik.

The Central Committee's meeting soon degenerated into a struggle for power between Novotny and Dubcek. This was not a matter to which the Russians could be indifferent. On 8 December the Soviet Party boss, Brezhnev, made a flying visit to Prague, in an attempt to support the Soviet ambassador there, N. Stepan Chervonenko, who had been trying to maintain Novotny in office, both as President and as Party Chief. Possibly to his surprise, Brezhnev met with the united opposition of Czecho-slovakia's communist progressives. He decided diplomatically not to swim against the tide, and declared: 'Comrades, this is your problem.' On his way to Moscow, he stopped off at Bratislava, where he met and apparently approved of Alexander Dubcek.

The outcome of the Czechoslovak inner Party struggle belongs to recent history. With the customary unanimity, Dubcek was elected to succeed Novotny as first secretary in January 1968. Two months later, Novotny was forced to step down from the Presidency of the Republic as well. Dubcek now moved very fast; with the advantage of hindsight, one might say, *too* fast. Dubcek had every apparent reason to think he was safe.

His talk with Brezhnev at Bratislava had gone well; one of the first telegrams congratulating him on achieving the top Party post had come from Brezhnev himself; and when he had visited Moscow at the end of January, the communiqué recorded 'full identity of views on all questions discussed'. All this evidently encouraged him to feel that he could carry out the reforms he had long had in mind, aiming at his concept of 'liberal communism'.

On 22 February, at a meeting celebrating the 20th anniversary of the communist coup in Czechoslovakia, Dubcek made the promises people expected of him—the 'widest possible democratization', the correction of past mistakes and the rehabilitation of political victims of the Stalinist era. On 28 February Czechoslovak journalists called for genuine press freedom; and next day the first issue of *Literarni Listy*, a new weekly journal of the Writers' Union, made its appearance. On 5 March, the Party Praesidium relieved one of the hard-liners, Jiri Hendrych, of responsibility for ideology, and gave his job to a reformer, Josef Stacek. A few days later, there were special commemoration ceremonies for the Masaryks, father and son. (The father, Tomas, had been Czechoslovakia's first President, and the son, Jan, had been Foreign Minister, until his death in mysterious circumstances while he was being interrogated by the communists.)

By mid-March, the Russians were getting worried about Czechoslovakia. An unprecedented wind of freedom was blowing through the Czechoslovak press. Even high officials were being criticized, and newspaper attacks on Novotny were one of the main causes of his final downfall from the Presidency of the Republic. This kind of freedom was regarded in the Soviet Union as incompatible with the Party's control. The last thing Dubcek wanted to do, however, was to antagonize the Russians; and on 16 March, in a speech at Brno, he reaffirmed his government's support for the alliance with the Soviet Union as the basis of foreign policy. But this was not quite enough to reassure the Russians. One high official after another was being dismissed and replaced by reformers who felt their hour had come. A Defence Ministry general committed suicide, and another fled to the United States on hearing that his parliamentary immunity was about to be lifted. On 29 March Brezhnev gave a dark warning of the dangers of 'imperialist' subversion of communist countries. Dubcek's reforming ways, however, had turned into a flood. Even if he wished to stop it, it is probable that he could not. On 1 April, when the Czechoslovak Party's central committee resumed an interrupted meeting, he said: 'We must continue to build up our army and improve it according to socialist principles; as a defensive barrier against the enemy outside, the imperialist aggressors. We must build it up as a firm link in the alliance of the armies of the Warsaw Treaty.' Two days later the Defence Minister, General Lomsky, resigned, and on 4 April a new Praesidium of the Communist Party was elected. Gone were all, or nearly all, the hard-liners; in their place, Dubcek had flanked himself with men animated by a reforming zeal that matched his own. Over them all presided General Svoboda, who had been elected President of the Republic in place of Novotny. Though in his seventies, Svoboda was still full of vigour. He had organized resistance to the Nazis when they occupied Czechoslovakia in 1939. He was later to stand up to the Russians.

The momentum of events started increasing with the publication on 9 April of the Czechoslovak Party's Action Programme. The reforms announced far surpassed anything that was available to the Soviet people after fifty-one years of communism. The functions of the National Assembly were proclaimed, freedom of speech and of the press were guaranteed; and judicial reforms were promised, including the rehabilitation of all victims of injustice in the recent past. The Action Programme was certainly a major turning point. More crucial still, however, was the proclamation of 15 June 1968 by the National Front—the 'coalition' of the Communist Parties of Slovakia and of Czechoslovakia as a whole with the remnants of other parties—the Czechoslovak Socialist party, the Czechoslovak People's party, the Slovak Revival party and the Slovak Freedom party. Until the June proclamation, these remnants had no autonomous importance, since all took their orders from the Communists. Indeed, the proclamation reaffirmed the leading role of the Communist Party along with support for the alliance with the Soviet Union and other communist countries and for active cooperation with all 'democratic, progressive socialist and peace forces' in the world. 'Anti-communist and anti-Soviet propaganda' was condemned, as was 'political activity directed against the ... programme of the National Front'.

In two important respects, however, the National Front proclamation was a revolutionary departure from communist rigidity. One was the statement that socialist State power must not be a monopoly of any party or parties, but must be accessible to all citizens. The second was the announcement that the Front was to be a forum for a 'confrontation of various interests and views'. This, I think, was really the point of no return for Alexander Dubcek. For the principle of the monopoly of power of the ruling Communist Party was an absolute requirement in Moscow's eyes. What Dubcek had tried to do was consistent with the logic of 'liberalization'; but it demonstrated that it is not possible to liberalize communism. The ruling party either has or has not the monopoly of power; that is the meaning of totalitarianism, whether of the Right or of the Left. If freedom of speech and of the press is allowed, it is meaningless unless it includes freedom of dissent; and the freedom of dissent comprises the right to say that the ruling party should move out and make way for others.

It seems certain that the formation of the National Front was the last straw, in the eyes of Brezhnev and his colleagues. Already, the Action Programme had breached totalitarian principles in several respects. For instance, by a pledge to curtail the powers of the secret police. 'We must guarantee,' the Programme said, 'to every citizen who has not committed an offence against the State that his political conviction and opinion . . . are of no concern to the State security bodies'. Moreover, it was laid down that the secret police 'must not be used to resolve domestic political questions'. Its functions were restricted to 'punishable offences' and the safeguarding of public order. True, such formulae could be stretched to include the kind of 'crime' that had cost dissidents their lives in the past, but the Russians clearly lost confidence that the definition would be widely enough interpreted. Another privilege, denied to Soviet citizens and therefore by implication intolerable if granted to others, was the right to foreign travel which was restored by the Action Programme.

94

In the two months or so that separated the Action Programme from the National Front proclamation, the Russians waged a war of words against Czechoslovakia's new rulers. On 6 May, when a new Czechoslovak ambassador presented his credentials in Moscow, President Podgorny had referred to 'anti-socialist' elements in Czechoslovakia. Two days later, the leaders of the East European parties that remained faithful to Moscow—the Polish, East German, Hungarian and Bulgarian—had been summoned to a meeting in Moscow; from which, of course, the Czechoslovak and Rumanians were excluded. The following day had brought reports that the Czechoslovak frontier with Poland was closed, and that Soviet troop movements were taking place on the Polish side. A spate of articles in the Soviet press condemned developments in Czechoslovakia, in various periphrases. On 17 May, the Soviet Defence Minister, Marshal Grechko, and the Prime Minister, Kosygin, visited Czechoslovakia.

Alarmed, the Czechoslovak leaders multiplied their reassurances. On 4 June, Dubcek declared in Brno that 'our whole policy is based on our relations with the Soviet Union'; and a few days later President Svoboda referred to 'the firm and invincible friendship and alliance with the Soviet Union'. Later that month, however, the Warsaw Pact announced that 'command staff exercises' were to take place in Czechoslovakia and Poland, and it was clear to everybody that the military pressure was on. The exercises began, in fact, on 19 June, four days after the proclamation of the National Front. They ended on 30 June; and two days later an evaluation meeting for Warsaw Pact journalists was held. But though the meeting took place in the Czechoslovak town of Milovice, the Czechoslovak journalists were not invited.

And so it went on, with a crescendo of vituperation against Czechoslovakia in the press of the Soviet Union and countries that supported the Russians, because they feared either Soviet pressure or the contagion of Czechoslovakia's liberal ideas at home. Reports of the discovery of secret armed caches on Czechoslovak soil, and of NATO and CIA plots heightened the tension. The climax of this war of nerves came on 15 July when leaders of the Soviet, Polish, Hungarian, East German and Bulgarian parties, meeting in Warsaw, issued a virtual ultimatum

95

to Czechoslovakia in the form of a document known as the
'Warsaw Letter'. Ominously, the signatories declared that they
were not prepared to stand aside while 'hostile forces push your
country off the road to socialism and create a threat of tearing
away Czechoslovakia from the socialist community'.

The Warsaw Letter called for the wholesale abandonment of
Dubcek's programme of democratic reform. Specifically, it
made the following demands:

1. Stern measures against right-wing and anti-socialist forces.
2. All political activities against socialism to cease.
3. The Party to seize all mass media and use them in the
interests of the working class and socialism. A return to Marxism-
Leninism and 'democratic centralism' — that is, firm control from
above.

Politely but firmly, the Czechoslovak leaders rejected the
Warsaw Letter. In retrospect, one of the most cynically illuminating
aspects of the whole crisis was the fact that the Russians, at one
late stage, allowed the Czechoslovaks and the rest of the world to
believe that Dubcek and his colleagues had got away with it, and
would henceforth be left in peace. On 29 July, talks between the
Soviet Politburo and the Czechoslovak Praesidium opened at the
border village of Cierna Nad Tisou.

On 1 August, for the first time in weeks, *Pravda* carried no
attacks on Czechoslovakia. The reason, it appeared, was that the
Cierna talks had reached an amicable conclusion. A short joint
communiqué referred to 'the atmosphere of frankness, sincerity
and mutual understanding' that had prevailed. President Svoboda,
in a broadcast to the nation, declared that the current programme
would continue. Next day, Dubcek thanked the people for their
'wise and circumspect attitude'. On the 3rd, the Czechoslovak
leaders met those of other Warsaw Pact member-States — except
Rumania — at Bratislava, and once again, a friendly communiqué
resulted. After signing it, Dubcek declared: 'We achieved what
we had promised and we did a good job.' It looked as though the
whole crisis was dissolving in a burst of socialist sunshine. And
on the 3rd Prague radio announced that the last Soviet troops
had left Czechoslovak territory. The threat seemed to be over.

Quite suddenly, however, the crisis began all over again. On 8 August, no doubt unwisely, *Literarni Listy* published an article attacking the Russians for interference in Czechoslovak affairs and another warning the Russians that they had forfeited Czechoslovakia's friendship. On 10 August, the Party paper *Rude Pravo*, published new Party statutes asserting the right of an outvoted minority to adhere to its views, guaranteeing secrecy of the vote and limiting individual terms of office. Before and after the publication of these draft statutes, three important visitors came to Prague. The first was President Tito of Yugoslavia, who was greeted with wild enthusiasm. The second was Ulbricht of East Germany—whose controlled press had been even more vituperative than Russia's in its earlier denunciations of Dubcek's policies. A few days later, yet another distinguished visitor arrived: Ceausescu of Rumania. There was no disguising the fact that Ceausescu, like Tito, was greeted with great and spontaneous rapture, while cold silence, or dutiful clapping, was all that Ulbricht could muster.

While Ceausescu was still in Prague, the Soviet press turned the heat on again, with a warning against under-estimating the importance and finality of the Cierna talks and the Bratislava Declaration. On 20 August, the East German party paper, *Neues Deutschland*, declared that socialist internationalism includes a readiness to enlist help from the fraternal countries. That day, the Soviet central committee met in Moscow. It was Czechoslovakia's last day of its new found freedom. At 11 p.m., Soviet troops, with accompanying forces from Poland, East Germany, Hungary and Bulgaria, crossed the Czechoslovak border. Announcing the invasion in the early hours of 21 August, Prague radio declared: 'This happened without the knowledge of the President of the Republic, of the Chairman of the National Assembly, the Premier and the first Secretary of the Czechoslovak Party central committee.'

Did the Russians allow the Czechs to suppose that they had won the day in order to achieve complete surprise when they did invade? This seemed the most likely explanation: a similar smoke-screen was laid in 1956, when the Russians negotiated with the Hungarian General Maleter and his colleagues about the withdrawal of Russian troops. It was clear that a long period of meticulous preparation had preceded the Soviet occupation of Czechoslovakia. This period would have encompassed the meetings at Cierna and Bratislava. It is possible, on the other hand, that the Russians believed they had persuaded Dubcek and his colleagues to halt their programme of headlong democratization. They might therefore have decided to call off the projected invasion—until the publication of the draft Party Statutes on 10 August; which must have come as a demonstration that the programme was still continuing.

From the point of view that interests us particularly—the future of communist power—perhaps the most important outcome of the Soviet occupation of Czechoslovakia was a new doctrine of intervention. First proposed by the head of *Pravda*'s propaganda department, S. Kovalev, in that newspaper on 26 September 1968, it was confirmed and elaborated by the Party boss, Brezhnev, at the fifth congress of the Polish Communist Party in November. As reported in *Pravda* of 13 November, Brezhnev's statement was a remarkable example of squaring a doctrinal circle. On the one hand, he reaffirmed respect for sovereignty; on the other, he claimed the right to intervene in a socialist country where socialism was deemed to be threatened.

First, this is what Brezhnev said on *sovereignty*:

Socialist States stand for strict respect for the sovereignty of all countries. We are resolutely opposed to interference in the affairs of any States, to violation of their sovereignty.

In contrast, this is what Brezhnev said to justify *intervention* in certain circumstances:

When internal and external supporters hostile to socialism attempt to turn the development of any socialist country in the direction of the restoration of the capitalist system, when a threat arises to the cause of socialism in that country, a threat to the security of the socialist commonwealth as a whole— it already becomes not only a problem for the people of that country but also a general problem, the concern of all socialist countries.

The implication of Brezhnev's statement, and of Kovalev's

earlier article, are menacing and far-reaching. Kovalev had swept aside the criticisms made of the intervention of the five Warsaw Pact armies in Czechoslovakia as groundless, since they were isolated from 'the general context of past struggle in the modern world'. Brezhnev's definition of sovereignty was clearly peculiar to the communist mind. It implied that once a country was 'socialist', and accepted as such by the Soviet Union, then it could *never* be allowed to change its political system, whatever the views of the majority of its people. Sovereignty, then, had nothing to do with such concepts as the inviolability of frontiers and the right of a legal government to make whatever reforms it considered necessary. Instead, sovereignty is re-interpreted to mean the inviolability of a socialist system. *153 791*

Through a chronological irony the United Nations special committee on the question of defining aggression met in Geneva in June 1968. The Soviet delegation had been expected to present a new draft definition of aggression. At that time, of course, the forthcoming Soviet aggression against Czechoslovakia was in the air, and the Soviet delegates had nothing to present. The special committee met again in New York on 26 February 1969, and this time the Soviet delegation, headed by V. M. Chkhikvadze, director of the Soviet Institute of State and Law and member of the World Council of Peace, did present a new draft definition of aggression. Interestingly, this omitted clauses previously proposed by the Russians but which had been quoted in condemnation of the Soviet invasion of Czechoslovakia. Chkhikvadze indeed admitted that 'new developments which characterize present international relations' had been taken into account in the drafting. The earlier Soviet draft, presented in 1953 and again in 1956, had included an Article 1 (d) on the landing of forces 'inside the boundaries of another State without the permission of the Government of the latter, or the violation of the conditions of such permission, particularly as regards the length of their stay or the extension of the area in which they may stay'. This was now dropped in the new draft. Also dropped were definitions of circumstances which do *not* justify aggression, including Article 6 A (d): 'Any revolutionary or counter-revolutionary movement, civil war disorders or strikes.' Another

99

Article dropped was 6 A (e), which ruled out aggression in connection with 'the establishment of maintenance in any State of any political, economic or social system'. Yet another clause omitted in the new Soviet draft was Article 7, which condemned the concentration of troops near frontiers; such as the Warsaw Pact manoeuvres on the Czechoslovak border before the aggression of 21 August 1968.

In the Preamble to the new draft, moreover, the Russians made an ingenious attempt to justify their new doctrine of 'limited sovereignty', by stating that 'the use of force by a State to encroach upon the social and political achievement of the people of other States is incompatible with the principle of peaceful co-existence of States with different social systems'. At first reading, this might suggest that the Russians were condemning themselves. However, they have always maintained that by occupying Czechoslovakia they were defending, not encroaching upon, social and political achievements. Apart from the support of governments that might themselves be threatened with a Soviet occupation if they challenged the Russian definition of aggression, the Russians stood virtually alone in their juridical approach. Following the *fait accompli* and defending it, the Soviet jurists had served notice on the world that any communist State that attempted to modify its system could expect to be invaded by Soviet forces—if it were geographically and in other respects convenient for an invasion to take place.

4. *The Rest*

Tito's Yugoslavia stands slightly outside the mainstream of communist regimes. Unlike the other satellite leaders of Eastern Europe, Marshal Tito came to power by his own virtually unaided efforts—not at the point of Russian bayonets; though the presence of Stalin's forces in the area was perhaps a support for him at the beginning. In 1947, however, he successfully defied Stalin and was solemnly 'excommunicated' from the Cominform. Khrushchev tried to win him back, and partially succeeded. Yugoslavia is not a member of the Warsaw Pact, but sends observers to Comecon. In international politics Tito has consistently striven, with considerable success, to maintain a neutralist, non-aligned position between the power blocs of East and West. With Nasser of Egypt and the late Pandit Nehru of India, Tito belonged to a triumvirate of neutral leaders, and wielded influence out of all proportion to the military or industrial strength of his country.

Today—in 1970—Yugoslavia presents a paradoxical picture. On the one hand, it remains a communist country, with a monopolistic ruling party—the League of Yugoslav Communists. On the other hand, economic reforms at home and western links abroad have combined to produce a curious half-way house. From some angles, Yugoslavia looks strangely like a capitalist country; in others, it is still determinedly 'socialist'. The question is, whether the capitalist side will gradually encroach on the socialist side, so that it is no longer possible to consider Yugoslavia a communist country. For the ruling party this is clearly a cruel dilemma. Its monopoly of power is justified—as in other communist countries—by the need to guide its country towards a communist future of abundance and equality for all. But can it continue to justify that monopoly if, in fact, Yugoslavia is moving away from socialism?

Having freed himself from Moscow's direct tutelage, Tito has found it easier than other communist dictators to introduce liberal reforms. But political discussion, though freer than in most other communist countries, has painful and visible limits. Milovan Djilas, once Tito's constant companion, fell foul of the regime for pointing out that it had developed an inhuman bureaucracy which he called *The New Class*—the title of a highly successful book he smuggled out of Yugoslavia for publication abroad. For his pains he spent years in prison. Some of the features of life of which Djilas had complained have since been remedied. But freedom of dissent is still curtailed, as Mihajlo Mihajlov, a young university lecturer, discovered when he attempted to publish a short work entitled *A Summer in the USSR*. He too was gaoled.

Despite such residual intolerance—which could easily worsen once Tito has gone—there can be no doubt that in the communist world today, Yugoslavia is 'different'. In common with other East European countries, a system of rigid centralized planning had been imposed on Yugoslavia during the Stalinist period. The break with the Cominform brought both external and internal consequences. Externally, Tito had to turn to the United States and other Western countries for economic aid. Internally, the withdrawal of Soviet advisers made centralized planning difficult. Tito tried to solve this problem by de-centralizing—that is by giving individual units, such as farms and factories, responsibility for their own economic plans. Previously, even wages had been determined centrally by the allocation of a maximum wage fund. Any losses at the factory level were made good by State subsidies. After 1950, however, rigid planning made way for a type of 'indicative' planning rather reminiscent of French methods (and echoed later in Britain's National Economic Development Council). That is, the function of the planning organs was henceforth to project trends. Under the New Order, profit-making determined planning decisions.

That year—1950—also saw the first tentative steps towards workers' control of industries. Today each industrial enterprise is controlled by an elected Workers' Council, which in turn elects and dismisses directors and other executives. Foreign visitors are usually told that the workers 'own' the factories they operate. This is clearly untrue, by the test of the question: 'If the workers own the factories, can they sell them and pocket the proceeds?' The answer is that they cannot. Private enterprise has nevertheless made surprising headway in Yugoslavia's economy. To some extent, this has been due to Tito's decision to seek membership of the General Agreement on Tariffs and Trade (GATT), to which Yugoslavia was admitted in 1966. Since membership carries the obligation to allow foreign capital investment, the Yugoslav government announced on 15 March 1967, that foreign investors could become partners in Yugoslav enterprises—to the extent of up to fifty per cent. In two other respects, foreign influences are important in Yugoslavia's economy: the inflow of tourists, and the outflow of Yugoslav workers. Tourism has become the largest single source of foreign currency earnings. The State-run hotels, however, leave much to be desired. Even State tourist agencies have therefore taken to displaying signs advertising rooms in private houses.* For two or three years, privately operated businesses connected with tourism, such as restaurants, garages and even camping sites, have been allowed to operate. Once the government takes the fateful step of allowing privately run hotels, then logically, the next step should be privately owned factories. If that stage is reached, Yugoslavia will cease to be a socialist country though it may remain a communist one by virtue of the Party's monopoly of power. Ideology, however, will have ceased to be a viable instrument for the enforcement of public conformity; this process appears already to be far advanced.

The outflow of Yugoslav workers is important in several ways. For one thing it relieves the economy of a possible further burden of unemployment. For another, the remittances sent home by the Yugoslavs working in the West constitute the second largest foreign currency earner, after tourism. No other communist country allows its workers to seek employment outside their individual workers' paradises: in Yugoslavia's case the number is as high as 400,000.

As in industry, so in agriculture. In the Stalinist period, agriculture was collectivized on the Soviet model. It was, indeed, intensified after the break with the Cominform. But it soon became plain that this strict application of doctrine was counter-productive, and recognizing that it was, the Party started to redistribute land to the peasants, although it limited individual holdings to an uneconomic 25 acres (10 hectares). By the early 1960s, more than eighty per cent of Yugoslavia's agricultural land was in private hands. Taxes had been reduced, and peasants allowed to buy their own farming equipment. On the other hand, under a 1962 decree, cooperative and State farms continued to receive higher guaranteed prices than were available to private farmers. This decree was symptomatic of the ideological fixation of the party apparatus, which continued whenever possible to obstruct economic reforms. Thus private firms—such as small retail shops, taxi hire companies and artisan workshops—were

* *Problems of Communism*, March-April 1968, p. 42.

intermittently under State pressure. In 1962 and the first part of 1963, some 5,000 small private firms went out of business.

The ideological dichotomy, however, went on. In July 1965, important decentralizing reforms — already endorsed by the Party Congress and Parliament — passed into law. There was a strong capitalist tinge about these newest measures. The tax changes enabled enterprises to keep about 70 per cent of their profits and dispose of them as they saw fit — for instance, by investing in other enterprises. A principal effect of the reforms was therefore to stimulate the creation of a national capital market. About a hundred investment or commercial banks were set up — replacing twice that number of communal banks — to provide funds for capital expenditure and working expenses. The idea was that the enterprises should control banks in which they had made deposits, though no single enterprise could exercise more than ten per cent of voting rights. By this time, Yugoslavia was beginning to look very much like the kind of mixed economy familiar to dwellers in Western welfare States such as Sweden and Britain. The State, of course, continued to predominate, but a market economy was beginning to work — not only in the allocation of capital, but also in pricing and even in the labour market. By 1968, unemployment had risen to over 300,000 or nine per cent of the labour force.

Moreover, since the level of wages was no longer centrally determined, enormous variations in earnings were beginning to appear. For instance, a skilled worker might earn $400 a month, and a similarly skilled one elsewhere no more than $30 for similar work. The difference between the two might be simply that the first was working in a successful enterprise, and the second in an ailing one.* It was a fair criticism to say that while sticking to the ideological claim that Yugoslavia was building socialism, the country was reproducing some of the worst features of early capitalism in Western and other countries.

Another important recent event was the sudden downfall in 1966 of Alexander Rankovich, former Vice-president of the Republic and Tito's heir apparent. More importantly, Rankovich was the head of the Secret Police, and Tito made the sensational

* *Problems of Communism*, March-April 1968, p. 44.

decision to dismiss him on learning that his own residences had been 'bugged' by the Secret Police. The Yugoslav Central Committee met in July 1966, and the records later published showed that in addition to wielding the power of the Security Services, Rankovich was among the leaders of the Party faction determined to resist economic and political reforms. His removal did in fact lead to further democratization: the power of the Secret Police to probe into people's private affairs was reduced, and that of the Party to oversee the execution of individual economic decisions was likewise curtailed.

In June 1968, Yugoslavia had its share of the student unrest that has affected so many countries. In this case, the students of Belgrade University rioted over both university grievances and such wider political issues as the alleged social abuses of the self-management system in industry. If anything, however, Tito himself emerged stronger than ever out of a clash between the students and the authorities. For Yugoslavia in particular, the Soviet invasion of Czechoslovakia two months later was a traumatic experience. The rapid pace of liberalization in Czechoslovakia had led many of the reformers in Yugoslavia to hope that their country would no longer be as isolated as it had been in the communist world.

The Soviet occupation shattered these hopes, and made the Yugoslavs wonder whether it would be their turn next. Exposed though they were, however, the Yugoslavs were outspoken in their defence of Czechoslovakia and their criticisms of the Soviet leaders. Once again, a patriotic surge and the evident determination of the Yugoslav people to defend their freedom even if the great Soviet war machine invaded their country, strengthened Marshal Tito's unique personal prestige. But there was no inclination to seek safety in alignment with the West. The Yugoslavs let it be known that they felt comforted by the existence of Nato; but that they did not propose to ask for Nato's formal protection.

Defiant as ever, Marshal Tito opened the Ninth Party Congress on 11 March 1969, with a passionate denunciation of Soviet intervention in Yugoslavia, not only in Stalin's day, but since. He condemned the Soviet occupation of Czechoslovakia as an 'outright violation of the sovereignty of a socialist country'. By then, Tito was 76, and the shadow of the succession hung heavily over the proceedings. The Yugoslavs had made a determined effort to end their isolation, and to some extent had been successful. Some sixty-six foreign delegations attended the Congress, by invitation. Many of them were non-communist 'progressive' parties and organizations throughout the world; only thirty-two invitations had been sent to communist parties. No invitations had gone to the hard-liners—China, Albania, North Korea, North Vietnam and Cuba—all of which had supported the Soviet action against Czechoslovakia. The only ruling party that attended, however, was that of Rumania. The Soviet Union had been invited; and so had East Germany, Poland, Hungary, and Czechoslovakia. All declined. Bulgaria and Mongolia accepted, then changed their minds. So did the Communist Parties of India and Iran. In Eastern Europe, therefore, the Yugoslavs continued to be isolated, but less so in the left-wing world at large.

The Congress was marked by some important constitutional changes. The Central Committee was abolished and replaced by a streamlined Presidium of fifty-two members. Moreover, a fifteen-man Executive Bureau headed by Tito himself, was set up. The country's federal structure was strengthened by the creation of a new Chamber of Nationalities to be composed exclusively of delegates from the assemblies of Yugoslavia's six constituent republics and two autonomous provinces. Yugoslavia remained a one-party State, however, for in the May elections that followed the Party Congress by a few weeks, all candidates for election to the five Chambers of the Assembly were drawn from single lists prepared by the Party's mass organization, the Socialist Alliance of the Working Peoples of Yugoslavia.

In the press, dissent continued to be severely curtailed. Indirectly such papers as *Borba* ('Struggle'), the main daily, pressed for freedom of expression—usually by indirect means, such as attacks on press control in the Soviet Union and praise for the temporary freedom enjoyed by Czechoslovak journalists. Curiously, one publication that found itself in trouble was the intellectual Marxist magazine, *Praxis*, the editor of which, Professor G.

Petrovich, was expelled from the Party after the students' disturbances in June. With its tiny circulation of about 4,000, *Praxis* would not seem to have been much of a danger. Its influence among the students, however, was considerable, and its arguments were an embarrassment to the Party hierarchy. Indeed, the case of *Praxis* was symptomatic of Yugoslavia's dichotomy and dilemma. The *Praxis* group were true Marxists, but sought to purify Marxist theory and practice in the name of orthodoxy. The hierarchy, on the other hand, were out to change doctrine wherever it appeared to conflict with the pragmatic realities of Yugoslavia's situation. The distinction was important. One of the 'sins' of the *Praxis* people was that they kept saying that Yugoslavia was returning to capitalism. They may have been right. Yugoslavia is not yet a capitalist country; and it is certainly not a democratic one; but its socialist credentials are now under severe strain.

Cuba

More eccentric still than Yugoslavia is that outlying bastion of communism, Fidel Castro's Cuba. To a large extent, the eccentricity reflects the extraordinary personality of the *Líder Máximo*. Unlike the leaders of all other ruling communist parties, Fidel Castro is not a trained Marxist revolutionary. This is not to say that he is not a revolutionary: on the contrary, his taste and talent for revolution are superlative. But he has publicly revealed that he did not become a Marxist until after the 'bourgeois nationalist' revolution he led against the oppressive Batista regime had already succeeded. During his guerrilla struggle, the then Cuban Communist Party stayed aloof, and even in some respects collaborated with the dictator. Although the wrongs in Castro's dispute with the United States were not all on one side, the break between them made the island economically dependent on Soviet and other communist help. Gradually, expediency and his own authoritarian inclinations led him to set up a communist regime.

On 2 January 1969, Fidel Castro celebrated the tenth anniversary of the advent of his regime. This provided a good occasion for reappraisal. Within a year of Batista's downfall, Castro had virtually eliminated political freedom. By then, only political parties that directly supported Castro were tolerated; and in 1961 Castro's own 26 July Movement was amalgamated with the old Popular Socialist Party (that is, the Communist Party) and the revolutionary student directorate, to create a new political body called the Integrated Revolutionary Organizations. There were two further changes of name. In March 1962, the Revolutionary Organizations became the United Party of the Socialist Revolution; and in October 1965 this was renamed the Communist Party of Cuba.

During his struggle, Castro had repeatedly denounced dictatorship either of the Right or the Left. But the regime he created denies freedom of speech, of association and of the press, while *habeas corpus* is suspended. At the outset, Fidel Castro had shocked many of his American and European liberal supporters by executions of supporters of Batista. Less attention was aroused by purges within his own Communist Party, though these are doubly interesting both because they are characteristic of communist regimes, and because paradoxically their purpose has been to prevent old guard Communists gaining control of the ruling party. For instance, one of the most influential Communists, Aníbal Escalante, was purged with nearly forty associates in January 1968. Escalante himself was gaoled. The manner of his downfall was instructive. Under Batista, he had been Secretary-General of the old Popular Socialist Party at a time when it was standing aloof from Fidel Castro's struggle. When Castro was in power, the Russians soon found that he had no inclination to become a true satellite, despite his economic dependence on Soviet support. Either because Moscow asked him to do so, or because that is the way a communist leader behaves anyway, Escalante tried to gain control of the revolution from within by placing his own men in positions of trust, bypassing the faithful partisans who had fought with Fidel Castro in the Sierra Maestra.

Castro put a stop to this—for some years—by banishing Escalante to Prague. But when he came back he started all over again. By January 1968, Castro and his inner group had had enough. They summoned the Central Committee of the new Communist Party to denounce Escalante's so-called 'micro-faction'. Escalante was gaoled for fifteen years, and eight of his associates for twelve. All were expelled. Castro's brother Raúl later disclosed that Russian police advisers had been in touch with Escalante. Not unnaturally, the Escalante affair soured relations with the Russians for some time. To some extent, they improved after Castro had publicly expressed partial support for the Soviet occupation of Czechoslovakia. Fidel Castro, in fact, goes his own way, and the Russians are unlikely ever to bring him under control. His strength lies in his charismatic appeal to the Cuban masses. Whether they are carried away or merely stupefied by his tireless flow of words—speeches of five or six hours are not uncommon—may never be known. But it is certain that his style suits the people he rules. His exhortations, denunciations and enthusiasm are contagious. Broadly speaking, the Cubans will do, or try to do, what he asks of them. This is sometimes surprising, as in many respects Cuba's performance under communism has fallen far short of Castro's hopes and predictions.

His most striking achievement is probably in education. Between 22 and 29 per cent of the population were illiterate before the revolution. By 1965, the figure had dropped impressively to less than 4 per cent. Among the half-million Cubans who fled the island after 1960 were many technicians. Their departure, however, stimulated technical and higher education. In 1958–9, there were only 6,259 technical school pupils and 25,000 students; after ten years of the new Cuba, the respective figures stood at 29,975 and 40,147. In public health, too, the achievement was not negligible. In 1958, there were no rural health services. By the end of 1968, there were 47 rural hospitals and 56 dispensaries with free service. There were five times as many doctors as under Batista.

The price paid for these undeniable achievements, and for the relative fairness of the redistribution of incomes and resources, has been high. Part of it, as we have seen, was the loss of political liberties. But these affect only a small intellectual and middle-class section of the population. The working masses, whether in the town or countryside, are more affected by the fact that strikes are illegal, that the trade unions are State-run, and that the 'volunteers' who theoretically respond to Fidel Castro's continual appeals are in reality providing forced labour, since it is difficult to escape the many forms of direct or indirect compulsion, used by the regime. Against that, rents are low or non-existent and telephone calls are free.

Or are they? The price of such 'social justice' may perhaps be found in the disappointing performance of the economy. Shortly after taking power, Castro had denounced Cuba's dependence on sugar as 'a hateful result of capitalist exploitation'. He announced a programme of industrialization, but little headway was made because of the country's technical backwardness and the resistance of Cuba's East European allies to the demands the Cuban programme made on their own inadequate resources. After a visit to the Soviet Union in 1963, Castro evidently decided that he was trying to move too fast on the industrial front, and would need again to concentrate on sugar. Under the 1959 agrarian reform, the land was supposed to be distributed to the tillers, the large estates having been expropriated. In fact, however, very little of the land that had been seized was given to peasant owners. Before the revolution, small and medium farmers already owned fifty-seven per cent of all arable land; the percentage increased by only two points in the ensuing years. And it dropped suddenly to thirty per cent in 1963, when all the medium-sized farms were nationalized under the second agrarian reform. As in other communist countries, the small farmers provide a quite disproportionate contribution to the national food crops.

The net outcome of Cuba's agrarian measures has indeed been a general drop in agricultural production. In March 1962, a stringent system of food rationing was introduced, much of which was still in force in 1969. In 1964 the cotton crop was only one-sixth that of 1962, and there was a further drop in 1965. Milk and cheese, butter, chickens and eggs, pineapples, tobacco, coffee, maize and rice also fell between 1964 and 1965. Nor has the main crop—sugar—fared any better. The 1963 harvest, after four or five years of revolutionary rule, was the lowest on record: 3·8 million tons. Subsequently, the picture improved, and 1965 brought a total of 6 million tons of sugar produced; but the figure for the following year fell again, to 4·45 million tons, though it rose again to 6·1 millions in 1967. Castro has staked his reputation on achieving a target of 10 million tons for 1970.

There was a humiliating note in his decision, announced on 2 January 1969 during his tenth anniversary speech, that sugar rationing was to be introduced to cut the country's consumption by about a third. During 1968, in fact, living standards had continued to deteriorate, and lengthening queues for food and clothing drove the fact home.

For Fidel Castro, a vicious circle seemed to be built in to his system. For economic aid alone, in mid-1969, Cuba's debt to the Soviet Union was estimated at about $2,300 million, not counting the subsidizing of Cuban sugar exports—worth several hundred million dollars. If Cuba should indeed achieve an output of ten million tons of sugar in 1970, she might make a start in extricating herself from this prodigious burden of debt. But the agricultural history of the previous ten or eleven years suggested that this was hardly likely.

If socialism means shared austerity, then Cuba has achieved it. If it means affluence for all, then the goal is a long way off. In the meantime, Fidel Castro appears to be in unchallenged control over his country. Short of a successful assassination attempt, the prospect must be that he will remain in power for many years. If and when he goes, a more orthodox communist regime, more subservient to Soviet wishes, is a possibility; but any attempt at precise forecasting is vitiated by the uncertainties of communist policies as a whole.

Outside Cuba, Fidel Castro has attempted to kindle the fires of revolution, especially in Latin America, but even in Africa. These attempts have been remarkably unsuccessful, but they are considered elsewhere in this book.

North Vietnam

It is not easy to dissociate the late Ho Chi Minh's Democratic Republic of Vietnam from its interminable wars, first against the French from 1946 to 1954, and from 1958 on against South Vietnam and the United States. An attempt is worth making, however, if only because the heroic image of a gallant North Vietnamese David fighting the American Goliath has made it difficult for many people to see the North Vietnam regime as it is. Indeed, the notion that North Vietnam is an example of an 'Asian communism', by implication morally more tolerable than Russia's kind, has become widely accepted.* The truth is that the North Vietnamese Republic is one of the most viciously repressive communist regimes anywhere; nor does its economic system solve the country's problems of peasant poverty and overcrowding: it merely disguises their continued existence.

Ho Chi Minh's long career as a Marxist revolutionary began in France in the 1920s. After training in Moscow, he spent many years in China and South-East Asia as an agent of Russia's Comintern. In 1945, taking advantage of the collapse of Japan, he proclaimed the Democratic Republic of Vietnam. Almost immediately, he formally dissolved the Indochinese Communist Party, which he himself had founded in 1930. In consequence, many non-communist Vietnamese nationalists joined his movement. The dissolution of the Party was, however, a deception, just as Stalin's war-time dissolution of the Comintern had been, for the *Cominform Journal* revealed on 21 August 1953 that between 1946 and 1950 —when there was supposed to be no communist party in Vietnam —Party membership increased from 20,000 to 500,000.† In fact, the Party was resurrected in 1951, under the name of Dang Lao Dong Viet Nam (Vietnamese Workers' Party).

Since Ho's Republic was at war with France until 1954, and engaged in further hostilities from 1958, the true character of the regime emerges best from a study of what happened there between those years, when North Vietnam was theoretically at peace.‡ It is an instructive exercise. During those years of 'peace', North Vietnam —among other things —pushed through an unnecessarily brutal land reform programme; weathered a revolt of the intellectuals which ended in further repression; and even

---

* Mr Graham Greene, in a not unsympathetic review of my Penguin, *South-East Asia in Turmoil*, in the London *New Statesman* of 19 March 1965, tabled a loaded rhetorical question: 'I would have liked to ask this intelligent observer whether he sees any favourable future, save communism, for South-East Asia'. Since communism is not, in my view, a 'favourable future' for South-East Asia or anywhere else, Mr Greene's question was not one I could answer logically.

† P. G. Honey, *Communism in North Vietnam* (MIT Press, 1963), pp. 12–13.

‡ During the war against France, the Republic consisted of communist-controlled areas. The northern half of Vietnam was allocated to Ho under the Geneva settlement of 1954.

heard a 'secret speech' by Ho Chi Minh. The parallels with China, and more distantly with Russia, were striking.

The land reform scheme, in particular, was a slavish imitation of the Chinese model. In charge of it was the Chinese-trained Secretary-General of the ruling party, Truong Chinh (whose name, an assumed one, means 'Long March', in tribute to a legendary feat by Mao Tse-tung and his armed followers). It was marked by extorted confessions under torture, denunciations of 'landlords' for alleged crimes, and summary public trials without right of defence. Its toll in dead may have totalled 100,000.* These excesses proved counterproductive. In various places, peasants rose in revolt, and in Nghe Anh province, the revolt was on a large enough scale to shake the regime. Rather hastily, Ho removed Truong Chinh from executive control of the Party (though not from membership of the Politburo), and halted the land reform programme. But much harm had been done to North Vietnam's agriculture and the executed 'landlords'— many of whom were simply peasants slightly richer than their neighbours—stayed dead.

In one respect, North Vietnam's experience preceded China's. In 1956, when land reform was called off, the writers were allowed a brief moment of freedom from censorship. One of the free periodicals that appeared at this time was called *Nhan Van* (not to be confused with the party organ, *Nhan Dan*); another was named *Tram Hoa*, the meaning of which, 'One Hundred Flowers' echoed a slogan launched earlier in the year by Mao Tse-tung: 'Let a hundred flowers bloom, let a hundred schools contend'. China's own brief period of freedom, sanctioned by this slogan, took place, however, in 1957. These free periodicals attacked the policies of the North Vietnamese leadership. They were suppressed at the end of 1956.

In February 1957, when Mao was giving the Chinese intellec-

* This is the figure given by a French observer, Gérard Tongas, in *J'ai vécu dans l'Enfer Communiste au Nord Vietnam* (Debresse, Paris, 1961), p. 222. I myself visited North Vietnam shortly after the land reform programme had been called off and wrote what I believe to have been the first account of it in English, under the usual cloak of anonymity, in *The Economist* of 5 January 1957, p. 50. The best account in book form is in Hoang Van Chi, *From Colonialism to Communism* (Pall Mall, 1964).

tuals their temporary freedom, Ho was muzzling his. In that month, a congress on art and literature was held in North Vietnam. It was addressed by Truong Chinh, who seemed already to be back in favour, and who declared that art and literature had to be 'socialist' in content. A new and orthodox literary weekly, *Van*, was later created.

The North Vietnamese intellectuals, however, having tasted freedom, wanted more of it. The writers and cartoonists of *Van* began to attack and satirize the regime with audacity. The consequences, though delayed, were predictable. In February 1958, *Van* was closed down for a policy review. In April, three members of the editorial team were arrested for 'anti-regime activities'. They were later tried as 'spies for the US-Diem clique' and sentenced to long terms of imprisonment.

Ho's 'secret speech' appears to have been made about 31 May 1957 in circumstances recalling Mao's secret speech of February that year, and Khrushchev's of February 1956. The first the North Vietnamese heard about it was when Hanoi Radio broadcast an incomplete version of it on 7 July. The reason for the temporary secrecy seems to have been its gloomy content, for in it Ho referred to North Vietnam's 'many difficulties' which he attributed to inadequate production. He reminded his audience that the Soviet Union had had many years of austerity while building socialism. He too prescribed austerity, together with more labour discipline; and for good measure, he denounced 'speculators'.

As with Stalin and Mao, Ho Chi Minh was the object of constant and fulsome praise of the kind Khrushchev denounced in 1956 as the 'cult of personality'. No one who met him failed to come under the spell of his personal charm. Objectively, however, 'Uncle Ho' had a record of callous indifference to his people's sufferings and of slavish imitation of the worst aspects of Stalinism and Maoism.

The economic performance of Ho's Republic, likewise, recalls that of its communist Big Brothers. With massive economic aid from China and Russia, obtained in 1955, considerable progress was made in industrialization, while agriculture lagged. In recent years, North Vietnam's formidable war effort and the effects of American bombing have made valid estimates difficult if not impossible. There can be no doubt, however, that the setbacks to be expected in a small country at war have been aggravated by the regime's continuing efforts to establish a 'socialist' system. Ho Chi Minh, himself, addressing coal industry representatives on 15 November 1968, attributed the steady drop in coal production since 1965 not only to the war but to 'poor management and organization'. Too many workers, he complained, were doing 'administrative, managerial and indirectly productive work'.

Such excessive bureaucracy is not, perhaps, exclusive to communist systems, but it is nevertheless inherent in the usual 'socialist' approach to economic problems, of which the North Vietnamese regime provides typical examples. For instance, faced with declining food output, the party launched a new food policy in August 1968, calling for stricter Party control over distribution and, in time, the abolition of the 'free' market and the allocation of food according to labour. In North Vietnam, as in China and Russia, 'free-lance' farming on private plots had made a disproportionate contribution to local food supplies. In the midst of a food crisis, however, the North Vietnamese leaders were proposing to increase the number of non-productive Party workers detailed to keep an eye on the peasants.

In these and other ways, the striking thing about North Vietnam, for all the initial self-sufficiency of its struggle for independence, was its resemblance to other communist regimes.

5. *Competitive Subversion*

Subversion is a permanent aim of communists everywhere, whatever their Party. It is indeed one aim they share with Marxist fundamentalists of the New Left. Once a communist party is in power, of course, then subversion of the new order by a member of the ruling party becomes a punishable crime. But non-communist societies everywhere, whether or not they may be strictly termed 'capitalist', are fair game. In such societies, it is the duty of every party member to undermine the establishment, to cast doubts on the social order, to proselytize for Marxism, if necessary using violence, but working within the Constitution whatever the Party in its wisdom has decreed. What too many people still fail, or are unwilling, to grasp is that it is the continuing, self-imposed mission of the ruling communist parties to help local communist parties everywhere else to subvert the existing order. In other words, to hasten the inevitable revolution.

Among Western liberals, there is a strong resistance to such assertions, which are held to recall the worst days of the Cold War and of McCarthyism. This reluctance to face facts is indeed a tribute to the persistence and efficacy of the communist propaganda machine. It is also a function of the natural desire of ordinary, fair-minded people everywhere to live at peace. Among such people are many who would concede that things were thus in Lenin's day and Stalin's. But surely, they would argue, all this is over, now that individual communist parties no longer take their orders from Moscow, expending their energies in internecine feuds and being pulled this way and that by the rival pretensions of Moscow, Peking and Havana. The argument is not without force, and needs to be examined critically in the light of available evidence.

Clearly, communist subversion is no longer the threat it was in the days when Stalin could call out the French workers on strike, or order Indonesian communists to take up arms in a futile uprising against the local Nationalist authorities. But at least in Stalin's day there was a monolithic simplicity about the threat of international subversion. If the Security forces made a capture, they knew where the orders had come from, and the gold as well. Nowadays, the threat is diffuse, ambiguous, hard to isolate and identify. It comes from several directions. It is still a threat, but a more complicated one.

Lenin believed in world revolution; and so did Stalin, for all his talk of 'socialism in one country'. When Lenin created the Comintern in 1919, one of his main objectives was to foster local revolutions in Western dependencies and thus—as he thought—hasten the collapse of capitalism. But the Comintern was only one of the Soviet instruments of world revolution. One of the others was a network of front organizations, which Lenin conceived as 'transmission belts' to the masses. The term 'front' has two quite distinct meanings: to the layman, the meaning that is most familiar is that implied by such expressions as 'United Front' and 'Popular Front'; the 'National Liberation Front' of South Vietnam is an example, and recent history has given us many examples of 'Fatherland Fronts'—yet another variant. Essentially, this kind of front is a tactical, political alliance between the Communists and other parties, which are later discarded when they have fulfilled their purpose, from the communist point of view.

It is often forgotten that this 'united front' technique was used by the Bolsheviks at the birth of Soviet communism. For in November 1917, the Soviet government went into partnership with left-wing members of the Social Revolutionary Party. In the ensuing elections of 25 November 1917, the Communists—although already in power—filled only 175 seats in the Constituent Assembly, out of a total of 707. As soon as the Assembly met, it was dissolved by armed Communists. A few months later the Social Revolutionaries had been ejected from the government. In the 1930s, the French and Spanish communists formed Popular Fronts with Socialist and even non-socialist parties of the Left to gain a share in power. The same technique of the united front was used by Mao Tse-tung during the Chinese civil war. In Eastern Europe, various united fronts were set up after the Second World War by local Communists under Soviet protection. For the unwary or the unprotected, the united front is a political death trap.

The united front technique is still an essential weapon in the communist armoury, and willing partners are still to be found. The Chilean Socialist leader, Señor Allende, went into partnership with the local Communists, under the title of Revolutionary Popular Action Front (FRAP from the Spanish initials) in the Presidential election of 1964. Fortunately for him, he lost. The French left-of-centre politician, François Mitterrand, went into partnership with the Communist Party for the 1966 Presidential election; but he too had the good fortune to lose. In South Vietnam, the NLF is entirely dominated by the People's Revolutionary Party, an offshoot of the ruling Lao Dong (Workers', that is, communist) Party of North Vietnam; but it includes some non-communists, none of whom can hope to exert any influence on the course of events should the NLF come to power in Saigon.

The other kind of front—the 'front organization'—is essentially a long-term technique. It is not intended, as the united front is, to bring specific results in months or even years. It is an instrument for the continuing subversion of non-communist societies and the furtherance of Soviet policies. The idea came to Lenin in 1921. Communism, he thought, could be propagated through trade unions, co-operatives, youth and women's organizations, and so on. In March 1926, at a meeting of the Comintern executive committee, the veteran Finnish Communist, Otto Kuusinen, called for the creation of a 'whole solar system of organizations and smaller committees around the communist parties . . . actually working under the influence of the Party but not under its mechanical control'.* Many such fronts were set up in the 1920s and 1930s. They included the Red International of Trade Unions, the Communist Youth International and the International Workers' Aid Society. Vigorous and effective, they collapsed when the Soviet Union signed its notorious pact with Hitler's Germany in 1939. From 1945 on, the Russians created a whole range of new international front organizations. In some instances, the Communists took over organizations that had been set up at other people's initiative. At the outset, many non-communists, both individuals and groups, joined the international bodies, believing them to be non-political. By 1949, Moscow's control over them was total; and many of the original members resigned on realizing this fact. But the Russians have never eased up in their effort to recruit new generations of innocents for their membership. Today there are ten Soviet-controlled international front organizations. Brief notes on each appear in Appendix I (page 227).

Just how effective are the international front organizations? The quick answer is that they are much less effective than they used to be before the Sino-Soviet dispute came into the open, and before Havana developed independent subversive programmes of its own. But this is a broad answer, which needs qualification.

* *International Press Correspondence.* Vol. 6, vi, No. 28, April 1926.

The front organizations were at their strongest during the first few years after World War II, when the memory of the Russians as 'gallant allies' was still lively, and a natural, uncritical sympathy for them was exploited for all its possibilities by the communist parties. The virulence of their anti-Western propaganda during Stalin's period was, however, self-defeating. The captive audience of non-communist individuals and groups available in those earlier years vanished when the non-communists pulled out to found their own international bodies; and the Communists in the fronts were left largely, as it were, talking to themselves. Seeing the danger, Khrushchev softened the tone of speeches and resolutions, and many new recruits were drawn in.

By far the most effective of the Soviet-controlled fronts, over the years, has been the World Council of Peace (WCP), which by virtue of the magic word in its title has drawn in a wide range of pacifists, intellectuals, internationalists, churchmen and idealists, including at times world-famous figures, such as Professor J. D. Bernal and Bertrand Russell. Because the WCP has such a wide appeal, however the Communists have found it difficult to keep it under tight control. Its effectiveness should not be under-estimated, despite dissensions which at times have been embar-rassingly visible. In common with other front organizations, the WCP has always been ready to oblige with anti-colonial—that is, anti-Western—resolutions; it kept silent when the Russians subjugated Hungary and the Chinese oppressed the Tibetans. Similarly, Western nuclear tests have been condemned, but not a word came out in condemnation of the Soviet tests, even though these have included a test of a 60-megaton bomb. In the Arab-Israeli dispute, all its strictures have been reserved for the Israelis, the Arabs receiving praise and support. A major propaganda theme has, of course, been Vietnam. The Soviet line on the war has been supported at many meetings, with appropriate condem-nations of the Americans. The Stockholm Conference on Vietnam in July 1967 was partly sponsored by the WCP. The World Federation of Trade Unions is important in a different way. Because the major French and Italian trade union bodies (CGT and CGIL) are communist-controlled, the WFTU has a large follow-ing in Western Europe. It is efficiently organized, with highly-disciplined affiliates. It is also, on the other hand, vulnerable to exposure—a fact of which the rival International Confederation of Free Trade Unions (ICFTU) has often taken advantage.

The Youth and Student Front Organizations (YFDY and IUS) are always on the look-out for talented—and recruitable—youngsters, particularly in Africa and other under-developed areas. Student scholarships in communist countries are offered and cleared through the IUS. By its character, the International Organization of Journalists (IOJ) creates special opportunities for propaganda. In recent years, it has had a marked impact in certain African countries, by offering the kind of practical help which the press of newly independent countries badly needs—such as courses in journalism, and all the requirements of press agencies and newspapers, including money, machinery and other equipment, and trained personnel. The Radio and Television Front Organization (OIRT) works closely with the IOJ and has won the confidence of a number of African governments.

The remaining Soviet-controlled fronts are relatively in-effectual. The Women's International Democratic Federation has had little impact, even in countries whose women are still not emancipated, although it did hold a conference in Bamako, in Mali, in 1965. The Resistance Front (FIR) has a dwindling membership; the Lawyer's front (IADL) is sometimes useful to the Russians by setting up commissions of inquiry, for instance on the German or Vietnamese problems, pleading the Soviet case. The Scientific Workers' Front (WFSW) works closely with the WCP because of its special interest in nuclear disarmament.

The recent history of the front organizations has been interesting, and occasionally entertaining. It was largely through the front organizations' international conferences that the world became aware that the Russians now had a communist problem of their own—a *Chinese* communist problem. The spectacle of Chinese delegates thumping the table, grabbing the microphone, shouting to drown the Soviet spokesmen's voices, had a high audience-value against the grey background of monotonous anti-Western resolutions and speeches. But in Sofia in December 1966, things came to such a pass that the Chinese delegates to the

WFTU General Council meeting had to be forcibly expelled. Thereafter, the Chinese boycotted major front conferences, although they did not formally resign from any of them. Instead, they have been setting up front organizations of their own, or securing control over existing bodies. None of the Chinese-controlled bodies is of major importance, but the most important are the Afro-Asian Writers' Permanent Bureau and the Afro-Asian Journalists' Association.

The Soviet invasion of Czechoslovakia in 1968 was a traumatic experience for the Soviet-controlled front organizations, four of which have their headquarters in Prague. All four had watched in silence as the Soviet pressure built up against the Dubcek government. The Russian invasion, when it came, threw them into unprecedented disarray. The WFTU's Secretary-General, Louis Saillant, and its President, Renato Bitossi, publicly denounced the intervention. On 28 August, the WFTU Secretariat issued a statement endorsing the attitude of Saillant and Bitossi and 'condemning and deeply regretting' the action of the Soviet Union and its four Warsaw Pact partners. The WCP, clearly much embarrassed, found nothing to say until 10 September, when it issued a statement in Brussels expressing 'concern and anxiety'; but, in contrast with the WFTU, welcoming the agreement the Czechoslovak leaders had reached in Moscow. This qualified rebuke was noticeably milder than the attitude of a number of affiliated peace movements, which roundly denounced the invasion.

Since those days of crisis, however, the Russians have worked hard, and on the whole successfully, to restore their hold on the front organizations. Their tactic has been to persuade the fronts to avoid mentioning the occupation of Czechoslovakia as far as possible and concentrate on other themes, such as Vietnam, the Arab-Israel crisis, the government of the Colonels in Greece, European security and other subjects on which the fronts are willing to echo the Moscow line. This replacement of Dubcek by the relatively hard-line Dr Husak in April 1969 has helped the Russians. But the old days of total Moscow control have gone, and are likely never to return in a form that would have satisfied Stalin.

Two front organizations that stand apart from the others in the breadth of their subversive intent are the Solidarity Organizations – the Afro-Asian People's Solidarity Organization (AAPSO) and the Afro-Asian Latin American People's Solidarity Organization (AALAPSO). The People's Solidarity Movement was set up – at Moscow's instigation, though indirectly – because the Russians had not been invited to the original Afro-Asian conference held at Bandung in 1955. The Chinese, whose Asian credentials were unimpeachable, were of course at Bandung, but the general consensus was that the Soviet Union was a European Power. The Russians, whose colonial territories sprawled over Asia, argued that they were Asians as well as Europeans. Having been snubbed at the front door, they decided to try the back door.

The Bandung conference was at the 'Head of State' level. An Indian emissary, acting in fact though not in name as Moscow's agent, persuaded President Nasser of Egypt to call a 'people's' conference in Cairo at the end of 1957. The advantage of labelling it a 'people's' conference was that any party or group designated by the Russians, for instance, as representing a 'people' – as distinct from its government – would be eligible to attend. The outcome of this conference was the creation of the AAPSO. As a price for being accepted as 'Asians', the Russians had to share power with the Chinese and Egyptians in this new body. For some years, however, the AAPSO was of great value to the Soviet Communist Party in co-ordinating and spreading its influence in the Third World. But as the Sino-Soviet split developed in the 1960s, the value of the organization became dubious if not counter-productive. The Chinese opted out in 1967; the AAPSO is now firmly in Egyptian hands, but the Russians continue to take a close interest in it.

The AALAPSO has also had a chequered history. It was logical, once Cuba had emerged as a professed communist country, to extend the Afro-Asian People's Solidarity Movement to Latin America. This was the idea behind the Tri-Continental Conference that was called in Havana in January 1966. It was intended that the Tri-Continental Organization envisaged should replace the AAPSO, although the headquarters would continue to be in Cairo. But the Chinese and the Cubans each had their own reasons to oppose this proposal, the Chinese because of their boycott of the Cairo organization and their irretrievable break with Moscow, and the Cubans because they had revolutionary ambitions of their own which they thought would be furthered if the new organization were based in Havana. In the event, it was decided that the AAPSO should continue in Cairo, while the Afro-Asian Latin American People's Solidarity Organization would be set up with an interim Secretariat in Havana.

The Havana conference was crowned, as such gatherings usually are, with a spate of anti-Western resolutions, to which a Soviet delegation composed of central Asians duly subscribed. The immediate outcome was a wave of protests from Latin American governments with which Moscow had diplomatic relations. What they wanted to know was how the Russians could subscribe to calls for their overthrow, while maintaining a friendly relationship. To this, Moscow responded with a denial that the Soviet delegation at the Havana conference was officially representative of the Soviet Union. The incident was an example of a communist regime's ability to operate on two levels; and also, of course, of the dilemma that increasingly faces the Soviet leaders when Party and State interests appear to clash.

This dilemma is real enough but of comparatively recent origin. In Stalin's day, it was virtually impossible for the interests of the Party to clash with those of the government, for an obedient world communist movement was always ready to execute a somersault if the State interests of the Soviet Union required a change of Party line. The most famous example of this — though it was only one among many — was the abrupt change imposed on communist parties all over the world when Stalin and Hitler concluded a pact in 1939. Stalin's heirs are less fortunate in this respect. The long-term aims of Party and State probably continue to coincide, but short-term conflicts have become difficult to avoid. State interests dictate a broadening of diplomatic relations, with an accompanying increase in trade and cultural exchanges. In the long term, this policy also serves the Communist Party's aim of penetration and subversion by more or less constitutional method. The Party's aim is also, however, to restore — if possible — Moscow's control of the international communist movement.

But the Soviet Party can hardly hope to be accepted as the vanguard of world revolution if it dissociates itself from movements dedicated to revolutionary violence. The compulsion to pay at least lip service to revolutionary violence — occasionally, where safe to do so, with contributions in cash, material, advice and training — is the stronger for the relentless competition from the Chinese and Cubans, both of whom claim to have developed successful models of revolution.

It is important to realize that the Soviet dilemma is not a moral one: it concerns only the choice of tactics to serve a long-established strategy. Its nature can perhaps best be understood in contrast with the subversive practices of communist governments that are not comparably inhibited — those of China, North Vietnam and Cuba. In Mao's declining years, Peking's apparent belief in permanent revolution and revolutionary violence everywhere is total. In September 1965, the Defence Minister, Marshal Lin-piao, called for the extension to the entire world of the Maoist theory of 'encirclement of the cities from the countryside'. In this concept, the capitalist countries were 'the cities' and the Third World (that is, Asia, Africa and Latin America) was the 'countryside'. He proposed that the process of encirclement should be carried through by people's wars led by communists taking China's revolutionary war as a model. That this theory was geographically nonsensical did not matter. China was serving notice on the world that so far as it lay within her power, she would go on helping revolutionary movements, especially those prepared to fight guerrilla wars, all over the world and without an end in sight.

The Chinese, in fact, were already well established in the of business international subversion. As early as 1960, members of the *Armée de Libération Nationale Kamerounaise* were arrested on returning from China where they had received guerrilla training. Africans from many countries continued to receive such training in China. The Chinese have also provided instructors in sabotage, guerrilla warfare and terrorist techniques, in training camps in Tanzania, in Ghana (in Nkrumah's day) and in Congo-Brazzaville. On a number of occasions, however, the Chinese have gone too far, and their embassies — used, as communist embassies often are, as espionage and subversion centres — were closed down some years ago in Burundi, Dahomey, Upper Volta and the Central African Republic.

In South-East Asia, the Chinese have been relatively cautious, for all their talk of the American 'paper tiger' and their professed scorn of nuclear dangers. They have, for instance, done far less than the Russians to help the North Vietnamese and the South Vietnam's Viet Cong in their war against the South Vietnamese government and the United States. Caution was not, however, the only reason for this relative inactivity: the painful fact for the Chinese was that they were simply not in a position to provide advanced weaponry for the Vietnamese Communists. Instead, they shipped big quantities of small arms and coolie labour in large numbers. Elsewhere in South-East Asia, one must take care to distinguish between Chinese lip support and actual involvement. The Chinese press and radio report news of guerrilla movements in great detail and in terms that imply proprietary rights — for example by attributing any successes to the 'Thoughts' of Mao Tse-tung. In fact, geographical distances would make it difficult for the Chinese to intervene actively in support of guerrilla movement in the Philippines, or on the borders between Thailand and Malaysia, and Sarawak and Indonesia, where there are no Chinese embassies that could serve as subversive centres. Chinese influence is nevertheless strong over the Philippine Communist Party, the Sarawak Communist Organization, sections of the Indonesian Communist Party (PKI) and the remnants of the Malayan Communist guerrillas. In countries on China's doorstep, however, there is strong evidence that the Chinese *are* involved, in the sense of supplying money, arms or training, in Thailand, Laos and Burma; and in India, Pakistan, Nepal and even as far afield as Ceylon.

The Vietnamese communists, within their geographical limitations, are considerably less inhibited than the Big Brothers of the communist world. North Vietnam's territorial ambitions are not confined to South Vietnam but extend to the other former States of French Indo-China — Laos and Cambodia — and even to Thailand, where there is a large Vietnamese minority. In Laos, the Pathet Lao movement was created by Ho Chi Minh's agents, and is entirely under Hanoi's control. In Cambodia, the Vietnamese Communists have attempted to spark off local uprisings. In Thailand, where a small guerrilla war is in progress in the North-East, the North Vietnamese are involved in two ways. The Vietnamese minority conduct subversive actions in support of the insurgents; and in North Vietnam itself, there is a training school at Hoa Binh for the Thai Communist Party guerrillas, and training facilities for Laotians.

The other maverick of the communist world is Cuba. Fidel Castro got in *his* international revolutionary call three years ahead of the Chinese Lin-piao – in February 1962, in the so-called Second Declaration of Havana, which called on the Latin American peoples to overthrow their governments. Shortly after he achieved power in 1959, Fidel Castro created schools and training centres, where students from foreign countries could be taught the propaganda techniques of Marxism-Leninism and the tactics of sabotage and guerrilla warfare. Latin Americans naturally predominated, but many African students were also trained in Cuba. Among them were the successful revolutionaries who seized power in Zanzibar in December 1963. In Africa itself, Cuban instructors have been busy, at various times, in Congo-Leopoldville (Kinshasa), Congo-Brazzaville and Tanzania. In Latin America, Castro's revolutionary efforts have been constant since 1961, but with a remarkable lack of success. There were, however, near misses for Cuban methods in Venezuela in 1963 and in the Dominican Republic in April 1965. Castro's former lieutenant in the Cuban revolutionary war, the Argentine-born 'Che' Guevara, failed in his attempt to set up a guerrilla movement in Bolivia, and was captured and killed in 1967. Today, however, in the face of these set-backs, there are still Castroite revolutionary movements in Colombia, Venezuela, Guatemala, Uruguay, Argentina and Peru. Increasingly, however, the emphasis is on urban violence rather than rural uprisings.

The Soviet Union's policy in this dangerous field of violent subversion has been less fanatical, less consistent and more opportunistic than that of China, North Vietnam or Cuba. As we have seen (Part 1, 2), the Russians committed themselves to supporting 'national liberation movements' in 1960. But this commitment was, in practice, very widely interpreted. On the one hand, training facilities for terrorists and guerrillas, mostly from Africa, were and still are given in the Soviet Union and, with Soviet approval, in Bulgaria. But the Russians like to keep as many options open as possible. In 1960, when the Belgian Congo was rather suddenly granted independence, the Soviet and Czechoslovak diplomatic missions made an all-out bid to secure power for their nominees. But the attempt ended in failure, and all communist missions in Leopoldville were expelled in September 1960. Diplomatic relations were later resumed, but in November 1963, the Soviet embassy in Leopoldville was again expelled. This made the Russians cautious — for a time. In October 1964, however, two things happened that produced a change of tactics. In Moscow itself, Khrushchev was overthrown; and in the Sudan, the Abboud government was also thrown out of office. General Abboud had consistently refused suggestions from the communists and from such militant non-communist governments as those of Egypt (United Arab Republic) and Algeria to allow Sudanese territory to be used as a staging post for an arms air lift to the Congolese rebels. The new government, under El Khalifa, was of more militant temper and granted the permission withheld by its predecessor. For some time thereafter, arms were airlifted to the rebels from the United Arab Republic, Algeria and Ghana. The precise degree of Russian involvement is not publicly known, but the arms were of Soviet and Czechoslovak origin, and the planes that delivered them were Soviet-built transports.

Nor does this end the tale of Russia's involvement in subversion in Africa. Until Nkrumah's overthrow in February 1966, Ghana had provided the Soviet Union — and other communist countries and parties — with an ideal subsidiary centre of subversion. Nkrumah had pan-African ambitions of his own, which he attempted to further through an African Affairs Bureau. The Bureau controlled a number of training camps, in at least one of which Russian instructors were employed. (Here again, the subversion was competitive since Chinese instructors were employed in another camp, and a variety of instruction was provided by Cubans, among others.) The East Germans — of all the East European satellites the most dependent upon Soviet support—provided Nkrumah with training in intelligence methods. Another institution much used by the Russian and other communists was the Kwame Nkrumah Ideological Institute, which—on Russian advice—was used as the sole selecting ground for members of the President's Personal Security service. All these facilities were, however, swept away with Nkrumah himself in 1966, and the Soviet embassy was among the diplomatic missions expelled by the new military government.

Kenya, Mali and Guinea have also been the targets of Soviet subversion, and Guinea—though under a regime that owes much to Marxism-Leninism and to economic support from the Soviet bloc—is one of the countries from which a Soviet ambassador has been expelled. Partly as a result of such setbacks, Soviet policy in Africa has been markedly more cautious during the past three years. In particular, a sharper distinction has been drawn between African States that are already independent (even though their governments may not be to Moscow's taste) and what is loosely known as 'white Africa'—that is, the Portuguese dependencies, South Africa, South-West Africa, and Rhodesia. In all of these, liberation movements qualify for Russian approval, and support with training, arms, money and advice—in competition with help available from China, and the militant African member-States of the Organization for African Unity.

In South-East Asia too, Soviet policy has had its ups and downs. Russia's role in initiating the abortive insurrections of 1948 has been mentioned. Soviet arms helped the Vietnamese Communists defeat France in 1954. Some years later, Khrushchev was sending aircraft and technicians to a neutralist leader in Laos. But when the neutralist, Captain Kong Lae, started using the planes to attack his former communist allies, Khrushchev became alarmed and withdrew the planes. In the summer of 1964, Khrushchev gave the then British Foreign Secretary, Mr R. A. Butler (now Lord Butler) the impression that he was opting out of the Indo-China conflict altogether. Indeed, for the first seven years of the second Indo-China war, the Russians did virtually nothing to help the Vietnamese Communists. A major reason for this was doubtless the lesson Khrushchev had drawn from his confrontation with President Kennedy in Cuba in 1962, which had shown him the dangers of involving the Soviet Union in a situation that could lead to a possible nuclear conflict with the United States.

In Indo-China as in the Sudan, however, Khrushchev's successors showed themselves less cautious than he had been. In early 1965, the situation did indeed appear to support a bolder policy, for North Vietnam and its Southern offshoot, the National Liberation Front, seemed on the point of victory over the thoroughly demoralized South Vietnamese and their American advisers. Hoping perhaps for a decisive voice in any future peace talks, and also for a chance to demonstrate before the international communist movement that the Russians were more effective revolutionaries than the Chinese, the Soviet Premier, Kosygin, went to Hanoi and committed his government to a programme of massive military aid. On paper, it was not a bad calculation. But the South Vietnamese Communists upset it by attacking American military installations while Kosygin and his team were in Hanoi. The Americans retaliated by bombing attacks on North Vietnam, and the great escalation had begun.

The Russians could not, however, lose face by withdrawing their offer of military aid and indeed, they have continued to supply aid, on a high technological level and in great quantities, ever since. Here again there was an apparent contradiction between Soviet State and Party interests. State interest undoubtedly dictated the avoidance of any chance of a nuclear confrontation with the United States. Party interests favoured a revolutionary competition with China. In the end, because of the forbearance shown both in Washington and in Moscow, these conflicting interests were reconciled. Nuclear war was avoided, Moscow's revolutionary credentials were enhanced and China's relative impotence demonstrated.

In Latin America, the Soviet policy has been even more ambiguous and apparently confusing than elsewhere. Verbal support for armed insurrection is intermittent. It comes in the Soviet broadcasts in the Quechua language of the ancient Incas, calling on the Indians of the Andes to revolt against their 'oppressors'; in the Radio Peace and Progress programmes from

Moscow; in Soviet approval of a resolution passed at a conference in Havana in November 1964, calling for active support for revolutionary movements in several Latin American countries; and in Soviet support through Moscow's 'unofficial' delegation, for the stronger resolutions adopted by the Tri-Continental conference, also in Havana, in January 1966. Moreover, the Russians are undoubtedly involved in active support for some revolutionary guerrilla movements in Latin America.

There is no real evidence, however, that the Soviet ideologists have any genuine belief, much less faith, in violent revolution as a road to power in Latin America. For orthodox, Moscow-line, communist parties everywhere in the region, notably in Chile where the communists are relatively strong, Moscow's instructions where the Communists are relatively strong, Moscow's instructions are to concentrate on constitutional methods, such as united Democrats, and so on. Moreover, at the State-to-State level, the Russians are pressing for increased trade and closer diplomatic relations, but the Soviet dilemma is more acute in Latin America than elsewhere. In economic terms, Fidel Castro's Cuban regime is a Soviet satellite. In political terms, however, this is not the case: Fidel Castro goes his own way, defying Moscow and gaoling local Communists who appear to be taking their instructions from the Russians. In the crudest possible terms, the Russians would doubtless like to get value for their money—for Cuba is an enormously expensive burden to carry. They may reckon that in the long run, when and if Fidel Castro is out of power—they may yet bring this unruly satellite under control. Certainly, it is Russian money that makes it possible for Castro to support revolutionary subversion in other Latin American countries.

In the meantime, however, the Russians cannot afford to be outbid by this upstart revolutionary. Hence they make all the right revolutionary noises; hence, too, they support movements of their own. All this is 'competitive subversion'. It may well be that they wish to gain the guerrilla movements in Latin America under their control the better to stifle them. And it is fair to assume that they wish at all costs to avoid a second nuclear confrontation with the United States. The fact remains that they are founder-members, as it were, of the Tri-Continental Solidarity Organization in Havana. And this means that they must do something, and be seen to be doing something, in Latin America as elsewhere.

6. *The Outsiders*

It is customary among Kremlinologists, Pekinologists and less specialized students of communism, on both sides of the Atlantic, to classify the communist parties in opposition according to their supposed allegiance to Moscow or Peking. It is an absorbing and ingenious pastime, in which I too indulge from time to time. Its utility, as a barometer of Moscow's success or failure in its efforts to reunite the world communist movement under its leadership, is not to be underestimated. It is, however, an inexact science, since it is increasingly difficult to say whether a given party really does support Moscow or Peking in the sense of unconditional alignment. Support on specific issues—such as the nuclear Test Ban Treaty, the occupation of Czechoslovakia or the desirability of peasant guerrillas—tells us more about the domestic political context in which a party operates than about fundamental loyalties. For instance, the North Vietnamese Workers' Party sided with Peking in declining to sign the Test Ban Treaty, at a time when the Russians seemed to have lost interest in Indo-China, and when it looked as if the Chinese would be the only source of material support to them in their war against the United States. The same party, however, supported the Soviet occupation of Czechoslovakia—after three years of escalating Soviet military aid to North Vietnam initiated by Khrushchev's successors. In Indonesia, the late D. N. Aidit, Secretary-General of the Communist Party (PKI), deliberately cultivated ambiguity in his attitude towards the Sino-Soviet dispute, by appearing to support both the peasant revolution advocated by Peking *and* the 'constitutional' approach favoured by Moscow. This chapter will not therefore deal in any systematic way with party alignments in the great schism.

My own reading of the history of communism, especially since the death of Stalin, is that the Russians are unlikely to succeed fully in restoring the disciplined unity of the international communist movement under their leadership that was characteristic of the Lenin and Stalin periods. But their dogged efforts to do so should not be underestimated. Between 1964 and 1969 they made repeated attempts to summon a world communist conference. At the time of Khrushchev's overthrow, the Chinese were working ceaselessly, with money and propaganda, to win individual parties away from Moscow and set up pro-Peking parties or factions. In India, Brazil, Belgium and other countries, they were successful. The main object of the Russians in attempting to convene a world conference was to counter this alarming situation, if possible by persuading the world's communist parties to join them in condemning the Chinese party and even, should this be necessary, 'expel' it from the world movement.

In March 1965, after months of efforts, they persuaded eighteen parties to attend a 'consultative' meeting in Moscow. They had hoped twenty-six would be represented. Among the many parties that stayed away was the Rumanian, which was determined to assert its independence and non-alignment in the Sino-Soviet dispute, although Rumania was clearly in the Soviet orbit. The Italian party, though it sent delegates to Moscow, showed itself highly resistant to the idea of solemnly excommunicating the Chinese. And eventually it was the Italian view that prevailed over the Soviet.

After several postponements and an unsatisfactory gathering of European communist parties at Karlovy Vary (Carlsbad) in April 1967, seventy-five of the world's communist parties assembled in Moscow on 5 June 1969. By 18 June most of them had agreed to sign a Document that represented the residual common ground between the parties attending the conference. It was an anodyne text, interesting above all for what the Russians had been forced to leave out. A comparison with two earlier drafts smuggled out to Western capitals is illuminating. The first draft, dated 25 July 1968, in particular, justified the provision of arms and the training of volunteers for the guerrilla forces of the 'national liberation' movements, and called for a world anti-imperialist conference.

Both these points were dropped in the second draft, presented by the working group that met in Moscow from 10 to 18 March 1969 though it was announced after the meeting that a world anti-imperialist conference would be organized. Both drafts and the final Document of 18 June refrained from condemning Peking and indeed called for the admission of the Chinese People's Republic to the United Nations. True, the Document restored a semblance of unity to the world communist movement, but on conditions Stalin would have found intolerable, for it plainly stated that 'there is no leading centre of the international communist movement'. Even then, the independent-minded Italians refused to sign Parts I, II and IV of the Document. Only the most innocuous section, Part III, got their endorsement. This attitude was consistent with their earlier denunciations of the Soviet occupation of Czechoslovakia and their consistent defence of Yugoslavia's experimental socialism.

Moscow's price for achieving the voluntary unity of the parties that attended the conference was thus a diversity of views that was the opposite of the discipline they had sought to restore. From this, many Western commentators concluded that the conference was a failure. In fact, it was a half-failure. And, just as a glass of water that is half-empty is also half-full, so it might be said that the 1969 conference was a half-success for Moscow. Ceausescu of Rumania, for instance, signed the full Document. True, he reasserted the rights of individual parties and declared that 'the principle of internationalism' should not be invoked 'if it interferes in any way in the internal affairs of a socialist country or a fraternal party'. But this was a mild echo of the militant terms in which he had denounced the Soviet invasion of Czechoslovakia only ten months earlier. Moreover, Ceausescu pledged his party's readiness always to carry out its duties as a vanguard of the international front of communists.

More satisfactorily still, Husak of Czechoslovakia—Moscow's choice as the man to restore order and obedience after Dubcek's experiment with freedom—blamed the Soviet invasion on the Czechoslovak Party's loss of control over events. Nor did he use such emotive terms as 'Soviet invasion'. Instead, he chose a euphemism: 'the well-known events of August'. This must have been music in Russian ears. Indeed, Dr Husak rebuked other communist leaders for their criticism of Moscow, which he blamed on their ignorance of the true situation.

A number of parties, of course, had stayed away from the gathering of June 1969: the Chinese, North Vietnamese, North Koreans and Yugoslavs among them. But the message of the conference was that Stalin's East European empire stood restored and intact in the shadow of the Soviet Army. Those present had averted their eyes from Russia's misdeeds in fraternal Czechoslovakia. All they could see was a world threatened by wicked American imperialism.

What conclusion could be drawn from Moscow's apparent acceptance of the view that there was no longer a 'leading centre' of world communism? Certainly not that the international movement had ceased to be a problem. This would be quite unwarranted, since in every case Russia's efforts to restore full control could be expected to continue unabated. Admittedly, the problem is different in kind. It is no longer the acute and indeed terrifying problem of a monolithic world movement at Stalin's order at the time of the Soviet Union's maximum power and hostility, which forced the West to unite and sign the Atlantic Treaty in 1949. But it is a new and more complicated problem. Paradoxically, indeed, the reason why polycentric communism is a problem is inherent in the circumstances that made monolithic communism cease to be one.

In the first euphoria of the Bolshevik *coup d'état*, Lenin's belief in world revolution made sense. In May 1919, the first issue of the Comintern journal the *International Press Correspondence*) proclaimed that the whole of Europe would be Soviet 'before a year has passed'. It was, in fact, the year of collapsed revolutionary hopes, with the abortive Spartacist rising in Berlin; the five-month life of Bela Kun's Soviet Republic of Hungary; the fiasco of the Bavarian Soviet Republic; and the ill-starred attempted uprising sponsored by the Austrian Communist Party. Though obliged to defer his hopes, however, Lenin went on working for world revolution through the Comintern. And so did Stalin, despite the realistic slogan of 'socialism in one country'.

The communist case continued to be plausible in the 1930s. The collapse of the Wall Street stock market in 1929 and the world depression that followed seemed to support the Marxist-Leninist belief in the impending 'general crisis of capitalism'. And it made sense that Stalin should consolidate socialism in its original home at a time of hostile capitalist encirclement. The credibility of international communism was, of course, badly shaken by the Hitler-Stalin pact, but the memory of this unparalleled act of cynicism swiftly faded when the historical accident of Hitler's decision to invade the Soviet Union made Stalin the West's gallant ally. By 1948, when the Czechoslovak Communists incorporated their country into the Soviet empire under protection of Russian bayonets, many of the non-communists in the West who had developed an emotional tolerance for communism during the war had begun to have second thoughts. In general, however, the non-ruling communist parties stomached the judicial murders in Eastern Europe and the creation of Stalin's satellite empire in the name of historical necessity.

The dissolution of the world communist monolith was, however, inherent in the cold war, and would probably have happened even if Stalin had lived a few more years.* The total and relentless hostility of Soviet propaganda, faithfully echoed by communist parties all over the world, served to isolate communism as the unmistakable enemy. This view was powerfully supported by such incidents as the abortive communist revolution in Greece, the Soviet boycott of the Marshall Aid programme, and the Korean War, together with the revelations of life in the Soviet Union by defectors, especially Victor Kravchenko (*I Chose Freedom*). The identification of the Soviet Union as an enemy and communist parties everywhere as that enemy's instruments, had two consequences. On the one hand, there were the fence-sitters and opportunists, the pusillanimous, who believed that communism, especially after Mao Tse-tung's advent to power in China, was 'the winning side', and were therefore tempted to join it if only for personal reinsurance. The great majority of people in Western countries, however,

* For further discussion of some of these arguments, see Kevin Devlin, *The Decline of Leninism in Western Europe, 1 & 2,* 27 November 1967 and 15 January 1968, Radio Free Europe Research, Munich.

reacted by deciding that 'something' had to be done about communism. This was the time of the birth of specialized publications devoted to anti-communist analyses, such as *Est & Ouest** in Paris, of the birth of the Congress for Cultural Freedom and of similar or complementary organizations in many countries. On the international front, Nato was born. Nationally, the Western intelligence services diverted their main efforts from the defeated enemy—German Nazism—to the active one, Soviet communism; and discreet government departments were set up to analyse, interpret and counter communist propaganda and activities. In France, de Gaulle labelled the French Communist Party '*les séparatistes*', and the label was seen to correspond with the truth. The power of monolithic communism was such that Stalin could decree a strike in France or Italy. But the seeds of weakness and dissolution were there too: government and security services were alerted, and so was public opinion although a long process of political education lay ahead. Thereafter, any group or individual that supported communism laid itself open to a charge of moral or actual treason.

This situation was unfortunately exploited and abused—most notably in the United States—by such unscrupulous demagogues as the late Senator Joseph McCarthy, but the starkness of the choice open to the citizens was undeniable. *For those who understood the nature of the enemy,* neutrality was the equivalent of support: if one was not for communism, one was bound to be against it. The late John Foster Dulles was right when he declared that 'neutralism is immoral'; unfortunate though that phrase was, since it gave offence to the leaders of newly independent countries, then trying to assert their independence of colonial rule by embarking on a policy of non-alignment between the hostile military blocs of East and West.

The political threat to monolithic communism implicit in the cold war was enormously increased by Western economic successes. With the enlightened aid made available by the United States under the Marshall Plan, Western Europe rose phoenix-like from the ashes of the war. The contrast between the boom-

* Originally entitled BEIPI (Bulletin de l'Association d'Etudes et d'Informations Politiques Internationales).

ing prosperity of Western capitalism and the organized scarcity of Eastern communism was dramatically evident to anybody crossing the checkpoints between West and East Berlin. Moreover, Western capitalism was demonstrating an astonishing and unexpected capacity to cure its own ailments and deficiencies. In Britain, the Labour government introduced welfare socialism (and, for better or worse, nationalized major industries) without revolutionary violence. In Western Europe, especially, full employment became an article of faith. The lessons of John Maynard Keynes had been learnt, and there was to be no return to the depressed 1930s. There were trade cycles still, but ways of ironing out the extremes of boom and depression had been found. Inflation was a problem, but to many people it was an acceptable price to pay for prosperity and full employment. In Western Germany and Japan, the wealth-creating capacity of private enterprise was stunningly demonstrated. And the economists of the Kennedy and Johnson eras in the United States showed that, for all America's social problems, it was possible to continue to expand the Gross National Product at a rate that frustrated all Soviet efforts to compete. In economic terms, indeed, it was the communist world that was in crisis in the late 1950s and in the decade of the 1960s, with the collapse of China's efforts at instant communism and the general breakdown of the system of centralized planning in Eastern Europe, most notably in Czechoslovakia. In Western Europe, in contrast, the European common market, by removing internal barriers to economic expansion, contributed to a startling rise in living standards.

In this situation, which I have necessarily over-simplified, the non-ruling communist parties inevitably faced a crisis of credibility. They would have faced it anyway, even if Stalin had still been alive; but the crisis was made far more acute by Khrushchev's denunciation of Stalin at the 20th Party Congress in Moscow, and by the Soviet repression of the Hungarian uprising. The dilemma that faced the leadership of the communist parties, particularly in Western countries, was essentially this: if they continued to support Moscow unconditionally, they would find themselves increasingly isolated in the eyes of local public opinion, and probably suffer a dwindling membership; if, on the other hand, they dissociated themselves from Moscow, their chances of gaining public support would be greatly improved, but they would weaken still further the claims of Marxism-Leninism to be a universally valid political philosophy. The advantage of the first course was that it would enable the party leadership to maintain a disciplined party, even if it were smaller in numbers. The advantage of the second course was that the Party's prospects of achieving power would be improved.

Let us now look at the way the three largest non-ruling communist parties faced up to the dilemma, and how two of them in particular behaved at a time of revolutionary crisis. The parties I have in mind are those of France, Italy and Indonesia. (In November 1965, the Indonesian party was the largest of the three, but its failure at a critical time resulted in near-annihilation.)

Broadly speaking, the French Communist Party (PCF) has always been ready to support Moscow. True, there were timid disagreements at the time of Khrushchev's denunciation of Stalin on 1956 and of his overthrow in the 'palace revolution' of October 1964; but these were nothing compared with the party's startling denunciation of the Russian invasion of Czechoslovakia in 1968. Even on this issue, however, the PCF soon started back-pedalling; until the central committee met on 13 and 14 October 1969, when the Secretary-General, Waldeck-Rochet, energetically denounced a member of the Politburo for maintaining his anti-Soviet attitude. The dissident, Roger Garandy, was spared on that occasion. But he was driven from the Politburo in February 1970, and expelled from the Party itself in May. Moscow's view had prevailed.

During the phase of monolithic communism, this was always the way disagreements in the international communist movement ended. What distinguished the PCF from other parties after 1956 was that it went on deferring to the Russians.* During this long post-Stalin period, the electoral support of the French Communist Party remained more or less the same, with approximately five million French voters ready to elect communist candidates to municipal councils or the National Assembly. But this apparently immovable voting strength told us more about the persistence of

* See *Est & Ouest*, Paris, 1–15 September 1968, p. 13.

the left-wing protest vote in France than about the real strength of the Communist Party. In fact, between 1946 and 1965, the membership of the Party declined from just over 804,000 to about 265,000. From 1946 — when the Communists left the French post-war government — until 1965, when they reached an electoral arrangement with the non-communist Left, led by François Mitterrand, for the specific purpose of defeating General de Gaulle in the presidential election of 1966 — the French Communist Party was the leper of national politics. No other political party would have anything to do with it. Although the Party took part in elections and usually returned a powerful body of deputies to the National Assembly, it was in effect an outcast.

The French Communists began seriously to re-examine their doctrine at their 17th Congress in 1964, which followed the death of Thorez, who had kept the Party on its narrow pro-Moscow line ever since its creation in the 1920s. His successor, Waldeck-Rochet, has proved himself more adaptable. His dilemma was a cruel one: on the one hand he wished to give his party a less ossified image by detaching it from its slavish subservience to Moscow and to ideological tenets that were looking decreasingly credible as time went on; on the other, there was a danger that if the Party became too obviously bourgeois and reassuring to the average Frenchman, it would lose its revolutionary appeal and perhaps be outflanked from the Left. Subsequent events have shown that the dilemma has not been satisfactorily restored; and indeed a solution seems logically unattainable, since it is hardly possible to be revolutionary and non-revolutionary at the same time. Waldeck-Rochet's attempts to resolve the dilemma, however, were ingenious. He himself, or the Party as a body, made statements that appeared to show that important ideological points were being modified. But subsequent explanations by the new Party boss made it clear that the modifications were not as radical as they appeared.

For instance, the doctrine that the Communist Party alone was qualified to preside over the advent of socialism was ostentatiously abandoned; but the need for a temporary 'dictatorship of the proletariat' — which simply means the dictatorship of the communist party — was subsequently reaffirmed. Similarly, violent revolution was tacitly abandoned in favour of a parliamentary and pacific path to socialism; but the right of the masses to use 'popular violence' if the bourgeoisie and reactionary forces themselves resisted the proposed socialist changes by force was explicitly stated. There was a similar ambiguity or duality about the Party's references to democratic rights. On the assumption that a socialist government was in power (that is, a government of the Communists in coalition with other left-wingers) the democratic right of the 'minority' in opposition would be guaranteed – but only 'in the framework of the new legality democratically established by the majority'. In other words, the communist-led government would draw up the rules, and the non-communists would have to abide by them or suffer the consequences. It would be a mistake, therefore, to conclude that the French Communist Party had ceased to be a totalitarian organization. Should a socialist regime be established through democratic elections, it would be there permanently – just as it would be if the Communists should come to power through revolutionary violence.

The French Party's abandonment of the violent path to power is, however, an important change. And its behaviour during the crisis of May and June 1968 showed that the change was a real one. Here was, it might be thought, an almost perfect pre-revolutionary situation. Students and agitators of different ages had taken to the streets. Law and order were breaking down, and armed clashes were taking place against the forces of order. More significantly still, from a Marxist standpoint, the workers began spontaneously to seize their factories and go on strike. If the French Communist Party had still been truly revolutionary in the Leninist sense, it would have taken advantage of these rare and unforeseen circumstances to attempt to seize power. Instead, it snubbed the revolutionary students, took over the spontaneous strike movement through its trade union organization, the General Confederation of Labour (CGT), and steered the revolutionary workers' movement toward a traditional demand for industrial advantages. In effect, it emerged as the saviour of the Gaullist regime, and the fact that the regime had nothing to fear from the Communists was made plain to the authorities, either tacitly or explicitly. True, the Party defended its passive attitude by claiming that it was not falling into the trap of violent action that would have given the government an excuse for suppressing the workers and imposing a military dictatorship. Nevertheless, Waldeck-Rochet saw fit to claim in an electoral broadcast reported in *L'Humanité* of 12 June 1968 that: '. . . the Communist Party has appeared as a party of order and of political wisdom . . . ' The claim was undoubtedly justified.

The greater flexibility displayed by the French Communists during the past few years has undoubtedly been very largely due to the influence of the Italian communist leadership. Thorez, the French Stalinist, had attacked the Italian Communist Party as revisionists. But when Italy's communist-controlled Trade Union organization (CGIL) met its French counterpart, the CGT, in Paris in December 1964, the French began to accept the Italian view that, for instance, toward the European Common Market, a policy of blind hostility was counter-productive. Instead, the French Communists began to agitate, as the Italians had been doing, in favour of greater representation of the workers in the organs of the European Economic Community. In May 1965, the Italian Party leader, Luigi Longo, met Waldeck-Rochet in Geneva and later claimed that he had won the Frenchman over to his tactical approach to the common market problem.

Italian influence is also visible in the softening of the French Party's attitude towards Nato. In Thorez's day, it was one of blanket hostility. General de Gaulle, however, took some of the wind out of communist sails when he began to disengage France from the Atlantic Alliance. This faced the French communists with the need to adopt an attitude that could be distinguished from the General's. They therefore criticised de Gaulle for wishing to retain France's *force de frappe* and solidarity with the United States. Instead, they proposed France's withdrawal from Nato in 1969 (when the Treaty would come up for revision) and the dissolution of all military pacts (by implication, including the Warsaw Pact), and the search for a new system of European collective security.

The Italian Communists have indeed been the great 'revisionists' of the communist world; which is another way of saying that they have been more adept than any other party at adapting themselves to the changed circumstances of the world after Stalin. It was the late Palmiro Togliatti who coined the term 'polycentrism', which was as good a description as any of the state of affairs that was bound to develop once Khrushchev had denounced Stalin in 1956 and espoused the doctrine of 'different national roads to socialism'. Togliatti was a master-organizer and politician. For many years, as we have seen, he was not merely faithful but abjectly obedient to Moscow. He stood by while other foreign Communists in exile in Moscow were tortured or done to death on Stalin's orders; he didn't even attempt to rescue his brother-in-law, Paolo Robotti, * from his sufferings in Stalin's gaols. If Khrushchev had not denounced Stalin in 1956, it is more than likely that Togliatti would have gone on singing the dead dictator's praises. And in that event, the Italian Communist Party might have declined as severely as did the French. But Khrushchev did denounce Stalin, and Togliatti — unlike Thorez — took note of this important fact and drew the logical consequences. Polycentrism was one of these: if the Russians were no longer to be relied upon to preserve the myth of Party infallibility then Togliatti had no option but to take his distance from Moscow, on pain of a disastrous decline in his own party's appeal. Events proved him right. True, the membership of the Italian Party declined from just over two million to 1,577,497 — about 28 per cent — between 1950 and 1965. But in comparison, the French Party's membership declined by about 67 per cent, from about 804,000 to 265,000 over a comparable period. At best, the electoral appeal of the French Party remained static; whereas the communist vote in Italy continued to grow.

When Togliatti died, in August 1964, he was in Russia where he had gone to discuss ideological points and tactics for the international communist movement, with Khrushchev and other Soviet leaders. In preparation for his talks, he had consigned a few thoughts to paper in what was later known as the 'Yalta Memorandum', from the place of his death. The Italian Communist Party later decided to publish this document, reportedly

* Kevin Devlin, 'The Party in Italy', *Problems of Communism*, September-October 1965.

against the wishes of the Soviet leadership. From that time, it became known as 'Togliatti's Testament'. It was a bold and significant decision on the part of the Italian Party leaders, for the Memorandum as Togliatti had drafted it was a clear ideological challenge to Moscow leadership. It is indeed improbable that Togliatti, had he lived, would have published it as it stood. Clearly, it reflected his own thinking, but it was also a conference document—a statement of points which Togliatti hoped to persuade the Russians to accept. It was therefore stated in what, for Togliatti, were rather crude terms. Himself a master of subtle dialectical prose, it is likely that he would have softened the terminology before publication, doubtless taking account of Russian views. Still, Togliatti's heirs went ahead, and thereafter were bound by his words and their decision to publish them.

In his 'Testament', Togliatti criticised the Soviet Union's slowness in reversing Stalin's suppression of individual freedom, reaffirmed his support for full autonomy for the individual Communist Parties and doubted the usefulness of an international communist conference—which Moscow was trying to convene—if its object was to be a denunciation of the Chinese. Perhaps the most important passage, in the Italian context, was the following:

> The old atheist propaganda is useless to us. The problem of religious consciousness, its content, its roots in the masses and ways of passing beyond it must be considered in a different way from in the past, if we wish to reach the religious masses and be understood by them.

There should, Togliatti argued, be free discussion between communist and non-communist writers, artists and scientists, who should not all be regarded as 'our enemies' or 'agents of our enemies', and deeper study should be given to the problem of the possibility of a peaceful transition to socialism.

What Togliatti was proposing, in other words, was that the Italian Communist Party should become, or seem to become, a political party like any other, apparently respectful of parliamentary legality and the democratic spirit. A party that would cease to antagonize all non-communists by dropping its systematic hostility toward them and holding itself ready for a meeting of minds. A party, moreover, ready for a dialogue with Christians in a Catholic country, and no longer open to the charge of atheism.

Togliatti's successor as Party boss, Luigi Longo, like him a veteran of the Comintern and of the Spanish Civil War, lacked the master's charisma. But he has carried on along the path framed by Togliatti, ably assisted by a dynamic and younger lieutenant, Enrico Berlinguer. Inevitably, since the Party has liberalized its approach to the outside world, it has had to relax its traditional internal discipline, and has suffered consequent dissensions. On the right wing of the party, Giorgio Amendola, a member of the Politburo, makes speeches that sound social democratic rather than communist. Indeed, when a foreign friend once asked him why he did not leave the Party, he replied ruefully: 'Because it's so cold outside'. To the Left, another Politburo member, Pietro Ingrao, calls for a platform that would attract the wild youngsters of Italy's New Left. In the old days, doubtless Amendola and Ingrao would have been forced to confess their deviations and toe the line or be purged out of the Party. In the new, post-Togliatti party, they are allowed to make their speeches and keep their seats on the Politburo.

With an efficient organization, a wide range of fund-raising devices, and publicity techniques that have been compared to those of Madison Avenue, the Italian Communist Party has built up its electoral appeal to the stage where it is no longer fanciful to suppose that it could come to power by democratic means. In the general election of May 1968, the Party increased its vote to nearly 27 per cent of the total with more than 8·5 million votes. To these, for practical purposes, one might add more than 1·4 million votes cast for the Communist Party's allies, the Socialist Party of Proletarian Unity. To have done this at a time of declining membership of the Party itself is an impressive and frightening achievement. How much of this success is due to the Party's new 'image', to its new ideological flexibility or to its effective publicity techniques is hard to determine. A fair share of the credit or blame for communist advances must be awarded to the late Pope John XXIII, who initiated a new

Vatican policy of relative tolerance towards the Communists, and of Church abstention from politics, while his new social policy for the working man (as expounded in his 1961 encyclical, *Mater et Magistra*), gave the Italian Communists an opportunity of which they fully availed themselves, to argue that in essentils, the Communist Party and the Church were pursuing similar objectives. At one time, the Church had declared that communism was a heresy, and to vote communist a sin, to be confessed. Under Pope John, this anathema and interdiction ceased, and Pope Paul VI has carried on his predecessor's policy of tolerance. The change in the Church's policy has probably been worth a million votes to the Communist Party, many of them from women voters who used to listen to their Parish priests and now listen to their husbands instead.* The Communist Party's gain has of course been the ruling Christian Democrats' loss — and the change in voting patterns has reflected the decline and corruption of the Christian Democrats.

In this situation, the interesting question is whether, given the changes in the international communist movement and the Italian Party in particular, there should be alarm or indifference at the prospect that the Communist Party might come to power in Italy. (I shall leave any rejoicing to the Communists themselves, and their supporters.) To answer this question, one must ask a further one: whether the changes in the Italian Party are real or apparent. My own view, which I believe the evidence supports, is that the changes are not real but apparent. In fact, the changes concern the *tactics* of achieving power: *doctrine* remains virtually intact. The Italian Communists have abandoned violent revolution because they no longer believe that the Leninist method is suitable to Italian conditions. They have repudiated Moscow's infallibility, because the Russians themselves have forfeited their claim. They advocate a dialogue with non-communists, including Catholics, because this improves their chances of achieving power by reassuring those who used to fear them and taking advantage of the new attitude of tolerance within the Vatican.

In home policy, they still advocate 'socialism', though now in

* See five articles on Italian Communism by Gaia Servadio, in the London *Evening Standard*, 5-9 May 1969.

easy stages. In foreign affairs, they still advocate policies that would be beneficial to the Soviet Union and disastrous to the West. Even Amendola, although regarded as a right-wing rebel within the Party, favours support for the Soviet Communist Party on international issues. The Italian abandonment of the old policy of hostility toward the Common Market is misleading, and intended to mislead. The new policy of a 'take-over' of the European institutions on behalf of the 'European working class'—which is, in effect, what the Italian Communists do advocate—is unlikely to be achieved; but if it were, it would simply make the European Economic Community unworkable, unless other European governments went communist as well. And in that event, the EEC as a whole would become an economic satellite of the Soviet Union. Moreover, the Italian Communists have made it clear that should they come to power, they would take Italy out of Nato. Objectively, as the Communists are fond of saying, the Italian Party, while contesting Moscow's absolute leadership, is serving the foreign policy interests of the Soviet Union.

A last point of tactics deserves mention. Unlike the French Communist Party, the Italian Party now officially admits that a socialist regime, installed through democratic elections, could subsequently be voted out of power. This amounts to saying that the Italian Communists would not cling to power even if they lost the formal support of the majority in an elected assembly. On paper, this is undoubtedly a very reassuring undertaking and its intention is undoubtedly to reassure. Can one, however, have any faith in a promise of this kind from a party with the record of the Italian Communist Party? To give such a reassurance is Machiavellian and tactically effective. But it provides no solid grounds for supposing that the Communists, once in power, would allow themselves to be dislodged.

Let us now turn to the largest 'outsider' of them all—the Indonesian Communist Party (PKI), which, until the autumn of 1965, was the most numerous communist party in the world, apart from the ruling parties of China and the Soviet Union. Apart from a membership of about three million, the Indonesian Party had some twenty million supporters in various mass organizations. About 3·5 million of these were in the Trade Union group, SOBSI, and nine million in the Peasant Front (BTI). The Youth and Women's associations had about 1·5 million members apiece. The Party's power was thus, at least on paper, formidable. So commanding, indeed, was the Party's position in Indonesian life that its leaders were tempted to make a bid for power. It was a very near thing, but the bid failed and the outcome was the near-extinction of the Indonesian Communist Party for the second time in a generation.

The first time was in 1948, when the Indonesian Communists, on Moscow's orders, staged an armed uprising, which was swiftly crushed by the Army of the young Republic, and in which the then Party leader, Musso, lost his life. Under D. N. Aidit, who became the leader in 1953, and who might be called the Togliatti of Indonesia, the Party made a remarkable come-back. Turning his back on the revolutionary violence, Aidit advocated the creation of a mass party and the adoption of a 'national' Indonesian platform. It suited President Sukarno to allow the Communist Party to grow in numbers and influence, as a counter to the essentially anti-communist Army, which the President distrusted.

One factor in Aidit's success was his skill in handling the problems caused by the Sino-Soviet dispute. His willingness to participate in the government and in State organisms was in line with Khrushchev's advocacy of constitutional methods. But in many speeches, Aidit laid emphasis on identification of his Party with the peasants, as prescribed by Mao Tse-tung. During the 'Confrontation' crisis between Indonesia and Malaysia, the Indonesian Communists tried hard but unsuccessfully to persuade Sukarno to 'arm the workers and peasants' – ostensibly to help him 'crush Malaysia', but doubtless in the hope that an armed proletariat and peasantry would enable the Communist Party to defeat the Army in the event of a show-down. In the meantime, the Party made considerable progress in infiltrating the armed forces.

The timing of the attempted *coup d'état* that smashed communist hopes for the second time, was closely linked to the state of President Sukarno's health. Chinese doctors, brought from

Peking at the President's request, examined him late in July and pronounced that the kidney complaint from which he suffered would result in paralysis or death. The Communists decided that this was the time to act: to delay action might mean that the President would die or be disabled and they would lose his protection. An Army takeover seemed the likely outcome, and they wished to forestall it. Aidit, who had personally accompanied the Chinese doctors, cutting short a tour of communist countries, called a series of Politburo meetings in July and August, at which the *coup d'état* was planned. It was agreed that the Communists themselves should stay in the background in the early stages. A dissatisfied Army officer, Lieutenant-Colonel Untung of the Palace Guard, was encouraged to seize power and physically liquidate the most prominent anti-communist military leaders, on the pretext of protecting the President from an alleged plot by a 'Council of generals' with the supposed backing of the American Central Intelligence Agency. The President himself was to be placed under some kind of restriction, and a revolutionary council, on which the Communists would be represented by nominees, was to be set up.

The decision to act is believed to have been taken at a Communist Party meeting on 17 August—Indonesia's National Day. The plan was, in fact, put into action on the evening of 30 September, when President Sukarno collapsed while addressing a public meeting. The first stages went according to plan. A squad of Untung's Palace Guards were ordered to kidnap the leading eight generals. Only six of them, however, could be found: all were murdered after bestial tortures. The two others escaped. One was the Defence Minister, General Nasution; the other, a more obscure soldier, General Suharto, then commander of the Strategic Reserve. Early on 1 October Untung's rebels took over Djakarta Radio and proclaimed a '30 September Movement'. Simultaneously, they set up a Revolutionary Council, most of whose members were unknown, but which included some Communists and many fellow-travellers. Later, at his trial, Colonel Untung was to admit that his political programme had been drafted by a member of the Communist Party. The failure to capture Nasution and above all Suharto, who quickly and decisively took over as Army Chief of Staff from one of the murdered generals, was fatal to communist plans. Untung was captured and sentenced to death. Aidit was found in hiding and shot by the Army; so was one of his principal assistants, Njoto, who had been the Communist Party's first government minister. A mass slaughter of Communists and suspected sympathizers followed in Java, Sumatra, Bali and other islands. In five months, between October 1965 and February 1966, between 300,000 and 500,000 people were butchered.

Aidit's failure was complete and illuminating. But the failure itself was not the main point of interest, in the context of this book. In fact, the attempted coup very nearly succeeded. But it is impossible to tell whether Indonesia would be under communist rule today if Nasution and Suharto had been murdered along with their six colleagues. Aidit's diagnosis was shaky. Although arms for his peasants had been sent by a clandestine route from communist China, Aidit could not claim to have fully armed the workers and peasants. Nor was there, in a true sense, a revolutionary situation in Indonesia. Moreover, Aidit, who had been listening to Sukarno when he collapsed in the Djakarta Stadium, had given the order to act on the mistaken assumption that the President was about to die. Had he stayed in the Stadium instead of slipping out to meet his followers, he would have known that the President had resumed his speech after a brief rest.

The real point, however, is that Aidit, who had built up a mass party and taken advantage of constitutional openings, in the end decided on an unconstitutional seizure of power. The facts of the situation, if differently interpreted, might have led him, on the contrary, to hold his hand. In a much more revolutionary situation, the French Communist Party decided in 1968 not to risk a clash with the Army that might have been fateful. The lesson is surely that in the age of polycentrism, individual communist parties, while no longer taking their tactical orders from Moscow, act as opportunity appears to dictate. One party might decide to try its luck with a *coup d'état*; another might call a general strike and do nothing else; a third might go all the way along the parliamentary road because the end in sight appears to be power in one form or another. But the ultimate end envisaged, whether the Indonesian, French, or Italian examples are used as models, is fundamentally the same: the establishment of a socialist regime. True, the Italian Party, in line with its continued attempt to reassure non-communist voters, has lavished praise on the Yugoslav experiment—just as it praised the heady liberalism of the Dubcek experiment in Czechoslovakia—while it lasted. But should the Italian Party ever come to power, it would face the same dilemma as Mr Dubcek did. To liberalize excessively would mean inviting other parties to take its place. Should it decide not to resist if voted out of office, the problem to Italy and the world might not be insoluble; but there is absolutely no guarantee that this would be the Party's decision. In the final analysis, the only safeguard to socialist reforms is the continuance in office of the party that initiates them. And this implies the monopoly of power of a ruling party. The totalitarian logic of communism is inescapable.

7. *The Fundamentalists*

What the 'Fundamentalists' have in common, above all, is a nostalgia for the pure Marxist dream of an earlier generation. I use the term 'Fundamentalists' to describe a large and inchoate category of outsiders, embracing such older groups as the Trotskyists, and ranging over the various bodies rather loosely known as the 'New Left'. Each of the Fundamentalist groups, old and new, believes itself to be the repository of the fundamental truths of Marxism-Leninism, modified in some cases by new accretions, such as Maoism, Guevarism, and the re-interpretations of Marxism in the light of the industrial and technological society, by the German-American philosopher, Herbert Marcuse. Broadly speaking, the Fundamentalists attack the established communist regimes, especially those of the Soviet Union and its satellites, as a bureaucratic and police-State betrayal of the original principles of Marxism-Leninism. The Trotskyists do so because they believe Trotsky was the logical heir to Lenin, and point to Stalin as the great betrayer of the Revolution. This belief has led the Trotskyists to make common cause with the New Left groups which, in certain respects, are not necessarily in agreement with the Trotskyists. On the whole, however, the New Left, whether consciously or not, traces its spiritual ancestry back to the violent school of Anarchism headed by Mikhail Bakunin—a contemporary of Karl Marx who parted company with him and became his rival in the First International. Bakunin's name, however, is rarely invoked by those who practise what he preached.

The relevance of the Fundamentalist groups to the subject-matter of this book is indirect but important. The fact that the Fundamentalists often denounce communism is deceptive: in some respects, they are more communist than the communists: and that, indeed, is what makes them Fundamentalists. Their importance lies in the challenge they present to the established communist orthodoxies. In the simplest terms, a new Left has arisen because the 'old' Left has largely ceased to appeal to those whose natural bent in politics is revolutionary. Quite possibly, the revolutionary strand in the human personality is ineradicable. Every generation throws up its revolutionary young, whose bent may derive from idealism or a taste for violence and adventure, or simply from a natural rebelliousness against established authority. One and two generations ago, such people turned to Marx or Lenin, or latterly to Mao Tse-tung. Today, Stalinism has ruined communism for them. Mao has at least the revolutionary appeal of the youthful Red Guards. But their real hero is 'Che' Guevara.

From the communist standpoint, this challenge from the Left is a serious matter. As in a capitalist business, a loss of customers threatens bankruptcy of the enterprise. But to the non-communist the spectacle of civil war within the extreme Left is only mildly comforting—it has happened so many times before.

For many people the New Left means rebellious students, and the association of ideas is valid; but there is more to it than that. In Britain, the New Left may be said to have begun in 1956, when the disillusionment caused by Khrushchev's denunciation of Stalin started an exodus from the Communist Party which reached its climax after the Soviet invasion of Hungary later that year. Some of the disillusioned ex-Communists later joined forces with left-wing socialists to produce a bi-monthly, *New*

Left Review, a merger of two periodicals, *New Reasoner* and *Universities and Left Review*. A more permanent literary expression of New Left philosophy is the New Left's *May Day Manifesto*, first published in May 1967 and revised under the editorship of Raymond Williams as a Penguin Special in 1968. The work of socialists, mainly from the universities, the *May Day Manifesto 1968* is well written and closely reasoned. Though critical of the Soviet Union, it advocates policies that would serve that country's interests, such as the detachment of Britain from the United States, the disbandment of Nato and the abandonment of a special international role for sterling.

In the increasingly violent protests, both in the British universities and in the streets, during the past few years, three Trotskyist bodies—the International Socialism Group, the Socialist Labour League and the International Marxist Group—have competed with the British Communist Party and the minuscule Maoist 'Communist Party of Britain (Marxist-Leninist)'. There has also been acute competition between the Trotskyists and the orthodox Communists within the Radical Student Alliance, a left-wing ginger group in the Universities; and the pro-Hanoi Vietnam Solidarity Campaign is in the hands of the Trotskyists. Over the years the Campaign for Nuclear Disarmament (CND) has attracted members of the New Left, some of whom later turned to illegal action in the so-called Committee of 100—now disbanded.

In continental Western Europe, the most significant development has been the emergence of the Syndicalist Student Movement. According to a charter adopted by the French National Student Union (UNEF) in 1946, the student is 'a young intellectual worker'. No longer does he study to please his parents or to fit himself for a career of personal advancement. Since 1946, his studies are for the good of society, and he is entitled to be paid for his work. If dissatisfied with his grant or his conditions of work, he may take industrial action—that is, go on strike. If those other workers—at the factory bench or the assembly line—are involved in industrial or political disputes, it is up to the new syndicalist student-worker to express his solidarity with other proletarians. The idea was appealing, and it caught on in neighbouring countries—Germany, Belgium, Holland and Britain. Indeed student syndicalists are to be found in Canada, Ireland, Luxembourg, Portugal, Spain, Switzerland and the United States—where the left-wing Students for Democratic Society (SDS) has become the spearhead of the protest movement in the American universities.

However it is perhaps more relevant to our purpose to consider the ideological challenge offered by the New Left. In a sense, of course, there is no universally accepted ideology of the New Left. What we are concerned with is the work of contemporary revolutionary prophets who have most powerfully influenced the Fundamentalists. One of these influences is undoubtedly that of Mao Tse-tung, whose revolutionary assets are considerable: a heroic legend, a successful peasant revolution in the most populated country in the world, a reputation as a poet that enhances his romantic appeal. Above all, perhaps, Mao's attraction lies in the irrational decisions of his latter years, in the slogan of 'permanent revolution' and in the sanctioned excesses of the Red Guards. Mao sanctions revolutionary violence, and sanctions it for its own sake. Moreover, he has attacked bureaucratism and the apparatus of the ruling Communist Party he himself helped to create. He is neo-anarchism impersonate.

Mao, on the other hand, is also an old man. High though his prestige stands, his revolutionary appeal cannot compare with that of Che Guevara. Physically attractive, with an agreeable personality, his concern for suffering humanity symbolized by a medical degree, successful in Cuba's guerrilla war, Guevara had an asset denied to Mao: the aura of martyrdom in his last action in Bolivia, killed after his capture, whether by the Bolivian security forces or the CIA is immaterial. Already the Guevara myth is probably invincible, for, as the French sociologist Georges Sorel remarked two generations ago, the power of a political myth bears no relation to its inherent credibility. In sober fact, Che Guevara won his Cuban successes in small tactical actions in highly favourable circumstances. As he himself recorded in his account of the Cuban Revolution, few of the actions in which he was involved engaged more than two or three dozen men on his side. In the end, the Cuban revolutionaries found they were pushing against an open door: the corrupt and inefficient dictatorship of Batista collapsed of its own accord, and Fidel Castro marched in triumph into Havana.

Both Castro and Guevara seem nevertheless to have thought that they had found the infallible recipe for revolutionary success anywhere in the world, and especially in Latin America. But when Guevara attempted to mount a peasant insurrection in Bolivia, he met with failure and death. His *Bolivian Diaries*, written with that engaging candour that is one of Guevara's attractions, make it plain that his leadership was uninspiring and his organization inefficient. Neither he nor most of his original band of supporters spoke Quechua, the language of the ancient Incas and of the Andean peasants, who were indifferent or hostile to the revolutionaries in their midst. Understandably, the Moscow-line leader of the Bolivian Communist Party, Mario Monje, refused to have anything to do with him. Before the guerrillas fought their first engagement with the Bolivian security forces, they numbered only fifty-one; and of these, eighteen or nineteen were Cubans. Moreover, the number steadily decreased after that.

Those are the facts; but it would take more than facts to shake the Guevara myth. In New York, London and Berlin, the student revolutionaries brandish giant pictures of the 'Che', as they intimidate the moderates and defy the authorities. At least part of the answer of the puzzle must be sought in the fact that Che Guevara did at least try to live as he preached. But the preaching itself is important in terms of revolutionary appeal. It carries a simple and optimistic message. It is easy enough for the sophisticated and sceptical to find out that it is Utopian; but it is admirably suited to those in search of a hero. It may be summarized in the following selected quotations from his works and speeches:—

On the conditions for revolution. 'It is not necessary to wait until all conditions for making revolution exist; the insurrection can create them.' (*Guerrilla Warfare*, 1961, page 15). This dictum is, of course, heretical from the standpoint of orthodox Marxism-Leninism, and even from that of Maoism. It is, however, an enormously attractive slogan for young people whose impulse is revolutionary, and who are impatient with the restrictions imposed on them in the name of discipline and correct analysis by orthodox communist parties. To be fair to Guevara, he went on to write: 'Where a government has come into power through some form of popular vote, fraudulent or not, and maintains at least an appearance of constitutional legality, the guerrilla outbreak cannot be promoted, since the possibilities of peaceful struggle have not yet been exhausted.'

Justification of force. 'When the forces of oppression come to maintain themselves in power against established law, peace is considered already broken.' (*Guerrilla Warfare*, page 15). This concept was modified and sharpened (as were other ideas from *Guerrilla Warfare*) in a speech by Guevara in Algiers in September 1963, in the following passage: 'The dictatorship always tries to maintain itself without showing too obviously that it is using force; to oblige it to unmask itself, to show itself in its true colours of a violent dictatorship of the reactionary classes, contributes to show the people their true nature and will deepen the struggle to the point where it will no longer be possible to pull back.' (Translated from the French text, *Le Socialisme et L'Homme*, Paris, 1968, page 58.)

One of the points that emerged from recent student disturbances, especially in Paris in May 1968, was the students' argument that the authorities are using force to maintain themselves in power, and that all the students are doing is to defend themselves against that force. The importance of the paragraph just quoted is that it is an incitement to provocation of the authorities.

The role of the working class. 'In underdeveloped [Latin] America the countryside is the basic area for armed fighting'. This quotation from page 15 of *Guerrilla Warfare* is complemented on the following page in these words: 'This is a fundamental of strategy. It ought to be noted by those who maintain dogmatically that the struggle of the masses is centred in city movements, entirely forgetting the immense participation of the country people in the life of all the underdeveloped parts of America.'

This passage also is heretical by the standards of Marxism-Leninism, and even outdistances Mao Tse-tung in denying a special revolutionary role to the proletariat. It should be noted, however, that the second Havana Declaration, which Guevara quotes with approval on pages 51 and 52 of '*Le Socialisme et l'Homme*, explained that the peasantry, by reason of its lack of culture, would have to accept the revolutionary and political leadership of the working class and of the revolutionary intellectuals. In effect, Guevara was telling student revolutionaries that it was up to them to lead the revolution.

On terrorism. Although Guevara does not use these terms, he distinguishes between *disruptive* and *coercive* terrorism in the following passage from *Guerrilla Warfare*, pages 93–4: 'We sincerely believe that terrorism is of negative value, that it by no means produces the desired effect, that it can turn a people against a revolutionary movement, and that it can bring a loss of lives to its agents out of proportion to what it produces. On the other hand, attempts to take the lives of particular persons are to be made, though only in very special circumstances; this tactic should be used where it will eliminate a leader of the oppression. What ought never to be done is to employ specially trained, heroic, self-sacrificing human beings in eliminating a little assassin whose death can provoke the destruction in reprisals of all the revolutionaries employed and even more.' What Guevara is sanctioning is selective terrorism by the elimination of individuals.

Vietnam and American Imperialism. 'Let us sum up in this way our aspirations to victory: destruction of imperialism through the elimination of its strongest bastion—the imperialist domination of the United States of North America. To adopt as a tactical mission the gradual liberation of the peoples, one by one or in groups, by obliging the enemy to sustain a difficult struggle on a terrain that is not his own, by liquidating his subsistence bases which are his dependent territories'. (Translated from French text of *To Create Two, Three, Numerous Vietnams*, published in April 1967 as a special supplement to the Havana review, 'Tricontinental', page 131, *Le Socialisme et l'Homme*.)

In an earlier passage in the same article, Guevara explained what he had in mind in these words: 'America, the continent forgotten in the latest political struggles of liberation, which is beginning to make itself heard through the Tricontinental, through the voice of the vanguard of its people, which is the Cuban Revolution, will have a much more important task: that of creating the world's second or third Vietnam.'

There is an obvious similarity between this Messianic call to action and the famous call by Marshal Lin-piao of China in September 1965, for the 'countryside' of the world to encircle and overcome the 'cities' of the world. But the point is that in his 1967 articles Guevara provided a rallying cry for all aspiring revolutionaries who saw the United States as the great imperialist enemy, and found in Vietnam a cause which they can passionately espouse.

Régis Debray shared with Guevara an admiration for the great leader of the Cuban Revolution, Fidel Castro. Here too is a glamorous revolutionary figure, with such assets as youth, a fair intellect (he is a Normalien), and the special advantage of martyrdom through a trial that became a *cause célèbre*, and an interminable prison sentence in Bolivia.

In his little work, *Revolution in the Revolution?* Debray went even further than Guevara in his revolutionary heresy. The key passages in his book occur in Part II, entitled 'The Principal Lesson for the Present', in which he answers a series of questions concerning the Party, the guerrillas, and the relationship between them and the leader, (pages 95–116 in the English edition of 1967, or pages 99–125 in the French edition of the same year). Debray's revolutionary message may be summarized as follows:

All peaceful tactics, such as the united front, are rejected, in favour of unlimited armed struggle;

The guerrillas are to be independent of the communist party, whose role is to be secondary until military victory has been achieved;

Party members are urged to abandon the cities for the countryside;

The political and military leadership are to be vested in one man; until victory has been achieved politics must remain subservient to military considerations.

Although Debray, in common with Guevara, was writing as an advocate of peasant insurrections, his message appeals to rebellious students in the towns, for he utterly rejects the discipline and political control of a party, and even Mao's 'united front' with non-communist parties. Not only does he sanction violence, but he sees no possibility of an alternative course. And although he does not, of course, use the term 'demagogue', he invites a charismatic figure to come forward and lead the revolution. Debray's message is instant revolution.

With Frantz Fanon, Utopia is reserved for the coloured peoples of the world, for the 'colonized masses' or 'natives'. Fanon too, like Guevara, had the advantage of an early death—in his case of leukaemia at the early age of thirty-seven. He too was a doctor—a psychiatrist—and a French-speaking Negro from Martinique, who settled in Algeria and threw in his lot with the revolutionaries of the Front de Libération Nationale (FLN).

His best-known and most influential book, *Les Damnés de la Terre*, is a powerful and disturbing work, a hymn of hate, which sees no hope for the oppressed except in the unbridled use of violence. His entire philosophy is contained in the following passages selected from *Les Damnés de la Terre*:

'The cause is the consequence; you are rich because you are white, you are white because you are rich. This is why Marxist analysis should always be slightly stretched every time we have to do with the colonial problem.

'Everything up to and including the very nature of pre-capitalist society, so well explained by Marx, must here be thought out again. The serf is in essence different from the knight but a reference to divine right is necessary to legitimize this statutory difference. In the colonies, the foreigner coming from another country imposed his rule by means of guns and machines. In defiance of his successful transplantation, in spite of his appropriation, the settler still remains a foreigner. It is neither the fact of owning factories, nor estates, nor a bank balance which distinguishes the governing classes. The governing race is first and foremost those who come from elsewhere, those who are unlike the original inhabitants, "the others".' (From the original English text published in France in 1963, pages 32–3; another edition of the same translation has since appeared in Penguin Books under the title, *The Wretched of the Earth*.)

'The violence which has ruled over the ordering of the colonial world, which has ceaselessly drummed the rhythm for the destruction of native social forms and broken up without reserve the systems of reference of the economy, the customs of dress and external life, that same violence will be claimed taken over by the native at the moment when, deciding to embody history in his own person, he surges into the forbidden quarters.' (page 33).

'Violence alone, violence committed by the people, violence organized and educated by its leaders, makes it possible for the masses to understand social truths and give the key to them.' (page 117.)

If one may summarize and paraphrase Fanon's message in a few simple sentences, what he is saying is this: 'You are a coloured man. You are oppressed. Your oppressor is the white man. Kill him.' What happens *after* the white oppressor has been killed is nowhere specified. No message could be starker or more nihilistic.

The first edition of Fanon's *Les Damnés de la Terre* came with a preface by Jean-Paul Sartre, who, in his later middle age, must be accounted one of the most powerful influences within the New Left. The left-bank sage of Existentialism, once the most reliable of fellow-travellers, he became disillusioned with communism some years ago. Since then, he has moved considerably further to the left than meets with the approval of the increasingly conservative French Communist Party. Let us consider examples of Sartre in word and Sartre in deed.

Here are some brief quotations from Sartre's preface:

'In order to triumph, the nationalist revolution must be socialist; if its career is cut short, if the native bourgeoisie takes over power, the new State, in spite of its formal sovereignty, remains in the hands of the imperialists.'

'Our worthiest souls contain racial prejudice.'

'They would do well to read Fanon; for he shows clearly that this irrepressible violence is neither sound and fury, nor the resurrection of savage instincts, nor even the effect of resentment. It is man re-creating himself.'

'The child of violence, at every moment he draws from it his humanity. We were men at his expense, he makes himself man at ours: a different man, of higher quality.'

And now, what of Sartre's motivation? Finding Western society collectively guilty of the 'crimes' described by Fanon, he sanctions the destruction of society in the name of expiation. 'This book had not the slightest need of a preface,' he writes, 'all the less because it is not addressed to us. Yet I have written one, in order to bring the argument to its conclusion; for we in Europe too are being decolonized: that is to say that the settler which is in every one of us is being savagely rooted out ... You know well enough that we are exploiters. You know too that we have laid hands on first the gold and metals, then the petroleum of the "new continents", and that we have brought them back to the old countries.... Formerly our continent was buoyed up by other means: the Parthenon, Chartres, the Rights of Man, or the swastika. Now we know what these are worth, and the only chance of our being saved from shipwreck is the very Christian sentiment of guilt. You can see it's the end. Europe is springing leaks everywhere.'

Sartre goes on to castigate the 'liberals', and the toughs of the 'tender Left', and to accuse them of trying to stave off the day of reckoning by putting 'at the head of our affairs a Grand Magician whose business it is to keep us all in the dark at all costs'.

Jean-Paul Sartre was of course on the side of the students behind the barricades in May 1968 — most notably in the interview he gave to *Le Nouvel Observateur* on 19 June 1968, in which he:

Approved of the violence of the students as 'counter-violence' against the repression of society;

argued that in the last analysis any attempt at a right-wing military takeover would be defeated if the workers simply stayed at home, since paratroopers cannot run factories;

attacked Raymond Aron for declaring that students must defer to their professors, and challenged him to submit to cross-examination by the students.

A rival philosopher whose name was much bandied about in recent student disturbances in various countries is Professor Herbert Marcuse.

Unlike Fanon and Guevara, Herbert Marcuse, as a writer, is obscure, prolix and turgid. This may have delayed the onset of his international influence, but obscurity is not necessarily a handicap in a philosopher. Marx too was a difficult writer; and the success of the Delphic oracle in Greek antiquity showed the advantages of ambiguity. Marcuse's two most important books are *Eros and Civilization* (1955) and *One-Dimensional Man* (1964).* The first was an optimistic refutation of Freud, in which Marcuse postulated and forecast a non-repressive culture, making possible the 'humanitarian ideals of socialism'. In the second work, published nine years later, Marcuse is all pessimism: the new forms of social control involved by advanced capitalist countries are seen as all-pervasive. Only revolution can dispose of them.

There is much in Marcuse's analysis of industrial societies that is penetrating and disturbing. As modern societies industrialize, they may choose between two roads to the future. One is the harnessing of industry so that man's vital needs are satisfied, misery reduced and hunger gradually eliminated, leaving men with the leisure to live their own lives as they see fit. He complains that this choice was never made, either in capitalist or 'socialist' industrial societies, both of which have opted instead for industrialization and technology for their own sakes. It is the reign of 'planned waste'. Thus goods are designed to wear out shortly after purchase, so that the machines may be kept busy replacing them. In the West, especially, a vast advertising industry is constantly engaged in the creation of false needs. The compulsion to satisfy these needs perpetuates toil and drudgery. Acquisitive capitalism expands outwards, so that American capital invades Europe, Latin America and Asia; and the war in Vietnam escalates. Hence a vested interest in the maintenance and expansion of an enormous defence industry, one purpose of which is to put money into the pockets of the workers, with which the unnecessary goods produced by other industries may be bought.

In the Soviet Union and other 'socialist' societies, the stage of 'planned waste' has not yet been reached. Since these initially revolutionary societies seized the means of production, they might have chosen to develop on the right lines. But they did not, since the bureaucracies in power were impelled to retain that power — which they would have lost if true communism had been allowed to develop. Moreover, the need to compete with the capitalist

---

* For a devastating analysis and demolition of Marcuse's philosophy see Maurice Cranston, in *Encounter*, March 1969.

societies stimulates a comparably aggressive expansion of technology and the defence industries.

In one sense, therefore, Marcuse is a Marxist fundamentalist. He concedes that Marx was right in his day to argue that the capitalists were exploiting the workers and must be overthrown and dispossessed. But he parts company with today's Marxists when he asserts that the necessary revolution can no longer be left to the workers. Looking at the advanced capitalist societies as they are now, he notes the fact that the workers are no longer revolutionary. This unsatisfactory state of affairs he explains with two concepts, 'the ironing out of contradictions', and 'the containment of social change'. As capitalist affluence has spread, the worker buys cars and other items once considered luxuries: workers' wives have washing machines; and workers' daughters wear cosmetics that make them indistinguishable from the daughters of their bosses. In the new industrial society, thought and behaviour become one-dimensional. The workers and the Establishment share the same values and the same false needs. The workers may suppose themselves to be free, since they can read any newspaper they please or attend entertainment of their choice. But this is not a true tolerance: Marcuse calls it 'repressive tolerance', since the 'needs' which the people feel have been created for them by technology and are designed to sap their revolutionary spirit.

It is, of course, possible to agree with much of Marcuse's analysis, and reach utterly different conclusions. One may even choose to rejoice at the spread of affluence and the 'ironing out of contradictions', and to doubt whether the 'containment of social change' is a tragedy. But Marcuse, for his part, is compulsively nostalgic for his lost revolution. If the people are happy, or seem to be happy, that can only be because they are unaware of the truth as Marcuse sees it. No good looking to the 'socialist' regimes, whose bureaucracies have deprived the people of revolutionary happiness. No good looking to the workers, who believe themselves to be contented. Only one group of people offers hope: the students, who have not yet been corrupted by the technological society, and who constitute an elite that can give a revolutionary example to the poor and the oppressed. Their role is to provoke the police, as the essential representatives of the system of 'repressive tolerance', and force them to show themselves in their true colours. Without actually advocating violence, he invokes the natural right of the oppressed to use violence, since 'by doing so they do not start a new chain of violence, but try to break an established one'.

While Marcuse thus blesses violence, he also advocates selective intolerance. This is not, however, what he calls it. His name for it is 'partisan tolerance' — as presented in one of his later essays, *A Critique of Pure Tolerance*. Specifically, he advocates the withdrawal of the right of free speech and assembly from groups and movements advocating aggressive policies or discrimination on grounds of race or colour; rigid opposition to teaching in universities or colleges designed to maintain society along its present course; and intolerance toward scientific research in the interest of 'deterrence'.

Beyond that, Marcuse's prescriptions for social change are vague or non-existent. The students — aware of their 'alienation' from society as the workers no longer are — are to spearhead his revolution. And free speech is to be denied to those who defend society as it now is. But we are not told how the humanitarian socialist society of Marcuse's dreams is to be installed. As Maurice Cranston says, 'He calls not only for terror, but for a reign of terror. He asks for the suppression of conservatives, for the suppression of conservative speech, even of conservative thought. This calls for the creation of institutions of repression which must exist for as long as conservative thoughts are likely to continue to exist in anyone's mind. Marcuse is therefore calling for something uncannily like the State-that-is-to-wither-away (but not wither away very soon) which is at once the most conspicuous and the most harmless feature of orthodox Marxist ideology. For all his attacks on Stalinism, Marcuse himself is calling for the very things that make Stalinism odious.'

It is only mildly incongruous to switch from Marcuse to the youthful revolutionary Daniel Cohn-Bendit. In May 1968, when 'Danny the Red' had his moment of glory in the Sorbonne and the streets of Paris, Marcuse was seventy and Cohn-Bendit nearly fifty years younger, but consciously or otherwise, the young man was acting out the old man's teaching. Daniel Cohn-Bendit enjoyed the fleeting satisfaction of having almost, but not quite, dislodged the mighty General de Gaulle. Unabashed by the triumph of the forces of repression, he and another Cohn-Bendit — Gabriel — took five weeks off from revolution to produce a book now available in English under the title '*Obsolete Communism*' (Penguin).* Much of Cohn-Bendit's work, indeed, is an impassioned denunciation of bureaucratic Bolshevism, and an attempt to re-capture the revolutionary fervour of the early days in 1917. The authors end by appealing to the reader to go to the cinema and throw tomatoes or eggs at the first advertisement that appears on the screen. More cryptically, the reader is advised to quote 'find new relations with your girl friend, love differently, deny the family'! Daniel Cohn-Bendit has shown that he means business.

Communist attitudes to the New Left are illuminating. That the Communists should hate a movement so anarchic and unpredictable was inevitable; but they also fear it. The Soviet literary Establishment has not dared to expose its readers to the philosophy of Herbert Marcuse, at least in the master's own words. But *Pravda* denounced him on 30 May 1968, in a long article by its commentator Yuri Zhukov, under the title 'The Pseudo-Prophet Marcuse and his Disciples', and the more serious periodical *Voprosy Filosofii* ('Problems of Philosophy') carried a long critical analysis and attack on him in its issue of October that year. More directly significant was the attitude of the French Communist Party and its trade union organization, the CGT, toward the student disturbances of May 1968, to which I referred in the preceding chapter. When a thousand students marched from the Sorbonne to the Renault works at Boulogne-Billancourt, paralysed by a strike, the workers would not allow them into the factory area. 'Cohn-Bendit? Never heard of him', said Georges Séguy, the CGT Secretary-General. And on 3 May, Georges Marchais, at that time Number 2 in the Communist

---

* The English title unfortunately loses the ironical flavour of the original German, *Der Linksradikalismus — Gewaltkur gegen die Alterskrankheit des Kommunismus*, properly preserved in the French title, *Le Gauchisme: Remède à la Maladie Sénile du Communisme*. In the French and German versions, Cohn-Bendit's title was a satirical reference to Lenin's *The Infantile Disease of Leftism in Communism*.

Party, denounced 'the German Anarchist, Cohn-Bendit' in *L'Humanité*, and went on to say that 'such false revolutionaries must be energetically unmasked'. Clearly, if the communists take the New Left so seriously, then so should we. But for different reasons. The Communists are worried about a challenge to their revolutionary credentials, about a competition for the left-wing clientele. The concern of non-revolutionaries, whether our aim is to preserve or to reform society, is to avoid both the descent into revolutionary chaos threatened by the Neo-Anarchists, and the strangulation from within threatened by the orthodox Communists. With this concern as a point of departure, what are the prospects for the New Left?

If history offers guidance, it is improbable that the New Left will achieve anything but local and temporary successes. From the seizure of Munster in 1534, by that New Leftist of the sixteenth century, John of Leyden, to the libertarian revolution of the Spanish Anarchists in 1936, anarchic revolutions have rapidly turned into pitiless tyrannies and in the end been swamped by right-wing repressions. The Spanish example is illuminating. In the early stages of the Civil War, the Anarchists on the Republican side initially instituted the revolution of their choosing. Within eighteen months, however, the Spanish Communist Party, which had been numerically insignificant at the outset of the conflict, gained *de facto* control of the Republican government. In the end, of course, the libertarian revolution was crushed, along with the Republic itself, by General Franco.*
It seems to me unlikely that the New Left revolutionaries will come any closer to success in the advanced industrial nations, than they did in Paris in May and June 1968. It ought, perhaps, to be chastening to the New Left student leaders in France to note the professional ease with which the Communist Party gradually re-established its hold over both students' and teachers' organizations in the year that followed the disturbances. Nowhere was this success more striking than in the new University of Vincennes, outside Paris, in which the CPF swamped the student body with its representatives, many of them only nominally students who

---

* See Brian Crozier, 'Participatory Anarchy' in *Interplay* (New York) for June–July, 1969.

registered for courses for the sole purpose of saturation. The aftermath of the events of 1968 was indeed classically predictable: the eclipse of the moderate non-communist Left and of the anarchic Left as well, leaving the field almost entirely clear for the Communists. In Britain and the United States, as these lines were written, the prospect was of the eventual containment or repression of the revolutionaries.

In one sense, the communist rejection of Marcuse and Cohn-Bendit is well-founded. The Syndicalists may re-define students as workers, but their contribution to social wealth is potential, not actual. The community recognizes the fact by investing in them in the form of grants; but a grant is not a wage. One of the painful discoveries made by the New Left students in Paris in 1968 was that the sons of workers, enjoying a university education for the first time in their family history, were less revolutionary than *they* were. By and large, the student revolutionaries are sons and daughters of the well-to-do and the students as a whole are not, in the Marxian sense, a social class. This limits their revolutionary effectiveness.

Another limitation is that students grow up and cease to be students. Their capacity to see a revolution through is thereby hampered. Nor do ageing students necessarily retain their pristine revolutionary fervour; if one excepts the 'professional students' often subsidized by the various communist parties.

Students were, in fact, shaking governments or bringing unstable ones down long before the New Left was heard of, or at any rate before it had passed into current speech. In 1960, the South Korean and Turkish students were more successful than Danny the Red and his French militants, in that they actually did bring their governments down. Spectacular student riots in Seoul and other Korean cities preceded the downfall of President Syngman Rhee in April, 1960. The left-wing Korean students later believed, with good reason, that they had the democratic government of Dr John Chang where they wanted it, for their pressure prevented the National Assembly from approving anti-communist laws he had introduced. The delayed outcome of the April riots, however, was the overthrow of the Chang government in May 1961 by a military junta, which proceeded to decree even more drastic legislation. In Turkey, almost simultaneously, mass student demonstrations brought down the government of Mr Adnan Menderes. In the end, however, it was the armed forces that removed Menderes on 27 May 1960. Apart from the negative satisfaction of having provoked the final crisis of the Turkish government, the students were not beneficiaries of their own revolt. They had removed one group of men, and cleared the way for another; the regime went on, under temporary military rule.

The not inconsiderable successes won by the militant minority of students in various Western countries in 1968 and 1969 were due very largely to their capacity to canalize the genuine discontent and grievances of their more moderate fellow students. Overcrowding, especially in the larger universities, such as Berkeley in California and the Sorbonne in Paris; the insufficient number of teachers and lecturers in swiftly expanding education systems; administrative paternalism, from which some students feel alienated, in the Marcusean sense; the remoteness of the connection between certain academic disciplines—especially in the Arts—and the careers to which they may or may not lead; these are phenomena that are present in universities everywhere, in the 'socialist' countries as well as in the West. Essentially, the student radicals do not want to reform such conditions, but to overthrow the existing social order. But the existence of legitimate grievances plays into their hands. Initially, their carefully calculated acts of violence may 'alienate' the moderates. But the retaliatory force of the authorities, which they 'provoke', may cause the moderates to rally to the extremist cause; in protest, for instance, against police brutality. This was true of Paris in May 1968, and it has been true of certain American universities, notably Berkeley, and Columbia in New York.

In addition, the student radicals have been able to exploit for their own purposes such emotive issues as nuclear weapons, Vietnam (above all), and latterly the plight of Biafra. Since such issues are often major targets of communist propaganda* New Left agitation has opened fresh opportunities for manipulation

* Biafra was an exception, since the Soviet Union supported the Nigerian Federal Authorities in the Civil War.

167

by the communist parties. There is, in fact, a convergence of interests in such propaganda themes on the part of the otherwise divided and fragmented Left. It is 'competitive subversion' all over again.

At the very least, then, the emergence of a militant New Left has added to the existing problems of Western governments' security departments, special branches and ordinary police forces. In the long term, however, the extent of the threat represented by the New Left will be determined far more by the success or failure of governments and private authorities in removing exploitable grievances and issues than upon any intrinsic appeal of the New Left. This is clearly more likely to be achieved in the case of specific grievances such as the administration or curricula of the universities, than in that of intractable international issues, of which the Spanish Civil War in the 1930s and the Vietnam War in the 1960s are typical examples.

To some extent the New Left philosophers weaken the appeal of Marx, Lenin and Stalin. But the Communists have always shown capacity to weather such challenges and continue, by sheer persistence and organizational cohesion. The patience of organization men is their ultimate asset—the one which ensures that in the long run Lenin and Stalin are more dangerous than Bakunin.

As for Marcuse, he has at least the distinction of having contributed yet another false philosophy to mankind. The fact that it *is* false does not, of course, imply that it will lack followers. Its great weakness lies in that it is Utopian but does not offer a Utopia.

Part III: The Future

Part III: The Future

1. *The Soviet Power Base*

The most important power centre of communism has always been, and still is, the Soviet Union. If the communist system were overthrown in China, communism as a material force would be gravely but not mortally shaken. If the system collapsed in Russia, the wound would probably be mortal for communist governments everywhere. This generalization probably applies not only to Cuba, North Vietnam and North Korea, but even to China. And the capacity of individual communist parties to survive, except as factions of declining significance, would be drastically impaired.

What, then, is going to happen to communism in Russia? It is a question that cannot be answered without reference to the two main sources of physical power in the Soviet Union: the secret police and spy system (KGB), and the Army. It may well be asked: What about the Party? Is the Party not the sole centre of power in a communist system? In this context, however, I am concerned with *physical* power rather than authority. The *unarmed* combat power of a Brezhnev or a Khrushchev is perhaps not to be under-estimated. But the *armed* power of the police and security organs, not to mention the Army, is overwhelming in physical terms. The question, therefore, is whether in any foreseeable circumstances, that physical power is likely to be used against, instead of at the behest of, the Party, and indeed against the Revolution that put the Party in power in the first place.

The first thing to say about this proposition is that it is far less fanciful in respect of the Army than of the KGB. For the security services are in a very real sense the power instrument of the ruling group, the 'naked sword of the Revolution'. This is not to say that the KGB has invariably been as obedient and responsive an instrument as the Party leaders might have hoped. Finding

Beria too powerful, Stalin's successors liquidated him; he thus shared the fate of two predecessors whom Stalin had liquidated although he had nothing to fear from them. It is perhaps inevitable that an organization as vast as the KGB and with so arbitrary an attitude toward the use of the means of coercion at its disposal, should occasionally get out of hand, or be saddled with the blame for the Party's more outrageous policies. But, so far, the winner in any test of power has always been the Party. It was Stalin who liquidated Yagoda and Yezhov, not the other way round. It was Beria, not Khrushchev or Malenkov, whose life ended with the executioner's death shot. Some years later, the head and former head of the KGB—Semichastny and Shelepin respectively—helped the Party to remove Khrushchev. But they did not thereby achieve power for themselves.

It is therefore quite conceivable that circumstances might arise in which the KGB would intervene to ensure the victory of one leader or group within the Party in preference to those in power at the time. What seems to be almost inconceivable is that the KGB would attempt to overthrow the Revolution. For the KGB personifies that revolution more than any other single phenomenon in the Soviet Union. If it ever intervenes again in internal power politics it is always likely to be on the side of revolutionary 'purity'—that is, of coercion and repression. One cannot see the KGB attempting to restore capitalism or institute democratic freedom.

These remarks do not necessarily apply to the Soviet armed forces, which at times have shown themselves impatient of Party control and have attempted to shake themselves free of it. In this connection, the removal of Marshal Zhukov in November 1957 is worth recalling. The greatest and most famous of the Soviet commanders, Georgi Zhukov won his fame with the defence of Moscow against the Nazi invaders, in December 1941, and signed the document recording Germany's surrender in May 1945. Envying his success and prestige, Stalin removed him from his job as Commander-in-Chief of the Soviet Army and posted him to a minor command at Odessa. He rubbed in his displeasure by depriving the Marshal of his candidate-membership of the Party's Central Committee.

These reverses occurred in 1946. As soon as Stalin died, Zhukov started his come-back. Before demotion, he had reached the top of the military hierarchy; now he began a rapid upward climb in politics. It started in March 1953 (the month of Stalin's death), with his appointment as First Deputy Defence Minister. Two years later, he became the first professional soldier to achieve political control over the armed forces, when he succeeded Marshal Bulganin—a political soldier—as Defence Minister. In 1953, he became a full member of the Central Committee, and in 1956, a candidate-member of the all-powerful Party Presidium.

For Khrushchev at that time, crisis was brewing. The ebullient First Secretary had enemies within the Presidium. One, obviously, was Malenkov, Stalin's protégé, whom Khrushchev had ousted as Premier in February 1955. With him were the 'young Stalinists', Pervukhin and Saburov, both of whom held Party and government posts and were building reputations as economic planners. Also against Khrushchev were the 'old Stalinists', principally Molotov and Kaganovich. The former, Stalin's war-time Foreign Minister, had supported Khrushchev in his clash with Malenkov for the Premiership—which Khrushchev took over (from Bulganin) in addition to his job as Party boss.

The full details of the murky plot by which these men tried to overthrow Khrushchev in 1957 need not concern us here. To oversimplify, one might say that the 'old Stalinists' wanted Stalinism without Stalin—at home, heavy industry at the expense of living standards; and abroad, cautious consolidation of the Soviet bloc. They could not approve of Khrushchev's 'adventurism' in Eastern Europe, nor of his partial adoption of the policy for which Malenkov had been ostensibly overthrown: more consumer goods for the people, to promote stability at home and a better image at home through a rapidly rising living standard. Malenkov's policy was supported by the 'young Stalinists' who found Khrushchev's adoption of his rival's ideas unimpressive. Moreover, under Khrushchev's proposals (grandiloquently presented as 'Theses'), Pervukhin's State Economic Commission was to be abolished. Like Malenkov, therefore, Pervukhin had strong personal reasons for wishing to oust Khrushchev.

In February 1957, having weathered the crisis of the Soviet intervention of Hungary, Khrushchev summoned the Central Committee and presented his 'Theses', which, broadly speaking, called for the reorganization and decentralization of industry. This was the signal for the two anti-Khrushchev factions to get together. Khrushchev, they all agreed, was becoming too strong: the principle of 'collective leadership', which benefited them all, was at stake. He must be removed. The plotters met in the office of the Premier, Marshal Bulganin, whose personal involvement in the plot seems, however, to have been nominal. At some stage the malcontents were joined by Khrushchev's protégé, Shepilov, who was Foreign Minister from July 1956 to February 1957. Khrushchev was later to describe him as a 'shameful double-dealer'.

On 18 June, the Malenkov-Molotov group forced a meeting of the Presidium, with Bulganin in the chair. Three members, possibly favourable to Khrushchev, were out of Moscow, and in their absence, the hostile group knew they had a majority. They called upon Khrushchev to step down as First Secretary in Molotov's favour, and demanded Malenkov's reappointment as Premier.

That day, the anti-Khrushchev group thought victory was inevitably theirs. But they had counted without Khrushchev's nerve and guile, and without the help he received from two unexpected quarters: from his friend Serov, the then head of the KGB; and from a distinguished soldier who had not, until then, 'meddled' in politics—Marshal Zhukov. Between them, these powerful interventions were decisive.

For months past, Khrushchev had been packing the Central Committee with his own supporters. Instead of bowing to the Presidium majority's views, as they expected, he declared that he had no power to resign from a post to which he had been elected by the Central Committee—which, he said, must be summoned to deal with the case. The trouble, for Khrushchev, was that members of the Central Committee were in distant places. Knowing this, Molotov and Malenkov tried to force the issue there and then. Khrushchev however, had a determined supporter in Mrs Furtseva, a close friend and Secretary of the

Central Committee. Possibly through her, news of the Presidium meeting reached other members. It is said, though without definite proof, that she filibustered to give members time to reach Moscow. More interesting, perhaps, is the story that Zhukov assigned military planes to transport the more remote members to the capital. Here again, truth is not easy to come by, but there is circumstantial evidence to support the story, for the annual air display that was to have been held at that time near Moscow was abruptly cancelled.

By 22 June, 309 members of the Central Committee were in Moscow, and the meeting began. It lasted seven days. In the end, Khrushchev emerged with a decisive majority (though the subsequent claim that nobody supported the plotters must be discounted). Collectively, the plotters were branded the 'anti-Party group'. In Stalin's day, they would have been physically liquidated. But Khrushchev was a milder man. Molotov, Kaganovich, Malenkov, Saburov and Shepilov were all given minor jobs in distant places. Other members of the group were punished in various ways.

At the same Central Committee plenum in June, evidently as a reward for services rendered, Khrushchev promoted Zhukov to full membership of the reorganized Presidium. At that time, there is no doubt that the most popular man in Moscow and the country as a whole was not Khrushchev but Zhukov. As the war-time hero of Moscow and Stalingrad, his prestige stood higher in the popular imagination than that of Khrushchev, a relative upstart. With his honest peasant's face and his barrel chest, every available square inch occupied by medals and insignia, he looked the part of the military strongman, should this have been his ambition. Nor was modesty among his noticeable qualities: he tended to strut and posture. With Stalin dead and officially 'debunked', Zhukov's name was being built up as first among the military leaders of the Soviet Union during the 'great patriotic war'.

Doubtless Zhukov loved all this. It is improbable that he sought personal power; or that if he had, and had achieved it, he would have radically changed the Soviet system, for he had been a loyal Party member since 1919. What is certain, however, is that

175

he made determined and systematic efforts to reduce the Party's power over the Army. This was a crucial issue. From the outset, Lenin kept the Red Army under Party control through Military Commissars. If the military commander gave an order disapproved of by the Military Commissars, they simply countermanded it; in extreme cases, they could order his arrest.

This system, though essential to the Party's totalitarian power, reduced the morale and efficiency of the Armed Forces and at times, under the stress of war, it was diluted (although in 1941, it was strengthened to stem a wave of desertions). Zhukov's view, as a highly successful professional soldier, was that the Political Commissars should be kept firmly in a humble place, to help in maintaining morale and in training recruits, but without power over officers, especially superior officers—and above all over Zhukov himself. Many career officers complained of criticisms by relatively junior Commissars, and Zhukov supported them.

In April 1957, the Party took action to reaffirm its contested political power in the Army. That month, the Central Committee Secretariat issued a new 'Instruction to Organizations of the CPSU in the Soviet Army and Navy', which confirmed the Party's right to intervene, including the right of Party representatives to criticize their officers. Once again, the career officers grumbled, and once again Zhukov supported them.

It did not take Khrushchev long, after the crisis of June that year, to decide that he could no longer tolerate the attitude of the career officers and that the way to silence them was to strike at Zhukov. From his standpoint, he was right. Zhukov may not have been plotting to seize power, nor was he at that stage a potential Bonaparte. But it stood to reason that if he successfully opposed all Party encroachments, so that the time came when the Party had no power left over the Armed Forces, the latter would become an autonomous force able, in certain circumstances, to overthrow the Party leadership and even the system itself. Zhukov himself was becoming too prominent, too pleased with himself, for Khrushchev's comfort.

The fact—if true—that Zhukov had saved Khrushchev by flying Central Committee members to Moscow may have supported a claim on Khrushchev's gratitude but would not have weighed as a serious factor in his calculations. On the contrary, the flying operation (if true, as I presume it to be) showed that Zhukov was not averse from using Army power for political purposes (however justified these may have seemed at the time). If he could do this once, he could do it again; and the next time, it might be against Khrushchev.

Khrushchev timed his blow superbly. Zhukov was on a visit to Yugoslavia and Albania. On 26 October, the eve of his return, he was dismissed as Defence Minister. He also lost his membership of the central Committee and Presidium. Formal charges against him alleged that he had opposed Party control of the armed forces and neglected their political education, had promoted the 'cult of personality' (his own), been guilty of adventurism in foreign affairs, and shared Stalin's responsibility for Soviet unreadiness when Hitler attacked Russia in 1941. His colleague, Marshal Konev, viciously attacked him in the press. In November, a decree on the 'improvement of Party work in the Soviet Army and Navy' was published. Once again, the Party's power, wielded by Khrushchev, was supreme.

In other ways, too, Khrushchev's timing was brilliant. If Zhukov had been allowed to return from Albania and take the salute in the Fortieth Anniversary military parade on November 7, it would have been difficult for Khrushchev to act against him for months. Moreover, the shock of his dismissal was attenuated by the anniversary celebrations and the successful orbiting of Russia's first two earth satellites, which, coming shortly after the launching of an intercontinental missile, demonstrated the devastating power of Khrushchev's empire.

Inconclusive though the Zhukov affair was, it did show that circumstances could arise in which the Soviet Communist Party felt itself threatened by a leading soldier. Nor is this the only example of friction between the Party and the Army. The most spectacular example of all does not help us very much, either. It was that of Marshal Tukhachevsky, executed on Stalin's orders in 1937 for alleged treason and military conspiracy. Forged evidence of contacts with the Nazis was used to justify his arrest; but it was not produced in court, and he was found guilty of all charges on

Stalin's unsubstantiated statements.* His memory was rehabilitated in 1958.

There is much evidence, notably in Khrushchev's speeches and irrepressible asides, of discontent within the Army early in 1960, when partial demobilization measures and a reduction of the military budget were announced. The delayed outcome of latent tensions at that time was the removal of Marshal Golikov, head of the Chief Political Administration and a career officer, and his replacement by a Party stalwart, Epishev, whose appointment in May 1962 was marked by his formal transfer to the Army with the rank of general.†

The issue of political or professional control of the armed forces came up again in 1967 when the career officer, Marshal Malinovsky, Defence Minister, died. It was widely rumoured in Moscow at the time that he was to be succeeded by a Party man, Ustinov, but in the event the job went to Marshal Grechko, another career officer. As though to mark the point that this concession to the professionals did not mean any weakening of Party control, the head of the KGB, Andropov, was promoted to candidate member of the Politburo (formerly the Party Presidium) in June, two months after Grechko's appointment. Grechko himself, however, was not similarly honoured.

These Byzantine manoeuvres are more important than they may seem. They confirm the primacy of the Party, not only over the armed forces, but also over the secret police. At the 20th Party congress, in 1956, Khrushchev had promised to strengthen the subordination of the police to the Party. It is consistent with this policy that the head of the KGB must never be a member of the Secretariat, which deals with current Party administration and keeps an eye on the activities of every organ of the State and government. Thus, when Shelepin was elected a Party Secretary at the Central Committee's plenum after the 22nd Party congress, he lost his job as head of the KGB (to Semichastny). Again, when Andropov took over from Semichastny in 1967, he had to leave the Secretariat; his election as candidate-member of the Politburo

* Robert Conquest, *The Great Terror* (Macmillan, 1968), p. 223.
† Branko Lazitch in *Est & Ouest*, 1–15 November 1968.

178

was, of course, a promotion, but only a notional one, since candidate-members have no real power.

The handling of the Czechoslovak crisis of 1968–69 throws light, of a kind, on Grechko's position. The Warsaw Pact armies made a brilliantly planned and executed job of the occupation of Czechoslovakia in August 1968. In the ensuing months, the Soviet Communist Party, broadly speaking, made a thorough mess of the political side of the operation. In the end, it was the Army that came to the fore again to save the politicians from the consequences of their own ineptness: Marshal Grechko flew to Prague after anti-Russian rioting at the end of March and threatened to use Soviet troops in the event of further disorders. On 17 April, the reforming boss of the Czechoslovak Communist Party, Dubcek, was replaced by Dr Husak, who was willing to toe the Soviet line.

There are tantalizing straws in the wind to suggest that a trial of strength may have taken place at this time, between the Soviet Party and Army. One of these straws – it was no more than that – was a series of announcements in Moscow of the deaths of Soviet generals. In the first six months of 1969, forty-six such deaths were announced. In themselves, the deaths of so many generals were not all that surprising. At the end of the Second World War Russia had 11,000 generals: it was only natural that they should start dying off nearly twenty-five years later. A diligent commentator, in the *Sunday Times* of 11 May 1968, worked out that at the same stage of the previous year, thirty-seven generals had died, whereas at that date the 1969 figure was only thirty-three. But in the next few weeks, the number rose to forty-six, and by no means all of them were old men. The most striking thing about these deaths was that so many of them, according to the Soviet announcement, had taken place in 'tragic circumstances'. As a rule, this euphemism refers to an accident. But alternative 'tragic circumstances' could be imagined.

A more significant straw in the wind was the sudden cancellation, on 24 April 1969, of the traditional May Day parade of the Soviet armed forces in Moscow and other cities. With the exception of the war-time years, this was the first time the military parade had failed to take place on May Day since the

Communist Revolution. It is known, moreover, that the usual full-dress rehearsals had taken place. Whatever the reason, the cancellation was a humiliating blow to the Soviet military. And indeed, the combination of circumstances — Marshal Grechko's intervention in Prague, the deaths of relatively young generals and the cancellation of the military parade — suggest that a struggle for power of unusual intensity may have been taking place behind the walls of the Kremlin.

The striking point common to all these examples is that in the end, the Communist Party won the day. Any other outcome has indeed always looked exceedingly unlikely. For the Party has its own instrument — the KGB — right inside the armed forces, spying on the officers and reporting everything that may threaten, however mildly or indirectly, the Party's total control. The KGB has its own spying organ within the armed forces, the Third Directorate.* In addition, the Party's political control is enforced by the Chief Political Administration of the Soviet Army and Navy, responsible to the Central Committee, and at present headed by 'General' Epishev. These arrangements impose a pessimistic caution in assessing the chances of a successful Army *coup d'état* against the Party.

My conclusions so far may thus be summarized as follows. An anti-regime coup by the secret police is barely conceivable, since this would be tantamount to the suicide of the Party; a *coup d'état* by the Army is conceivable, but unlikely to succeed because of the KGB's stranglehold on the armed forces. In my view, little time need be expended in considering the alternative possibility that has occasionally been fashionable among Western liberals — that of a peaceful evolution of the Soviet system in a liberal direction; still less on the wild hope of left-wing Fundamentalists that a popular revolution will sweep the bureaucratic system away, 'liberating' the people from the stranglehold of the State.

Some liberalization is, of course, possible, but there will always come a time when the guardians of official orthodoxy call a halt and institute a fresh repression. There was a 'thaw' under Khrushchev, but it did not last long. The condition of the intellectuals under Khrushchev's successors has markedly worsened. As

* *The Times* (London), 14 November 1967.

for a 'liberal' revolution, of the kind that made a false start in Czechoslovakia, this seems a forlorn hope. That it went as far as it did was a reminder of Czechoslovakia's democratic past. But Russia's history offers no comparable democratic foundation upon which a liberal democracy might be built, if one excepts the ill-fated Kerensky period of 1917. If a Dubcek came to power in Russia—in itself an unlikely occurrence—he would not last as long as Dubcek did. Indeed, since Russia's rulers felt themselves threatened by the Dubcek experiment in Czechoslovakia, it is inconceivable that they would allow a similar experiment to get off the ground in the Soviet Union.*

Does this mean there is no hope for a change in Russia—*ever*? In political history, nothing is permanent. A Bonaparte, perhaps unknown today, perhaps unborn, could master a favourable situation, bending Party and secret police to his will. Such a situation could arise at a time of national emergency, for example an external military threat; from a total breakdown of the system; or if the ever-widening gap between theory and reality were to deprive ideology of its last shred of credibility. This last hypothesis needs expansion. As I mention in Part II, 1, the Soviet technological intelligentsia has already begun to question the relevance of Marxism-Leninism to the needs of Soviet society. Since the Communist Party still rests its case for a monopoly of power upon the correctness of Marxism-Leninism, the issue is important to the Soviet leadership. Typically, it has reacted in two ways: by repression (the traditional answer to the discontented), and by adopting non-Marxist measures in the name of Marxism-Leninism (as in the Liberman reforms). We are not yet in sight of the limit beyond which ideology can no longer be bent to suit the expedient needs of those in power.

If, however, the intellectuals can be sent to mental homes or labour camps, and if the intelligentsia may be similarly repressed, the same is not necessarily true of the armed forces as a whole at a time of rapid technological change. The situation that faces the Soviet Union in its permanent competition with the United States is that the prodigious American economy seems able to

* For an interesting international discussion of Russia's future, see *Interplay* (New York), May 1969.

sustain not only a rising standard of living but also the military-technological race with Russia. Russia, on the other hand, to hold its own in the military-technological race, is obliged to hold down living standards. (These do rise, of course, but more slowly than they might.) A revolutionary situation, of a kind, could arise if the Soviet armed forces came to feel that they could never catch up with the United States so long as the Soviet Union maintained its present system of State capitalism, and that Russia's national security was therefore in jeopardy.

At the time of the Cuban confrontation of 1962, such a situation seemed possible. In 1970, when these lines were written, published information suggested that the Russians were at least holding their own in the fateful race. All the indications were that during the preceding four or five years, the Soviet Union had gradually closed the gap, at least in respect of inter-continental ballistic missiles (ICBMs): the Russian force of ICBMs reportedly stood at 900 to 1,000, and the Americans were said to have 1,050 of them. There is no point in this context in speculating about existing and future terror weapons, such as the multiple independently targeted re-entry vehicle warheads (MIRV) or the fractional orbital bombardment system (FOBS). Whatever may have happened at the time of the May Day cancellation, there was no visible technological reason for discontent within the Soviet armed forces. Indeed, military expenditure was increasing under the 1968 budget. But this is not to say that a revolutionary situation for technological reasons, will never arise in the future.

In the context that concerns us, therefore, the prospect is a gloomy one. A Soviet government is not likely to be removed except through force and guile. Liberalization on a significant scale is too remote to bring comfort to outsiders. Any new government is unlikely to be less dependent on ideology (suitably modified) than its predecessors. The power of the secret police may fluctuate, but only within its own arbitrary latitude. No Bonaparte is in sight. The Soviet power base of world communism is intact, and the long-term struggle against the West continues undiminished.

2. *The Chinese Power Base*

In the 1950s, the conventional wisdom among students of communism was that the Sino-Soviet alliance was indestructible. Today the conventional wisdom is that the Sino-Soviet rift is beyond repair. I believe the conventional wisdom is wrong now, as it was then.

Conventional wisdom is not necessarily wrong, however, even when it has been accepted for a very long time. The conventional wisdom of the Chinese empire was that China should avoid having enemies both on the landward and seaward sides. This made sense, and it still does. One of the untrumpeted achievements of Mao Tse-tung is that he made enemies of both the super-Powers: America to the East and Russia to the West.

In the long run, for both strategic and economic reasons, Mao's foreign policy is untenable. In China's case, the connection between strategy and economics is peculiarly intimate. In 1949, when the Chinese People's Republic was born, China was emerging from thirty-eight years of revolution, civil strife and war, and centuries of arrested development. The population was vast and exploding; the arable land inadequate without massive injections of fertilizer; technology was backward and the raw materials of industry were remote from the industrial centres and hampered on their journey by an inadequate rail system. China needed aid from somewhere. America, the universal giver, was excluded by China's ideology and Mao's announced decision to lean to the Soviet side in the world schism. China badly needed Russia's economic aid, both for normal development and because – without Soviet know-how – her bid for Great Power status would be retarded. But dependence on another Power, including the Soviet Union, was hurtful to Mao's ancestral pride. When the Russians proved reluctant to pass on their military nuclear secrets to China, Mao threw caution to the winds and initiated the great quarrel. Self-reliance became the motto (and indeed there was now no other way) – but self-reliance fed, in Mao's mind, by the untapped energies and collective genius of the Chinese people.

The outcome was disastrous: at home, industrial development was held up by the euphoria of the 'great leap forward' and the chaos of the cultural revolution; abroad, China's military weakness and the barbarities inflicted upon foreign diplomatic missions reduced her influence to zero. In one vital sector, it is true, development went ahead impressively — that of nuclear energy and missile production. It is not by coincidence that this sector was less affected than others by the cultural revolution although it did not entirely escape the attention of the Red Guards. The fact remains that when China had a major military crisis on her doorstep — America's intervention in Vietnam — the Chinese were incapable of competing with the Russians in the provision of advanced weapons to North Vietnam and the revolutionary guerrillas in the South.

One man who had the common sense to see that Mao's policies could not work, and the courage to say so, was Marshal Peng Teh-huai, the former Defence Minister, whose dismissal has already been mentioned (Part II, 2). Marshal Peng was above all a modernizer. He doubted whether Mao's theories of peasant guerrilla warfare had any permanent value. He wanted a professional army, whose job would be to train and fight, and not — as Mao wished to use it — pitch in with the agricultural workers to bring in the harvest. He saw little value in Mao's idea of a nation-in-arms, and was sceptical of the practical uses of a vast untrained militia. Above all, he wanted nuclear status for China, and quickly. Since Russia was China's only supplier of modern weapons, he wanted to keep in with the Russians. He had no time for the great leap forward, or for the Communes; and he went so far as to express his distaste for these innovations in a letter to the Soviet Communist Party, without consulting the Chinese Politburo. Khrushchev is believed to have encouraged him, and his refusal to apologize for intervening in Chinese affairs seems to have brought the latent Sino-Soviet dispute into the open.*

Peng, moreover, was not alone: he was the leader of an 'anti-Party' group in the Politburo, and had its support at the Lushan Party conference in August 1959, when he read out a memorandum attacking the Party's policy. While the conference was on, Peng also wrote a personal letter to Mao (the text of which

* For a full account of Peng Teh-huai's dismissal, see David A. Charles in *China Quarterly*, October-December 1961.

was quoted in a Chinese newspaper in August 1967). It was not a disrespectful letter, but it obviously deeply offended Mao. At that time, however, Mao was not strong enough politically to take his full revenge on Peng Teh-huai. In December 1958, he had stepped down from the chairmanship of the Republic to be replaced four months later by Liu Shao-ch'i, who—it turned out later—was not unsympathetic to Peng's views. The Marshal had nevertheless been too bold and in September 1959, he was dismissed as Defence Minister (though allowed to retain his membership of the Politburo). One of the many charges later hurled at Liu was that he had supported Peng Teh-huai, and indeed in January 1962 Liu had called for a reversal of the verdict on Peng.

The point of interest in the context of China's future is that Peng Teh-huai, who stood for good relations with 'revisionist' Russia, had many supporters in the Chinese Communist Party. Apart from the small 'anti-Party' group, he had backing from Liu Shao-ch'i, and therefore from many Party members, high and low, since Liu at that time controlled the Party apparatus. The fact that Liu allowed Peng to be dismissed in September 1959 is relatively unimportant: Liu may have disapproved of Mao's wilder policies, but he was committed to support them through Party discipline, and Peng's denunciations were therefore, at that time, an embarrassment to him. When it became clear, in 1966, that Mao was determined to bring Liu down and smash the whole apparatus of the Communist Party in the name of 'permanent revolution', many of Liu's supporters hastily deserted him to save their own skins. But such changes of front in a crisis do not necessarily reflect inner judgements. Broadly speaking, the difference between Liu and Peng on the one hand and Mao and his supporters on the other, was this: Liu and Peng were rational human beings who were determined to make communism work, in full awareness of the realities of China's poverty, backwardness and need for friends; whereas Mao's policies, by all objective standards, and making every allowance for Mao's 'Chineseness', are irrational, though logically consistent with his own career and known beliefs. If this interpretation is correct, as I believe it to be, then it must be assumed that at some time

185

after Mao's death or retirement, either Peng himself (if still alive) or people who think like him, will come to the fore again. A new phase of Sino-Soviet understanding therefore seems to me one of the probabilities in the years ahead; although the process could be seriously retarded if the frontier battles between the two Powers turned into a war.*

This is not, of course, to say that a Sino-Soviet rapprochement is likely *immediately* after Mao's departure. Nor should it be inferred that Mao's declared supporters are as insane as he is. Insanity is not an attribute one would apply to Chou En-lai, for instance. Nor is Mao's designated successor, Marshal Lin-piao necessarily as mad as he sounds. It is indeed legitimate to wonder whether Lin may not have consciously used Mao, by flattery and total adoption of his ideas, however crazy, as the most effective way of staking his own claim to power. Mao Tse-tung's speeches are now rarely published. He has been seen, though infrequently, at public rallies; his visitors have been few. Indeed, rumours of serious illness and even death, circulated late in 1969. This was the background to Lin-piao's decision to be the active champion of Mao's Thoughts.

All this is speculative. The fact remains that if Mao died or formally retired (an unlikely prospect) Lin-piao (or somebody else) would inherit a situation partly of Lin's own making, with several years of political and economic chaos behind him, with a new and untested party built upon the ruins of the old, and headed on a regional basis by revolutionary committees that may turn out to be ephemeral. Lin-piao's great asset is undoubtedly the Army which, though much divided by the dissensions of the cultural revolution, has enhanced its stature throughout the chaotic past few years. But will this fragile consumptive command the energy necessary to hold the ramshackle edifice together? Will he not be the prisoner of his own anarchic policies? Will he stand up

---

* In *The Coming War between Russia and China* (Secker & Warburg and Pan Books, 1969), Harrison Salisbury, former Moscow correspondent of the *New York Times*, argued that a nuclear conflict between the two communist great powers was almost inevitable. It seems to me, however, that he made insufficient allowance for Moscow's cautious realism. If (as he notes) the Russians believe Mao to be mad (a view I share), then surely they will see advantages in waiting for him to die or retire, since his successors may prove, from their standpoint, more reasonable.

to the inevitable centrifugal forces of China's regions and non-Han minorities? Alternatively, will he have the strength to reverse the policy of 'permanent revolution' and adopt the saner policies of Liu Shao-ch'i and Peng Teh-huai—and still remain in power?

The answers to all these questions are problematical. A lengthy period of weakness and possible disintegration must be accounted one of the possibilities in the period that immediately follows Mao's disappearance. Should this period be prolonged, Marshal Peng's chances of returning to office—and possibly to power— would be slight, because of advancing age (he was born in 1900). But deprived of Mao Tse-tung's presence, the 'permanent revolutionaries' will not necessarily hold out long against the modernizers and advocates of Soviet friendship.

My tentative conclusions so far may therefore be summarized as follows. Mao's disappearance is likely to be followed by a period of chaos, yielding to the emergence of a 'revisionist' group advocating friendship with Moscow. A further possibility must, however, be explored—that of a nationalist and anti-communist military *coup d'état*. Ever since Chiang Kai-shek's eviction from continental China in 1949, this has been the increasingly forlorn hope of his Kuomintang rump government on Formosa (Taiwan). A victorious Nationalist return to the mainland has never seemed likely, short of an American-sponsored invasion. The Americans, however, have consistently banned a Nationalist invasion of China, even at the time of the Korean War, and after, when the mutual antagonism between Washington and Peking was at its height. Nationalist guerrillas have operated on the mainland from time to time and have even had local successes; but there has been no general uprising in favour of the Nationalists. Although Formosa under Nationalist rule has become a showcase of rapid economic development, and has achieved an unusually successful land reform, there appears to be no mass support for Chiang Kai-shek on the mainland, where memories of the incompetence of his administrations are predominant. Since he has not achieved the mythical 'return to the mainland' by now, it is unlikely that he will achieve it in his remaining span of life.

It is generally agreed that Chiang will be succeeded by his son, General Chiang Ching-kuo, Defence Minister and head of the security service. But the son is unlikely to succeed where the father failed. Indeed, he is unlikely even to try. Partly educated in Moscow (at a time when the Soviet Communist Party was working closely with the Kuomintang), General Chiang is probably a man who would not be embarrassed at the prospect of a deal—either with the Soviet Union against China, or with China's own leaders, in a situation that would enable him to retain control over Formosa.

Is there, then, yet another possibility—that of an anti-communist *coup d'état* within the Chinese People's Liberation Army? Even in China the advent of a Bonaparte cannot be entirely ruled out, but the prospect seems even more remote there than in the Soviet Union. For if anything, the Chinese Army is even more politicized than the Russian. As in Russia after the Revolution, the indoctrination of the Army started early—as early as 1928, when political officers were installed at company, battalion, regiment and army level throughout the embryonic Chinese Red Army.* As the United Nations forces discovered during the Korean War, blind obedience, fanatical indoctrination and discipline without individual initiative were the characteristics of the Chinese Liberation Army; the Indians made a similar discovery when the Chinese attacked them in 1962.

The Chinese Army is in fact totally permeated by the Party. There are Party cells of three to five members in every company. In addition, each company (at the time of the Korean war) had perhaps half a dozen 'little youth groups', with membership restricted to candidates for membership of the Party itself, enrolled in the New Democracy Youth Corps. Screening was rigorous. During the Korean War, at any rate, the political officer had complete control over Party activities in the company, and his responsibility covered the loyalty, efficiency and even thought of every individual unit member. In China, as in Russia, the Party has nevertheless had trouble from time to time in the old issue of professionalism versus doctrinal purity. Since Mao Tse-tung has always laid down that 'redness' is more important than 'expertness', purity has normally triumphed.

* Samuel B. Griffith II, *The Chinese People's Liberation Army* (Weidenfeld, 1968), especially chapter fifteen, pp. 251 et seq.

In July and August 1962, there was some evidence of disaffection within the Army. An Army Day notice by the Political Department of the Honan Military District in Central China, for instance, called for efforts to expose the plots and crimes of Chiang Kai-shek and the American imperialists 'among the masses of the PLA Personnel and the militia'. In March 1963, the Central Committee of the Chinese Communist Party drew up new regulations for political work in the Army, designed to prevent 'important questions being decided by individuals' contrary to the Party line. This was a clear indication that some senior officers were still arguing that modern warfare, with all its complexity, made detailed control by Party committees even more unpractical than in the past.

After Peng Teh-huai's dismissal in 1959, the Minister of Public Security, General Lo Jui-ching, was appointed Chief of the General Staff and Vice-Minister of Defence (under Lin-piao), and his appointment was taken as a sign that the Party was determined to tighten its control on the Army through the presence of a top security police man (though Lo did have a military background, too). General Lo, however, was one of the many prominent figures swept away in the cultural revolution. The present Chief of the General Staff, General Huang Yung-sheng, owed his promotion to his success, as Commander of the Canton garrison, in controlling an area in which violence and factionalism were rife during the cultural revolution.

The prospects of a 'revolution from below'—as distinct from Mao Tse-tung's revolution from above from 1966 on—would have been remote indeed until the cultural revolution threw everything into turmoil. If anything, the security system in the Chinese People's Republic was even more all-pervasive than in the Soviet Union. As Edgar Snow put it in *The Other Side of the River*, 'China is now a living colossus none of whose organs, including the whole vast external surface or skin, can be touched without sending a message through the nervous system of the giant'.* Apart from a highly organized police, the Ministry of Public Security controlled 'people's security committees' led by Party stalwarts in factories, production brigades, communes and

* Page 350 in the Random House (New York) edition, 1962.

government offices. Each family, and each member of every family, was permanently under surveillance. In such conditions, a mass uprising was inconceivable. It is impossible to say how much of this vast security apparatus has survived the cultural revolution. But even assuming that it may have been gravely impaired, 'revolution from below' would seem unlikely to achieve anything apart from contributing to the possible anarchy that Mao's successor may inherit.

A weak Chinese central government, beset by regional anarchy, would be more likely than a strong one to return to policies of intimidation and repression. A stronger People's China, in which order was restored, and an orthodox Communist Party reconstituted, perhaps under the leadership of a supporter of Liu Shao-ch'i or Peng Teh-huai, might open up interesting perspectives. Even if friendly relations with Russia were resumed, a new form of revisionism could well seem an attractive way of expressing China's separateness and national pride. Yugoslavia, rather than the Soviet Union, could well become a model, though not of course a model to be slavishly imitated. The 'inveterate tendency of the Chinese peasant towards capitalism', which has repeatedly been noted by the Communist Party itself, could even, in the end, secure permanent official tolerance. (It has already been tolerated at different periods as an infallible way of alleviating temporary food shortages.) A land reform in reverse, with a redistribution of the land to co-operatives and even individuals, is not unthinkable. Nor is a system of workers' control in the factories. Once the Party has abandoned Mao's wild and Utopian theories, anything is possible. The Chinese are an industrious, practical and ingenious people. A shifting ideological cover could well be provided for a freer economic system. There is no doubt that a greater measure of economic freedom would imply some dilution of the Party's totalitarian control. But this seems a very remote prospect. And in China, as in Yugoslavia (and indeed in Russia itself), the custodians of power would need to ask themselves at all stages whether the point of no return was in sight, whether China was ceasing to be communist. If ever they thought it was, they would be under strong compulsion to tighten the screw once more.

From the viewpoint of the outside world, there is little comfort to be derived from the prospect of a stabilized People's Republic. At least during the cultural revolution, it could be said that Mao had reduced China to international impotence. A China in which centralized control had been re-established, and in which the economy had begun to expand again from the natural stimulus of greater private initiative, might again present dangers to the outside world—in particular to China's neighbours, such as Burma and Thailand, in which insurgent groups are more or less responsive to Peking's will, but even further afield, in Africa. Paradoxically, Lin-piao's call for revolutionary uprisings all over the world meant little during the phase of weakness to which his own policies contributed. But it could become significant if China's strength were growing.

3. *Moscow's Strategy for the 1970s*

Since Moscow remains the main power centre of communism, it is to Moscow that we must turn for clues to communist world strategy. This is another way of saying that Soviet world strategy and communist world strategy are essentially synonymous. To put it that way is, of course, to oversimplify a very complex picture. But broadly speaking, the proposition still stands up.

To be sure, the strategic interests of the Soviet Union often run against the tactical aspirations of local communist parties. But this was always true, even in Stalin's day and Lenin's. True again, Peking often works against Soviet interests, while Havana has tried hard, though rather unsuccessfully, to pursue a Latin American policy independent of Moscow's will; though, as we have seen, the efforts of rival centres of communism, while mutually competitive, invariably work against the interests of the non-communist world.

The point, however, is that the Soviet Union is the only communist world power. The means at Fidel Castro's disposal, if one excludes those that are provided by Soviet aid, are too puny to affect the balance of power, much though his use of them may add to the burdens of Latin American (and even of African) governments. Nor is China a world power in a meaningful sense. The advent of Chinese nuclear power, assuming an effective delivery system, may or may not affect this verdict. But in the immediate future, Peking's capacity to influence the world beyond China's boundaries seems likely to be limited to the intimidation of neighbouring countries and the relatively ineffectual subversion of distant ones. Russia alone has the weight and strength to make its power felt all over the world. It is therefore relevant to this study to consider the use that may be made of it in the next decade. This means, specifically, describing Soviet foreign policy, seeing how it affects the world communist movement and individual parties, and pointing to the strategic opportunities which we may expect the Soviet leadership to exploit in the 1970s.

There is much understandable confusion about Soviet foreign policy. Is it primarily an imperial phenomenon, a continuation of the foreign policy of Tsarist Russia? In that event, is the fact that Russia is a communist country irrelevant? Or alternatively, is a victory for Russia a victory for 'world communism'? The confusion is, I believe, unnecessary. In many respects, the Soviet Union's foreign policy is indeed a continuation of Russian imperial policy. But communist ideology is a far more efficient servant of the Russian State than Tsarist autocracy could ever be. For one thing, it 'exports' far better, and lends itself, as Tsarist autocracy could not to the same degree, to the recruitment or use of non-Russians in the service of Russian imperialism. In that sense, a Soviet diplomatic or military success is a victory for communism. For if communism is ever to spread over all or most of the world, the chances, overwhelmingly, are that the prevailing variety of communism will be the Soviet kind.

To ignore the communist aspect of Soviet imperialism is to take no account of the momentous change brought to Russia in 1917 by the advent of totalitarian Marxism as a State philosophy. The present rulers of the Soviet Union are heirs to that State philosophy as well as to the Tsars' dominions, greatly enlarged within living memory. Their imperial forebears include Ivan I of Russia, nicknamed 'Moneybag' for his parsimony, who extended the hegemony of Muscovy over surrounding States. They include Ivan the Terrible, who destroyed the Khanate of Kazan, conquered

Astrakhan and waged war on Sweden; and Alexander I who, besides defending Russia against Napoleon's *Grande Armée*, inspired the Holy Alliance and grabbed Finland, Bessarabia and much of the Caucasus. Even Nicholas II, the last of the Tsars, whom the Bolsheviks murdered, was among their imperial fore-runners, for it was he who carried Russia's eastward expansion to its furthermost points with the occupation of Port Arthur and Manchuria—until Russia's power blunted itself against the emerging might of Japan.

When Lenin seized power in 1917, he brought a message of hope to the oppressed dependent peoples in the Tsars' former territories. One of the first acts of his revolutionary government, on 15 November 1917, was to proclaim their right to secede and set up independent States. The hopes aroused were, however, illusory, and the Declaration of 15 November was an early example of semantic distortion under communism. In Khiva and Bohkara, in Azerbaidjan and Georgia, local leaders took Lenin at his word and set up independent republics. All were short-lived, for in Lenin's eyes, all were 'bourgeois nationalist', and that was not the kind of 'independence' he had in mind. By 1921, all had been overthrown and supplanted by administrations con-trolled from Moscow.

Then came Stalin. By the use or threat of military force or by international agreement in favourable conditions, Stalin pushed the Soviet State westward into eastern Poland, grabbed the Baltic States, seized Bessarabia and northern Bukovina, Ruthenia in Czechoslovakia, important areas of Finland, and East Prussia; in the Far East, he took over South Sakhalin and the Kuriles from Japan; and secured lease rights in Dairen and Port Arthur. Some of these acquisitions were new; others were restorations of Tsarist conquests.

During the Second World War, the victorious advances of the Soviet Army extended Stalin's control—which, though indirect, was absolute—over East Germany, Poland, Czechoslovakia, Rumania, Hungary, Bulgaria and Albania. For some years, Yugoslavia, though not 'liberated' by Russia, was effectively controlled by Moscow, until Tito successfully defied Stalin in 1948.

And this, in effect, is where we came in. Rash and ebullient as he was, Khrushchev left the Soviet empire weakened abroad and unsure of itself at home. His successors are duller men, less given to clowning but less likely, also, to cede vital points. We do not need to be told what Mr Kosygin and Mr Brezhnev are after: their deeds speak for themselves. At home, they have been clamping down on the intellectuals, strengthening the secret police and gradually restoring Stalin's reputation. Abroad, they have restored Moscow's authority where it was threatened, in Czechoslovakia, and preserved it elsewhere in eastern Europe (apart from Albania). They have persisted, with some success, with their efforts to restore Moscow's authority over the non-ruling communist parties and isolate China. Everywhere else, they have probed for weak points, using whatever means, or combination of means, seemed tactically appropriate: aid and trade; diplomacy; a naval presence in the Mediterranean and elsewhere; propaganda; the training—either overt or secret—of trade-unionists and party cadres, or saboteurs, terrorists and guerrilla fighters; or the sale or gift of arms, both open and clandestine. To this already formidable arsenal should be added a vast and expanding expenditure on military technology; espionage and—at the humdrum level—the bribery and corruption of local politicians.

To what end or ends, it may be asked, is this gigantic and continuing effort devoted? A favourite cliché of anti-communist organizations has the disadvantage of sounding exaggerated, emotive or even hysterical. The cliché—'world domination'—is, however, closer to the probable truth than any other two words I can think of. Let the Russians speak for themselves. In his report to the 23rd Congress of the Soviet Communist Party in 1966, Brezhnev pledged the party to 'do everything in its power to ensure that the world socialist system becomes still more powerful and advances from victory to victory'.

This pledge may sound relatively modest, on the scale of world domination. But 1966 was a comparatively muted year in Soviet international relations. Two years later, when the Soviet physicist, A. D. Sakharov, smuggled out to the West a pamphlet in which he appealed for friendship between the United States and the

Soviet Union,* the answer was swift and unambiguous. 'Socialism and capitalism,' said the government newspaper, *Izvestia*, 'the two fundamentally different world systems, are developing in diametrically opposed directions ... The struggle between two basic tendencies, two opposing world forces—capitalism and socialism—permeates the course of history in the last third of the century.' The writer, Viktor A. Cheprakov, went on to say that 'revolutionary currents, whose guiding force is found in the socialist countries, led by Marxist-Leninist parties, comprise the mighty power that will bring all countries into the orbit of socialism and open the way for harmonious socialist action on a global scale.'†

Whether all the Soviet leaders believe such statements to be literally true, and such aims attainable, is not of dominant relevance. The point is that the passage quoted is by an officially approved writer in the organ of Soviet State policy. 'All countries' are to be brought into 'the orbit of socialism'; and it is the Soviet Communist Party that decides what constitutes socialism. This is Soviet foreign policy, and all Soviet actions are consistent with a strategy of attaining the stated objective of a world system controlled from Moscow. As if to show that the *Izvestia* article was meant to be taken seriously, the Warsaw Pact forces invaded Czechoslovakia ten days after it was published on 11 August 1968.

Let us turn now from the general and sweeping aims of Soviet foreign policy to the real world, in all its perverse diversity. As the decade of the 1970s begins, fresh opportunities beckon the Soviet leaders. The 'socialist commonwealth' stands as a huge and apparently changeless patch on the world map. The Czechoslovaks' importunate taste for freedom threatened change near home, but was suppressed. Almost all other major areas, however, are in a state of flux.

This is something new, for the strategic map of the world remained virtually immobile for twenty years. The West's answer to Stalin's European threat was the Atlantic Treaty, signed in

---

* The pamphlet, *Progress, Co-existence and Intellectual Freedom*, is discussed in a different context in Part II, 1.

† For a discussion of this article, in the context of détente, see Elliot R. Goodman, in *Survey* (London), Winter-Spring 1969.

J

1949. That year, China passed into Mao Tse-tung's hands. Between 1949 and 1969, there were a number of dangerous international crises: an episodic one over Berlin in 1959–60, which petered out in anti-climax; a shooting micro-war over the Chinese offshore islands in the late 1950s; a dangerous nuclear confrontation in the Caribbean in 1962; two protracted wars in Indochina; a conventional war in Korea. But by and large, the map remained almost unchanged after each crisis—although North Vietnam did pass formally under communist rule in 1954.

Towards the end of the twenty-year period, however, important changes began. In the Near East, Israel smashed the Arab armies, demonstrating a capacity for independent action that undoubtedly astonished the Russians, but at the same time enabled them to increase the United Arab Republic's dependence upon the Soviet Union. In the United States, President Nixon committed his Administration to a policy of cautious military withdrawal from Vietnam. In Latin America, the collapse of 'Che' Guevara's attempt to spark off a guerrilla revolution in Bolivia demonstrated the vanity of Fidel Castro's regional ambitions and helped the Russians to increase their pressure upon his regime.

In Western Europe, two important political changes took place, the consequences of which cannot yet be precisely evaluated. In West Germany, the Christian Democrats, who had been in power ever since the elections of 1946, were turned out in favour of Willy Brandt's Social Democrats. This spelt the end of a twenty-three-year dominance of the party that had been most disposed to 'collaborate' with the victorious Allies, to align Bonn's policy with Washington's and uncompromisingly reject any overtures from communist East Germany under the Ulbricht regime—itself dependent on the Soviet military presence for political survival. The new Brandt government, however, let it be known that it was prepared to recognize the existence of two German States within the German nation, pending a final settlement.

While this formula stopped short of formal recognition of East Germany, it was far enough removed from the old policy of stern disapproval of any government that dared to recognize

East Germany (the 'Hallstein doctrine') to encourage a Russian hope that fresh opportunities were emerging in Bonn. Moreover, although the new West German Chancellor stood by the essential principle of self-determination for the German people that is, for reunification on Bonn's terms, he was willing to widen trade and cultural arrangements with East Germany. Equally encouraging, from Moscow's standpoint, was Brandt's decision to sign the nuclear non-proliferation Treaty, which the outgoing Kiesinger government had declined to sign, perhaps in order to retain a bargaining counter in future discussions on German unity. Essentially, the decision to sign removed Russia's fear that the West Germans might take over America's nuclear shield over Western Europe, should the United States ever tire of its Nato commitment.

In France, too, an important change took place in 1969. General de Gaulle, whose second tenure of power had lasted nearly eleven years, resigned. Although he was succeeded as President by the man who had been his Prime Minister until the 1968 crisis — Georges Pompidou — it was soon clear that Gaullism without de Gaulle was going to mean changes. And that the changes would probably be against Russian interests.

Broadly speaking, de Gaulle's foreign policy had suited the Russians well. It would be absurd, of course, to call him 'pro-communist': no one had denounced the French Communists with a more contemptuous venom than he during the days of the Rally of the French People; and during the Cuban missile crisis of 1962, he had unhesitatingly taken President Kennedy's side. But in Marxist terms he was non-ideological. He had snubbed the Americans, vetoed British entry into the European Economic Community and pulled France's forces out of Nato. Although unable to detach West Germany from the United States, he had asserted French political primacy over the Bonn government, and even given public recognition to the Oder-Neisse line — in effect sanctioning Soviet seizures of German territory later handed to Poland. Meanwhile, he had systematically improved French relations with Eastern Europe. Moreover, by banning shipments of arms to Israel, he indirectly helped Soviet policy in the Near East.

Pompidou's government was both intrinsically weaker than de Gaulle's—despite a big majority in Parliament—and less emotionally committed to systematically anti-Anglo-Saxon attitudes. Its weakness sprang from the new President's lack of a comparable *mystique* and the long-term incredibility of his being able to keep the various Gaullist factions—left, right and centre—united. For some months, Pompidou's foreign policy showed no perceptible sign of movement. Then, at a common market 'summit' meeting at The Hague, in November 1969, he opened the door which de Gaulle had slammed in British faces, by sanctioning talks that could lead to Britain's admission to the EEC. The effect of the changes in France and Germany was thus that it became desirable, as it has not been previously, for the Russians to explore the possibility of an understanding with Bonn, while making things difficult for Paris.

In Britain also, towards the end of the seventh decade, an important change took place. In January 1968, the Prime Minister, Harold Wilson, announced that British forces were to be withdrawn from the Far East (except Hong Kong) and from the Persian Gulf by the end of 1971 instead of by an unstated date in the mid-1970s. This opened up the prospect of a power vacuum over a vast area, especially after America's decision to withdraw from Vietnam. The question was: Who was to fill the vacuum? The British decision therefore created new opportunities for the Russians. It is too early to say how far the return to power of the Conservatives in June 1970, with a pledge to maintain a British military presence in the Far East, will frustrate Soviet plans.

The last factor in this world power equation is Japan. For more than twenty years after their defeat in the Second World War, secure under the American nuclear umbrella, the Japanese virtually opted out of power politics. By the mid-1960s, however, Japan had become the world's third industrial power (after the United States and the USSR), and a cautious debate began, on the possibility that Japan might play a role in the security of the Pacific region. America's interest in encouraging this trend was evident, although it was the MacArthur Constitution, imposed on Japan during the American occupation, that precluded Japan from becoming a nuclear power or indeed from becoming a military power at all. The trump in American hands was Okinawa, which, under American occupation, had been transformed into the biggest nuclear base in the Pacific, but whose return Japan insistently demanded.

Before becoming President, Richard Nixon had made it clear that the return of Okinawa might be conditional on Japan's involvement in Pacific defence. Accordingly, in November 1969, the American President and the Japanese Prime Minister, Mr Eisaku Sato, reached an agreement satisfactory to both sides. Okinawa was to revert to Japanese sovereignty by 1972. By that time, the Americans are to remove stocks of nuclear armaments from the island. (The development of American submarine nuclear launching facilities had, in any case, reduced Okinawa's importance in this respect.) The agreement, however, provided that if the Vietnam war had not been settled by 1972, there would be consultations between the two countries, to ensure that the restitution of Okinawa should not prejudice the chances of self-determination for the people of South Vietnam. Privately, Nixon and Sato were reported to have agreed on the need to reintroduce American nuclear weapons into Okinawa in the event of a grave international crisis.

Russia's world strategy for the 1970s is inherent in the changed situation just analysed, and in the activities described elsewhere in this book (especially in the chapters on the world communist movement and on subversion). It may be summarized as follows:

In Europe: to exploit Herr Brandt's readiness to improve relations with Eastern Europe to achieve at least *de facto* recognition of the Ulbricht regime; to split the Bonn-Paris axis; to detach the European members of Nato from their trans-Atlantic allies.

In the Middle East and in Africa: to continue the Soviet naval build-up in the Mediterranean and the Indian Ocean (filling the 'British' power vacuum in the Persian Gulf); to support actual or potential client States (Egypt, Algeria, Syria, Iraq, etc.); to compete with the Chinese in arming and training guerrillas.

In the Far East: to fill the 'American' power vacuum, if it develops according to expectations, pre-empting competitive bids from either China or Japan; just possibly, to strike a 'punitive' blow at China.

In Latin America: to complete the process —already advanced— of bringing Fidel Castro's foreign adventures under control, while improving their own capacity to subvert the governments with which they seek, in a parallel process, to improve State relations.

Although it may seem paradoxical, a search for détente is an essential element in these aggressive designs. Just as 'peaceful co-existence', in communist eyes, means the intensification of the international class struggle, short of a major war, so détente, in Russian eyes, means guarding against the risk of a nuclear confrontation with the United States and causing America's allies to reduce their defence budgets—leaving the Russians free to fish in troubled waters of their choosing.

In this context, the Soviet Union's achievement of nuclear and ballistic missile parity with the United States in the second half of the 1960s is a major technological change to set beside the geo-political changes I have listed. The achievement of parity made it possible for the Russians to embark on strategic arms limitation talks (SALT) with the Americans at Helsinki in 1969. Should the talks be successful, they could serve a mutually advantageous aim, by avoiding a new and ruinously expensive technological arms race between the super-powers involving the creation of anti-ballistic missile systems (ABMs), and such horrendous devices as multiple independently targetable re-entry vehicles (MIRVs).*

While they last, however, the SALT discussions serve additional political purposes. For instance, they help to encourage the belief that in the last resort, America and Russia will settle their strategic problems alone, Nato and other military pacts, such as Seato and Cento, having become irrelevant to America's security. The logical

---

* For a discussion of the advantages to Russia of an ABM system, see J. I. Coffey, 'Soviet ABM Policy: The Implications for the West' in *International Affairs* (London), April 1969.

end of this argument is that America will not risk nuclear war to protect Western Europe or its Asian allies. It is not by coincidence that 1969 was also the year in which Moscow launched two complementary diplomatic initiatives. At the world communist conference in June, Brezhnev called for an Asian collective security pact, specifically directed against China, but implicitly directed at America as well*. In Prague, at the end of October, the Warsaw Pact powers renewed the long-standing call for a European security conference in terms which, though less polemical than previous statements, implied the exclusion of the United States and Canada.

To analyse Soviet objectives and dissect Moscow's strategy is not of course to prejudge the outcome. My purpose in this chapter is to place the relatively amorphous issue of 'communism' in the hard and precise context of Soviet ambitions. In Russia's world design, the communist parties, both in power and in opposition, and the innumerable leftist groups, have a definite place. Ideally, from Moscow's standpoint, the world communist movement ought to be as disciplined and obedient as it was in Stalin's day. Parties ought to turn up in Moscow when summoned (as sixteen Asian parties failed to do in June 1969). But in the more sophisticated world of the 1960s and 1970s, readiness to sign Russian-drafted documents may be less important than responsiveness to Russian wishes in precise instances. Unanimous adoption of Soviet theses may be politically counter-productive in individual countries. In Stalin's time, the issue of opposing, say, the Soviet invasion of Czechoslovakia, had it arisen, would have been swiftly suppressed. Some forty years of unconditional obedience to Moscow, however, made it relatively easy to isolate non-ruling communist parties as the obvious tools of Soviet foreign policy. Today, to declare disapproval of Moscow over Czechoslovakia is a relatively cheap way of demonstrating 'independence' from the Kremlin and gaining respectively as a political party 'like any other'.

Whether the Russians see things in this light, it is difficult to say. Certainly, it would be a Machiavellian and intelligent course

* See Lawrence L. Whetten, 'Moscow's Anti-China Pact' in *The World Today* (London), September 1969.

for them to encourage the dissidence of, say, the Italian Communist Party on Czechoslovakia. Probably in Moscow, as well as within the non-ruling parties, the issue of overt or secret loyalty to Moscow is hotly debated. It is significant that the Stalinist old guard of the British Communist Party, led by the veteran theoretician R. Palme Dutt, tried hard, at the National Congress in November 1969, to have the Party's condemnation of the Soviet military intervention withdrawn; even though the attempt failed. Similar debates in the French, Italian, Swedish and other communist parties have been going on.

From the standpoint of Russia's world strategy, however, some questions are more relevant than public loyalty to Moscow. For instance:

—Is a communist party willing, whatever its public attitude, to help the Soviet Communist Party in specific ways, for example by carrying funds to the more inaccessible parties?
—Is public dissociation from Moscow likely to improve a party's chances of getting to power?
—Does a 'dissident' party advocate international policies which, if put into practice, would serve the ends of Soviet foreign policy?

By all these tests, the Italian party—the largest and most 'independent' party in the West—still qualifies as a 'Russian' party.

Nor should any illusions be entertained, as they undoubtedly have been in some quarters, about the value of the powerful French Communist Party as an instrument of Soviet policy, if not in appearance then—as Marxists say—'objectively'. Without doubt, the party and its trade-unionists of the Confédération Générale du Travail (CGT) helped to keep General de Gaulle in power in May and June 1968 by refusing to join the New Left students in revolutionary action. As a result, the non-communist Left virtually collapsed in France, leaving the Communists more powerful than for many years past. Moreover, with de Gaulle out of power, it became less desirable—from Moscow's point of view—to make things easy for the French government. Hence a wave of strikes and abductions which led the Premier, Chaban-

Delmas, in an exceptionally intransigent speech on 27 November 1969; to castigate the CGT's policy as 'a call to subversion by all possible means'. It would not be surprising to learn that Boris Ponomarev, the Soviet party secretary responsible for relations with the 'fraternal parties', congratulated the French party leader, Waldeck-Rochet, when he turned up in France with a large delegation after the French central committee had met in October.

The Russians have never, however, troubled themselves to help persecuted communist parties if, at a given time, Soviet State interests made it expedient to maintain good relations with the appropriate government. For years after the Soviet arms deal with Egypt in 1955, Egypt's Communists continued to languish in Nasser's gaols. Similarly, Stalin was on good terms with Chiang Kai-shek while the latter was waging war on Mao's communist guerrillas (an early cause of the Sino-Soviet rift). Again, the fate of the Tudeh ('Masses') party in Iran has for some time been of less interest to the Russians than the desire to improve relations with the Shah's government, which persecutes it.* Such examples could be multiplied, and show a remarkable continuity from Stalin's day to Brezhnev's.

One innovation of Khrushchev's was designed to meet the case of 'radical' governments in the newly independent or 'emergent' countries in which the local communist party was either very weak or non-existent. This was the idea of establishing 'fraternal links' with the existing ruling party. Khrushchev established such links with the Arab Socialist Union in the United Arab Republic (Egypt), with the Algerian Front de Libération Nationale, with Guinea's Parti Démocratique de Guinée and with Mali's Union Soudanaise. This device has evidently proved useful, for Khrushchev's successors have kept it up, despite occasional rows with the selected ruling parties.

Yet another device was used at the Moscow conference in June 1969. The Asian parties having declined to attend, the Russians created a 'Communist Party of East Pakistan', and

---

* A penetrating commentary on Russia's strategy and tactics in the Middle East, by Walter Laqueur, will be found in *Foreign Affairs* (New York), January 1969. See also Martin Edmonds and John Skit, 'Current Soviet Maritime Strategy and Nato', in *International Affairs* (London), also January 1969.

produced a delegation (led, ironically, by an Indian) who dutifully made anti-Chinese speeches.

Though clear about ultimate objectives, the Soviet leaders are almost infinitely flexible and pragmatic in tactics. A communist party may be used or abused, congratulated or sacrificed. If one does not exist, it can be created for the circumstance, at least on paper, as in East Pakistan or Lesotho. If it is banned, the local ruling party, if sufficiently anti-Western and incipiently revolutionary, will do. But the end envisaged is always the same: the advancement of Soviet interests. As these interests include, as a major priority, the advancement of Soviet communism, each Soviet setback and each success is a success or a setback for communism, since 'communism' acquires meaning only in the context of its power base.

4. Communism and Ourselves

It is going to be a long war. Any thought of a quick victory, any hope of the imminent collapse of the communist power system through its inherent contradictions or the challenge of rival forms of Marxism, must on the evidence be ruled out. This does not, on the other hand, imply a rapid extension of the system in the next few years, although in one precise area—South-East Asia—a geographical advance of communist power is likely. The further prospect is of a sprawling, untidy guerrilla war both within Western societies and in the underdeveloped areas, in which the combat lines will be indeterminate, the combatants difficult to identify, the duration unpredictable and the outcome uncertain.

I have already analysed the outlook in the two main power centres, Russia and China. Assuming a further long lease of life in the former and a rapprochement between the two as a longer-term prospect, the heartland of the communist empire seems likely to remain intact, and perhaps to be consolidated. (A factor that could upset this expectation might be a border war between Russia and China, in which the main imponderable would be America's attitude.) After the Czechoslovak experience, the chances of successful assertions of independence in Eastern Europe must be rated very low.

In Western Europe, three countries whose internal stability is at present in doubt are France, Italy and Spain. In France, the transition to Gaullism without de Gaulle has been smoother than many observers expected. The crisis of May-June 1968 provoked the collapse of the non-communist Left and demonstrated that the Communist Party has abandoned violent revolution, though it is still dedicated to permanent war against the existing system. The net effect of the crisis was, however, to deprive the Communists of potential coalition allies. It would be rash to predict the Pompidou regime's long-term prospects. It does, however, seem improbable that the New Left's revolutionary challenge, even if repeated—as it may be—will be more successful next time than it was in 1968.

In Italy, the principal danger is that the Communist Party may emerge in time as the strongest single political force (though not necessarily in command of an absolute majority at the polls). If this situation arose, and if the other parties failed to unite to keep the Communists out, it might fall to the Communist Party to lead a coalition government. At this stage one of two prospects would face Italy: either a more or less gradual legislative programme to promote communist measures constitutionally; or, more likely, an anti-communist *coup d'état* by the police and army. An 'Italy of the Colonels', though not an immediate prospect, cannot be ruled out.

In Spain, Franco has made careful dispositions for the survival of the Franquist State under a monarch. Should these fail, the likely prospect would be of widespread disorders, swiftly snuffed out by a military seizure of power. The outlook for a parliamentary democracy is too remote for serious consideration.

Beyond Europe, the most dangerous situation is undoubtedly in South-East Asia. At the time of writing, the outcome of the war in Vietnam was still not a foregone conclusion. In itself, President Nixon's policy of gradual military withdrawal and of 'Vietnamization' of the fighting was not inconsistent with the efficient prosecution of the war. Indeed, as Sir Robert Thompson, the former Head of the British Advisory Mission in Vietnam, has argued, a massive American involvement was not the best way to fight a war of subversion and terrorism.* By the second half of 1969, in fact, the Viet Cong and its allies from North Vietnam were relatively weak and demoralized. A total American withdrawal and complete Vietnamization would, however, leave the South Vietnamese forces alone to face a possible conventional invasion of South Vietnam by the tough and highly trained regulars of North Vietnam. If a full American evacuation took place too precipitately—say by the end of 1970—there could be no doubt of the eventual outcome.

In his speech of 3 November 1969, President Nixon plainly showed that he was aware of the dangers of precipitate withdrawal and determined to avoid them. If it is politically practicable for him to leave behind a relatively small force of *professional* troops (who would be less vulnerable to adverse public agitation than conscripts) for a long period—anything up to ten years—a gradual wearing down of the communist apparatus and strengthening of the South Vietnam State and its forces, are plausible possibilities.

It would, however, be unrealistic to ignore the alternative prospect—that of the extension of communist power from North to South Vietnam. In the light of the late Ho Chi Minh's long history of irredentist ambitions and of North Vietnam's actual incursions into neighbouring territories, it must be assumed that Hanoi's authority will in time extend over Laos, and possibly over Cambodia as well. (President Nixon's military intervention in Cambodia was short-lived; and South Vietnam's capacity to contain Hanoi's pressures is in doubt.)

The fate of other countries of continental South-East Asia will depend very largely upon Peking's strategic plans. Left to its own devices, with some assistance from the United States, Thailand seems capable of containing and defeating its local Communist guerrillas (who are supported by China and North Vietnam). But a victory for the 'people's revolutionary war' in Vietnam, especially if it were followed by an American strategic withdrawal, might stimulate a rapid growth of the 'people's war' industry in

* See, for instance, Robert Thompson, *No Exit from Vietnam* (Chatto & Windus, 1969).

China. Should this happen, the threat to Thailand and to Burma (which is less well equipped than Thailand to deal with such a threat) would significantly increase. A successful revolutionary war in Thailand would, in turn, revive the capacity of the Malayan Communist guerrillas—the remnants of whom are based on Southern Thailand—to threaten Malaysia and Singapore. The essential truth of the 'domino' theory seems to me to be incontrovertible.

In Africa communist successes have been limited. The scene of most intensive penetration was Ghana, until Nkrumah was overthrown. Operating bases of a kind have been set up in Congo-Brazzaville and Tanzania, and the competitive or complementary activities of the Russians, Chinese, Cubans and others are now aimed primarily at mounting guerrilla operations against the Portuguese territories, Rhodesia and South Africa. There seems no immediate prospect that these will succeed. In the long run, Soviet policy probably rests its major hopes upon the conversion of existing regimes into client States. The greatest success so far has been in the United Arab Republic, and determined efforts are being made elsewhere, notably in Algeria and Nigeria.

In Latin America, three great obstacles stand in the way of a further extension of communism: distance, the interventionist traditions of local military establishment, and the United States. The experience of the last few years suggests that Fidel Castro is not going to succeed in kindling revolutionary fires on the Cuban model in continental Latin America. What is known of the attempted Dominican rising in 1965 suggests, however, grounds for caution. Two features stand out: the planning of the attempted coup was a joint venture (returning communist infiltrators had been trained in Cuba and several East European countries); and considerable headway had been made in indoctrinating the armed forces. The current example of a 'progressive' *and* nationalist military junta in Peru shows that the military are not necessarily 'reactionary'. If as many higher officers are won over to communism in a major Latin American country as had been in Indonesia by 1965, an extremely menacing situation could develop. The new wave of urban terrorism should be seen in this perspective.

On the assumption of a geographical stalemate (apart from South-East Asia), let us now turn to possible responses to communism.

A powerful mental blockage inhibits most people from seeing communism as it really is.* The behaviour attributed to Communists seems to them so monstrous, so contrary to nature, that they are unwilling or unable to grasp it. Themselves incapable of comparable cruelty and duplicity, or of sustained hostility and hate, they take refuge in the consoling thought that 'it can't be true', or, if the truth of hostile allegations is accepted, that 'it cannot last' or, 'it is bound to change'. They lend a wishful ear to liberal commentators who assure them that affluence is bound to liberalize and soften the communist regimes. They readily accept the facile notion that the system they know—plural democracy—being of superior merit in its potential for the relative happiness of the greatest number, is bound to prevail over total tyrannies.

Every now and then, of course, such complacencies are shattered by some reminder of the ferocity of the communist beast. The recent past has brought several such reminders, including: the invasion of Czechoslovakia; the release of the British lecturer, Gerald Brooke, after the successful blackmailing of his government by the KGB; and the decision of the Russian writer Anatoli Kuznetsov, to seek refuge in the United Kingdom. During the whole of the period that spanned these three events, Mr Anthony Grey, Reuter's correspondent in Peking, was held in close confinement, an innocent hostage whose only crime was that his nationality was the same as that of the authorities in Hong Kong who had gaoled Chinese journalists for their part in communist-inspired riots.

In the face of such evidences of communist barbarism, normal people *do* react. 'Normal' newspapers run suitably indignant leaders; Parliamentarians make appropriate speeches; and readers express their sense of outrage in letters to the press.

But few two-year periods are as rich in reminders of such barbarism as 1968 and 1969. The inertia of normality tends

* To define 'normal' would be invidious. In this context, I am referring to people whose approach to politics and philosophy is not fanatical.

inexorably to reassert itself. In 1956, it was 'unthinkable' that the Soviet leaders, fresh from their denunciations of Stalin, should behave as he would have done in Hungary (and worse, in a sense, since *he* had refrained from invading Yugoslavia in 1947). In 1968, it was 'unthinkable' that the Soviet leaders should behave as their predecessors had twelve years earlier; but the indignation of normal people did not stop the Soviet Army from occupying Czechoslovakia. We may confidently expect the next outrage to be deemed 'unthinkable'—until it happens.

Nor is such reluctance to believe the worst of communism, in itself, dishonourable. Even in an age of receding faith, hope and charity are powerful constants of human nature. We hope communism will change for the better, and the behaviour of Communists improve. And we are charitable enough to seek excuses for the inexcusable.

But if it is not dishonourable to be hopeful and charitable, neither is it intelligent or courageous, where communism is concerned. And courage and intelligence are desperately needed qualities if communism is ever to be defeated, as it can and must. It is natural to hope that the problem will disappear of its own accord; but deeply misguided to count on it. The battle against communism is inescapable, and it will be won only if the objective of victory is kept constantly in view, however long it may take.

Such assertions may sound dogmatic, but the logic of the facts supports them. The dominant fact is the implacable hostility of all communist parties towards non-communist systems, and especially toward plural and representative democracies, which are termed 'capitalist' and 'imperialist'. This hostility was solemnly reaffirmed by the seventy-five parties that attended the international communist conference in Moscow in 1969. It is not logically defensible to be neutral toward an implacable and unscrupulous foe, whose constant objective is one's own destruction. Whether we want it or not, the war is on. It will end in our destruction unless the enemy is defeated. Nor does defeat necessarily imply the *enemy's* destruction: what is needed is an end to his capacity to damage or destroy *us*.

It may be useful to consider some arguments which together constitute the liberal conventional wisdom about communism.

In so doing, I shall recapitulate some of the main conclusions already reached in this book, and suggest further ones.

—Communism was admittedly a grave problem when the world communist movement was the obedient instrument of Stalin's foreign policy, but this is manifestly no longer the case; communism is therefore no longer a proper concern of governments.

COMMENT The fact that the world communist movement is less responsive to Moscow's will than it used to be does not mean that it has ceased to be useful to the Kremlin. The scale and persistence of Moscow's efforts to restore the unity of the movement under its leadership should not be underestimated, and are themselves a measure of the value the Russians place upon it. Whatever the reservations of individual communist parties about Moscow's leadership, many of them continue to serve the stated and unstated objectives of Soviet foreign policy, not merely by agitation and propaganda, but also by rendering specific clandestine services to the KGB.

This is of course particularly true of the ruling European parties, but it applies to many others as well. The East German, Czech and Bulgarian parties are deeply involved, for instance, in Russia's subversive operations in Africa. But every now and again, a piece of evidence comes to light showing that non-ruling parties are also doing Moscow's clandestine work. In April 1965, for instance, an Italian communist courier was arrested with a Spanish woman in Caracas on being found in possession of US $270,000 in notes destined for the Venezuelan Communist Party. Press reports came to light that suggested the Italian Communist Party had undertaken to be 'paymaster' to the Venezuelan party. Most of the Latin American parties have in fact continued to obey Moscow's instructions, which often run counter to Fidel Castro's wishes.

Every communist party everywhere is indeed a permanent centre of subversion, which either accepts Moscow's instructions or suggestions, or works independently towards objectives consonant with Moscow's wishes. Splinter groups that proclaim their solidarity with other communist centres, such as Peking or Havana, present additional problems. The fragmentation of the world communist movement is a matter for mild rejoicing to the extent that it has reduced Moscow's capacity to make mischief on a world scale. But it does not mean that the world communist movement has ceased to be a problem. On the contrary, in the age of competitive subversion, fragmentation has added to the burdens of the security services.

Nor should it be forgotten that each individual member of a communist party is a potential recruit to the Soviet espionage system. This is probably as true now as it was in Stalin's day. The most famous of Russia's spies, Richard Sorge, executed in Tokyo in 1944, was overtly a Nazi, but covertly a communist. Philby, the British double agent, became a communist in the 1930s and remained one in a remarkable career that carried him high into the upper hierarchy of the British Intelligence Service. Dr Klaus Fuchs, the German Jewish refugee who supplied British atomic secrets to Russia, was a Communist. Julius and Ethel Rosenberg, executed in America in 1953 for spying for the USSR, were Communists; so were Morris and Lona Cohen (better known as Peter John and Helen Joyce Kroger), gaoled in Britain in 1961 for spying, and released in 1969 in part-exchange for Gerald Brooke. This short list could be extended almost indefinitely. *

* For a good short account of Soviet espionage methods, see *The Soviet Spy Web*, by Edward Carran (Ampersand, London, 1961). Important though the Soviet espionage network is, the only aspect of it that is directly relevant to this study is the recruitment of foreign Communists as spies for the Soviet secret services. It is worth pointing out, however, that while ideological commitment facilitates recruitment, the absence of it does not inhibit the KGB's talent scouts, ever on the look-out for human weaknesses that may be exploited for blackmail purposes. The British Board of Trade published a pamphlet, *Security Advice about Visits to Communist Countries* in March 1969, to warn innocent business men of the sex traps that might be laid for them on their visits to Eastern Europe. Decoys of both sexes planted by local intelligence services tempt the unwary into compromising situations that may yield photographic evidence with which to blackmail the victims into working for the KGB or its East European associates. Although the Soviet Union's intelligence service inherited some of its methods from the Tsarist secret police, it is fair to comment that the communist regimes do not find such procedures repugnant, and indeed have developed and perfected them.

In addition to recruiting foreign Communists, the KGB operates a vast network of spies under the diplomatic cover of Soviet embassies—a practice that is imitated by other East European States. It would, of course, be naïve to suppose that the Western countries never use 'diplomatic cover' for their own spies. But the scale of comparable communist operations—as shown by the unnecessary size

It may be objected that in the cases I have named, recruiting took place many years earlier, before de-Stalinization and the emergence of 'national' communism. True; but it is probably only a matter of time before more recently recruited agents are exposed. For to the dedicated Communist, even if he has reservations about the Soviet system or current leadership, the Soviet Union must always remain the 'workers' fatherland', the original scene of the first successful Marxist-Leninist revolution and the home of 'socialism'. To doubt it would be to align himself either with the Trotskyists — who accept the myth of the revolutionary fatherland but reject Stalinism as a perversion of it — or with the despised Utopians. In the last analysis, doubters must quit the Party, even though some of the stayers may be Titoists.

To the Soviet Communist Party, it is clearly of enormous importance that such beliefs should be retained. But in sustaining the original myths, they are greatly helped by the need of true believers to cling to their beliefs in the face of every disappointment, setback and disillusioning event. Neither the strength of the beliefs nor the persistence of the Soviet Party and its agents in sustaining them in others should be under-estimated.

The conclusions are therefore inescapable. For many years yet, there will be a continuing need for vigilance on the part of Western security services and counter-espionage systems. But such police or semi-police activities will need to be supplemented by systematic study of communism and the international communist movement.

—Since the Sino-Soviet split developed, communism has been irrelevant to the study of the foreign policies of the Soviet Union and China. The behaviour of both, as great powers, is unaffected by the fact that they both have communist regimes.

COMMENT These are beguilingly simple propositions; but the element of truth in them should not obscure the fact that they are superficial. True, the Soviet Union and China do behave as great powers do, and it would be surprising if they did not. The

---

of their embassy staffs — dwarfs Western efforts. In 1968, no fewer than thirty embassy officials of communist countries were expelled on suspicion of spying. Ironically, half of those expelled had been accredited to other communist countries. In the communist world, 'dog eats dog'.

bond of communism was insufficient to preserve the Sino-Soviet alliance. The interests of the two powers are in conflict in various ways, notably over India and the Sino-Soviet border.

The fact that the dispute between Peking and Moscow is couched in ideological terms is, however, important in itself. The Chinese leaders may reproach their Russian ex-comrades with failing to give them nuclear secrets when they needed them, and with failing to stand up to the Americans over Cuba in 1962. But they also challenge Moscow's leadership of the world communist movement, and the orthodoxy of their Marxist-Leninist faith; just as they challenge Russia for the leadership of revolutionary movements in the Third World. The Russians cannot, and do not, ignore these challenges.

True, the ideological forms of the dispute cloak power motives. If the great majority of the world's communist parties, and of the Third World's guerrilla movements, accepted Peking's philosophical guidance instead of Moscow's, China's power would be correspondingly enhanced. But if Marxism-Leninism were not the State philosophy of both countries, it would not be possible for the dispute to be expressed in ideological terms; nor would the leadership of communist and other revolutionary movements be at stake. To leave communism out of account in any study of Sino-Soviet behaviour would therefore be to deal with only half the problem.

The truth of this proposition is perhaps best demonstrated by a *reductio ad absurdum*. Take the case of Vietnam. One of the major policy objectives of the Chinese People's Republic is the reduction, and if possible the physical removal, of the American military presence in South-East Asia. If Moscow's great power motive in that area were simply to oppose Peking, then the Russians might be expected to help the Americans maintain South Vietnam's ability to resist aggression from North Vietnam and its communist guerrillas in the South; and in general, to support American attempts to establish a *Pax Americana* in the Far East. Instead, the Soviet Union has given massive logistic support to the North Vietnamese.

Absurd? Agreed; but why? One reason why the proposition is absurd is that the Soviet Union has its own great power ambitions in South-East Asia, in opposition to China's, and in rivalry with America's. But another reason should not be overlooked. By helping North Vietnam with modern weapons, Russia demonstrated not only her technological superiority over China, but also her willingness to help a violent revolutionary movement far from her own borders and on China's doorstep. She thus displayed her revolutionary credentials, which the Chinese had challenged before the world communist movement and the revolutionary groups of the Third World. In so doing, incidentally, the Russians yet again made use of a militant communist party—that of North Vietnam—for their own policy purposes. If the Americans withdraw from Vietnam, the credit will go largely to Moscow for its vital supplies of advanced weapons and special training, and the achievement will have been won virtually without loss of Soviet life.

Nor should it be forgotten that in their approaches to Hanoi, the Russians were able to draw on the fund of their lengthy relationship with the North Vietnamese leader, Ho Chi Minh, who was trained in Moscow and was a Comintern agent when he set up the Indochina Communist Party in 1930.

— *The Western communist parties are either insignificant (for example in Britain and the United States), or are changing into ordinary political parties like the rest (for instance in Italy). Moreover they are increasingly independent of Moscow. Even if the Soviet Party remains dangerous, the Western parties need not be taken seriously.*

COMMENT   I have already examined at some length the proposition that the Italian Communist Party—the largest and most independent CP out of power—has ceased to be a threat (Part II, 6). Essentially, the argument is disposed of by the Party's history of subservience to Stalin, its expedient assertion of independence for electoral purposes, and the fact that the Party's foreign policies are substantially the same as Moscow's. In the present chapter, I have also given an example of the Italian Party's willingness to serve Moscow's clandestine needs by funding a Latin American communist party.

The case of the weaker Western parties, such as the British and American, is different. The Communist Party of the United States, to give it its full name, is now feeble to the point of impotence, as much because of its declining attraction as because of the harassment of the Federal Bureau of Investigation. Its membership probably does not exceed 5,000. A protracted attempt to force members to register as 'subversives' was, however, ruled unconstitutional by the Supreme Court in November 1965. Clearly, the subversive potential of the Party is much diminished, in comparison with fifteen or twenty years ago. When every allowance is made for the hysterical excesses of the McCarthy witch hunt of the 1950s, the investigations of the Committee on Un-American Activities did unearth evidence of the clandestine recruiting of Party members and their placement in positions of trust in industry and government. In those days, the Party's capacity to damage the United States, if only by providing potential spies for the Soviet Union, was disproportionate to its numbers and minimal electoral appeal. Today, however, one must assume that the Russians look elsewhere for spying talent, the Party being, it is said, riddled with informers. Feeble though it is, however, the American Communist Party drew advantage from the wave of opinion against the Vietnam war, and helped to channel Soviet, North Vietnamese and Viet-Cong propaganda. On its own, it would have been incapable of arousing public opinion on the Vietnamese issue, or any other.

Being fully legal, the British Communist Party is easy to observe. It has not always been free from police harassment however, and a flashback to its semi-clandestine period is a useful reminder of its essential character. In his autobiography, *I Believed*, the British ex-communist, Douglas Hyde, paints a lively picture of the Party's history during the Second World War. The main facts are, of course, familiar. In common with other Western parties, the British Communist Party faced an agonizing ideological dilemma when Hitler invaded Poland. Was this the long-awaited holy war against fascism? Or did Stalin's subsequent invasion of Poland from the East, under the protection of the Nazi-Soviet pact, mean that it was an 'imperialist' war, of no interest to the workers of the world?

There was no problem about the Hitler-Stalin alliance itself which, says Hyde, 'did not trouble the trained Marxist at all,' for: 'The Soviet leaders had a responsibility to the working-class of the world to defend the USSR and could, if necessary, for this reason make an alliance with the devil himself.'* But the hiatus of a fortnight between the German and Soviet aggressions against Poland threw the British comrades — and other communist parties — into a turmoil. They had already in effect labelled the war 'holy'; now came precise instructions from the Comintern that it was to be 'unholy'. The British communist leader, Harry Pollitt, refused to accept the new line, though he later publicly recanted. But the Central Committee did, and from that time, the Party worked day and night for Britain's defeat.

In this situation, the question of 'patriotism' did not arise, for the only sense in which the word held meaning for Communists was that it was 'patriotic' to work for a Soviet Britain. To defend the Soviet Union was patriotic, since the USSR was the home of the working-class and the bastion of communism. But if the Soviet Union decided that the war Britain was waging against Nazi Germany was 'imperialist', then everything had to be done to sabotage the British war effort.

And 'everything' was far from negligible. The *Daily Worker*† carried its quotidian message of defeatism. In the factories, communist shop-stewards called strikes on any pretext, including the flimsiest (such as, in one instance quoted by Hyde, a protest against the quality of the tea provided in the canteens). In Parliament and in the constituencies, secret members of the Party — crypto-communists — made anti-war speeches or introduced anti-war resolutions.

It was only a question of time before the *Daily Worker* was banned, and in anticipation of the ban (and of the outlawing of the Party itself, which did not come), the Party made its plans. Secret printing presses were ready; numbers went underground; wealthy crypto-communists helped with money and premises. A news agency — Industrial and General Information — was set up, to place communist-slanted news and features in the 'capitalist' press and distribute the Party line to members.

Then came the day, in June 1941, when Hitler's armies invaded the Soviet Union. Overnight, the British Communist Party —

* Douglas Hyde, *I Believed* (Heinemann, 1950), p. 68.
† Now the *Morning Star*.

along with CPs everywhere – changed its line. The 'imperialist' war became a holy war for the defence of the workers' fatherland. Instead of working for strikes and delays, the communist shop stewards started working for maximum production. Anglo-Soviet occasions were organized. Humble Party members carried posters of Churchill, the arch imperialist of the day before, in honour of Uncle Joe's gallant ally.

All this was thirty years ago. Meanwhile, the Party has weathered traumatic experiences: the denunciation of Stalin, the invasion of Hungary, the occupation of Czechoslovakia (which the Party denounced). Each of these experiences has provoked mass resignations. Always, however, the Party has preserved its cohesion and more or less rebuilt its numbers. The hard core that is left after the disillusioned have gone are the heirs not only to Marxism-Leninism as a philosophy, but to the October Revolution, Stalinism, and all that has been done in the name of communism in the Soviet Union. They cannot repudiate their past *and* remain communists.

What they try to do, actually, is to pretend the past never happened. It is fascinating to read the Party Programme over the years, and note the gradual elimination of eulogies to Stalin and the Soviet Union. All that is left now is a great void. The latest edition of the Programme, entitled 'The British Road to Socialism', omits ritual praise of the Soviet Union. But it also omits references to Soviet crimes, while rich in anti-imperialist venom. This is the only clue to the Party's long-standing allegiance to Moscow. But who can doubt that in another life-and-death crisis, the British Communists would behave as they did in 1939 – despite the Titoist leanings of its leader, John Gollan.

Less hypothetical, however, is the way they behave now. Although the political impact of the Party remains negligible and it is no longer represented in the House of Commons, (except, probably, by crypto-communists within the Labour Party), it is viciously potent in industry. Working through front organizations and special groups in specific industries, the Party has perfected the technique of unofficial strikes. As the former Prime Minister, Harold Wilson, told the House of Commons on 28 June 1966:

The House will be aware that the Communist Party, unlike the major political parties, has at its disposal an efficient and disciplined industrial apparatus controlled from Communist Party headquarters. No major strike occurs anywhere in this country in any sector of industry in which that apparatus fails to concern itself.*

To be fair, disruptive political strikes are today more likely to be the work of Maoist, Trotskyist or Anarchist groups than of the relatively sober Communist Party. But the Party remains a subversive organization working effectively and often in secret, to disrupt and weaken the existing system. The same is true, *mutatis mutandis*, of other communist parties throughout the non-communist world, irrespective of the degree of their public support for the Soviet Union.

Some further liberal fallacies about communism may be dealt with more summarily:

—*Communism is evolving. Already the excesses of Stalinism are merely painful memories. In time, even the Soviet leadership will realize that Dubcek of Czechoslovakia was right, and liberal communism will be born.*

COMMENT Less is heard of arguments of this type since the Soviet Army and its Czechoslovak nominees broke the Dubcek experiment. The point that tends to be overlooked by the liberals is that 'liberal communism' is a contradiction in terms. If a communist regime liberalizes to the extent that it surrenders its own monopoly of power, then it will in time yield to non-communists; in that event, communism would cease to be a problem in that particular country.

But communism is an absolutist and exclusive power system, which cannot exist without a monopoly of power. Just as no communist regime has ever come to power except through the exercise or threat of force, so there is still no recorded example of the overthrow of a communist regime. (True, communists have achieved office at the polls on a provincial level, e.g. in India, or on a municipal level, e.g. in Italy. But no communist party has yet

* For a full but succinct survey of Communist industrial tactics, see *The Agitators*: *Extremist Activities in British Industry*, published by the Economic League, London.

come to power anywhere on a national level by constitutional means. And where a communist administration has been removed from office, as in the Indian State of Kerala, force—i.e., the imposition of Governor's Rule from the Central Government—has been necessary.) Once a communist government is in, it is there, apparently, 'for keeps'. The conviction of an absolute historical right to rule is so deeply ingrained, and communist techniques of repression so highly perfected, that it is unlikely that any communist national government will ever be removed except by force, whether internally by revolution or *coup d'état*, or externally through war.

—Communism is an idea. You cannot fight it with weapons: the only way to defeat it is by winning people's hearts and minds.

COMMENT This hackneyed fallacy was frequently heard during the Vietnam war. The fallacy lies in the under-lying suggestion that local Communists won over people's hearts and minds by peaceful argument in a free market of ideas. In fact, the Communists have enforced conformity by relentless pressure, bullying and terrorism; by specious promises of future welfare and, where applicable, land reform; admittedly, also, by personal example and devotion to duty; and, in some cases, through popular revulsion against corrupt and brutal regimes. The example of Malaya showed that it is possible to defeat communist insurgency by physically protecting the people from communist bullying, by efficient and uncorrupt administration, by evident justice, and where applicable, by the conferment of political independence. In the end, such measures do win hearts and minds; but they are effective only if *bodies* too are protected by efficient security forces.

—Communism may be of little interest to advanced countries, but surely it is the best thing that could happen to backward countries—the only solution to poverty and underdevelopment?

COMMENT Nobody with knowledge of the economic and social plight of, for instance, India, should dismiss this argument out of hand. It rests, however, upon the proposition that 'communism' lifted Russia in a few decades from backwardness and poverty to the second world ranking in industry and science. The argument is boosted by reference to China's supposed progress under communism. In fact, however, Russia's industrial progress under communism was rather less rapid than America's under free enterprise. And China's progress does not begin to compare with Japan's. All the 'good' things achieved in the Soviet Union — from social welfare to lunar probes — can be matched by non-communist countries, none of which has paid a price comparable to Russia's in human suffering and death.

The notion that communist methods are specially suitable to Asian and African countries is pernicious. Communism does not solve problems so much as disguise, very effectively, the absence of solutions. China did, of course, make rapid industrial progress between 1949 and 1958; but stagnation or recession was the consequence of the Great Leap Forward, the creation of agricultural communes, the Cultural Revolution and other Maoist policies. The most rapid economic progress has been achieved by Asian countries that have allowed private enterprise to create wealth; for instance, Japan, Formosa, Thailand, Malaysia, Hong Kong and (in West Asia), the Lebanon and Israel.

— *The cold war is over. Now the West should ensure peace by seeking a détente with Russia. (In extreme forms, this argument is supplemented by casting doubts on the continued usefulness of Nato and other military alliances.)*

COMMENT As I hope I have shown (in Part II, 5, and elsewhere), the cold war is *not* over, although it takes milder forms than in Stalin's time. The point to grasp and remember is that the communist parties, in their unrelenting war on all non-communist systems, use an almost infinite variety of techniques: front organizations; the training of trade unionists and agitators; spying, terrorism and murder; the training of revolutionary guerrillas and the provision of arms and money; the *coup d'état*; the promotion of civil war; and, if considered safe, outright military aggression. Such methods are supplemented by State-to-State relations, trade treaties, economic and military aid, and so on. If the Communists appear to ease up on one form of pressure, it is only because at the time, other forms may appear more suitable.

Against this background, the suggestion (made fairly frequently until the occupation of Czechoslovakia silenced it for a time) that

Nato has outlived its usefulness, since the Russians have abandoned war as an instrument of policy in Europe, is dangerous. To the extent that the Soviet Union has reduced its military threat in Europe, the credit is due to Nato (which comprises the American, British and French nuclear deterrents). But if Nato were removed, the threat would increase.

None of the foregoing invalidates the suggestion that ways of reducing international tension should be sought. It is the duty of the major Powers to seek ways of avoiding nuclear war (while ready to face it without flinching if necessary as President Kennedy did in 1962); and of reducing armaments without a weakening of defensive capacity relatively to the communist Powers. But it is possible to do this without surrendering to the delusion that the hostility of the communist Powers has relented.

—*With the world communist movement in disarray, communism is losing its appeal and recruiting is falling off. The real problem is no longer communism but the New Left.*

COMMENT To some extent, these propositions have been examined in Part II, 5 and 7, and in the present chapter. The fragmentation of communism and the proliferation of new or revived left-wing groups (such as the Trotskyists and Anarchists) has certainly created new problems for the communists themselves. As far as non-communists are concerned, it has not removed the problem, but complicated it. In some countries (Britain is one of them) the communist party is going through lean times. At the Party Congress of November 1969, it was announced that membership had fallen by nearly 2,000 to 30,607 since the previous Congress in 1967. More worrying still, from the leadership's standpoint, membership of the Young Communist League had dropped from more than 6,000 to 3,850 during the same period. This dramatic fall of nearly thirty-six per cent undoubtedly reflects the shock of Czechoslovakia and shows that the denunciation of the Soviet invasion has not sufficed to remove youthful distrust of a party whose links with Moscow are part of its history. Likewise, however, the fall in recruiting reflects the romantic appeal of the New Left groups, whose promise of violence and excitement the relatively staid Communist Party is, at present, unable to match.

If the decline in recruiting continued, the British Party could, within a generation, be reduced to a dwindling group of ageing zealots. But it is much too early to assume that the decline will, in fact, continue. A similar drop in membership occurred after the repression in Hungary in 1956. But political memories are short, and the Party gradually rebuilt its strength. True, the New Left has grown since Hungary precipitated its creation. But there is an ephemeral air about its proliferating groups. Beside them, the Communists look, and are, more solid. Their patience, discipline and organizing capacity should never be underestimated, either by the New Left or by ourselves. In any long-term contest, trained Communists are the more likely to win even if, to do so, they have to infiltrate the fundamentalist groups and take them over from within. Meanwhile—in Britain, France and elsewhere—the problem of Marxist agitation in industry continues. In Britain, especially, the departure of Party members has not improved matters; for many of the departed members have joined the (Trotskyist) Socialist Labour League, which outdoes the Communist Party in industrial extremism.

While the declining appeal of communism as a faith and an ideology could seriously weaken the movement in the latter years of the century, the problem of those who, like Togliatti, have kept their zeal while losing their faith, remains. The danger from 'faithless zealots' is, indeed, likely to grow in the next decade. For if the appeal of communism really is declining, the zealots—whose motivation is power—are likely to redouble their efforts, since time is less obviously on their side than in the days of expanding membership and an unshakeable faith that communism was round the corner. These general remarks may not be universally applicable; but they seem particularly true of France, where communist voting strength remains high, and Italy, where it is growing, in both cases irrespective of actual membership.

It follows that while the New Left must be systematically studied and countered, this does not mean that similar studies and action in respect of the Communists ought to be abandoned. The new challenges the old, but has not yet ousted it.

For the liberal, communism presents an insoluble dilemma.

Should freedom of speech and of political action be permitted to those who would deny that freedom to others? A strong and self-confident society may allow itself the luxury of such tolerance, but only on condition that it is aware that tolerance of the intolerant is indeed a luxury.

The liberal doctrine that all ideas should be given a hearing sometimes degenerates into the implicit view that all ideas are equal. They are not. In the hands of totalitarians, ideas and words are as weapons in the hands of gangsters.

There must therefore be limits to tolerance. In the inescapable war that is in progress, whether we wish it or not, factories, government departments and defence installations are not the only bastions. Others include radio and television centres, publishing houses, newspapers and magazines, universities and other learned bodies. A well placed 'communicator' is as deadly in his way as a communist shop steward in his. A determined nucleus of television or newspaper executives may use their 'freedom of speech' to deny it to those who question totalitarian 'solutions'.

The great political divide of our time is between those who support collectivist-totalitarian objectives and those who oppose them. In a free society, to opt out, to turn a blind eye to industrial subversion, to leave unanswered the arguments of defenders of collectivist-totalitarian regimes or movements, is to side with an enemy by default.

Even for the liberal, there is no middle way, where communism is concerned. For it is the Communists who make the rules: if you are not for them, you must be against. In this situation, those who say communism is no longer a problem merely ensure that it is. Communism must, in fact, be fought continuously, for as soon as the counter-pressure eases, its own pressure, which is permanent, reasserts itself. In this war of attrition, he who laughs last will assuredly last longest.

In writing this 'peroration', I am acutely conscious that it will jar on liberal ears. Among normal, decent, unfanatical people, there is a certain prudishness, a *pudeur*, about being thought to be 'anti-communist'. This sentiment is understandable. A witch-hunt is an abhorrent device. The harm that McCarthy did was not limited to those whose careers he wrecked unjustly: it lay also in the fact that his demagogic excesses played into the hands of the Communists by discrediting 'anti-communism'.

A further difficulty lies in the remarkable success of the Communists in persuading many intellectuals that theirs is a movement of the Left and of 'the people' — so that even among those who cannot in conscience refrain from condemning, say, Stalin's crimes, there will be those who are emotionally disposed to find them more excusable than Hitler's. The first intellectual barrier to cross is that which protects communism and its derivatives in the name of 'the people'. The essential thing to grasp is that it is *totalitarian*, and that no group of people suffer more under the system than the intellectuals — in Russia, those who who would like to emulate Anatoli Kuznetsov and seek refuge in the West, avoiding both the grovelling conformity of a Writer's Union and the fate of Daniel and Sinyavsky.

Anti-communism is in fact necessary, though it may not always be tactically advisable so to label it. It is particularly necessary from the standpoint of liberals (in the British rather than the American sense of this internationally ambiguous term). For the current drift towards domestic anarchy and violence in the Western countries points to one of two extremes: collectivist dictatorship or right-wing reaction. It seems to me highly improbable that, in the last analysis, the advanced industrial societies will permit the former; only a discreet and intelligent anti-communism is likely to avoid the latter, which, to some liberals, is a less tolerable prospect than coercive socialism.

In a liberal context, anti-communism does not in any sense involve a witch-hunt or — except at times of grave emergency — a reduction of normal liberties. What it does call for is readiness on the part of those who want to defend a threatened way of life to take up the challenge; to answer totalitarian arguments; to counter totalitarian tactics in factories and universities. Above all, it calls for a sense of responsibility on the part of those in executive positions especially in the world of communications, and a discreet readiness to reduce the power of infiltrators to do their worst, for instance, by providing a platform for anti-totalitarians.

If the long war is lost, it will be because such things are not done, or not done in time.

Appendix: The International Front Organizations

Appendix: The International Front Organizations

WORLD FEDERATION OF TRADE UNIONS (WFTU)

The initiative for setting up the WFTU was taken by the British Trades Union Congress, which called a preparatory conference in London in February 1945. The first President was Sir Walter Citrine, but the communist Secretary-General, Louis Saillant, soon packed the Secretariat with Communists. In January 1949 the British TUC, the American CIO, and the Dutch MVV withdrew from the WFTU. The following November a non-communist international body, the International Confederation of Free Trade Unions (ICFTU), was formed. Originally, the WFTU had its headquarters in Paris, but the French government expelled it in 1951 for subversive activities. It moved to the Soviet sector of Vienna, then under four-power occupation. After Austria had regained its independence, the government ordered the expulsion of the WFTU for endangering Austrian neutrality. Since then the headquarters have been in Prague.

WORLD FEDERATION OF DEMOCRATIC YOUTH (WFDY)

The WFDY too was founded in London—in November 1945—but in this case the conveners were the World Youth Council, a communist-controlled body since disbanded. The occasion was labelled a World Youth Conference. It attracted many youth organizations, who had no idea about the ulterior purpose behind the conference. Soon the Communists captured all key posts. By 1950, most of the non-communists, realizing what had happened, had left; they founded a new and independent organization, the World Assembly of Youth (WAY). As with the WFTU, the WFDY was originally based in Paris but was expelled by the French government in 1951. Its headquarters are now in Budapest, although it moved briefly to Prague during the 1956 Hungarian uprising.

INTERNATIONAL UNION OF STUDENTS

Students of many countries and representing many shades of political and religious affiliation attended a world student congress in Prague in August 1946. There, they set up the IUS, in the belief that they were founding a 'representative organization of the democratic students of the whole world who work for progress'. Control soon fell to the Communists, and by 1951, many of the non-communists had left. The eye-opener, for most of them, had been the expulsion of the Yugoslav Union of Student Youth in February 1950, as a direct consequence of Tito's break with Stalin. In March 1967, the Yugoslavs reaffiliated as associate members. As for the non-communist unions, they are now represented by the International Student Conference with headquarters in Leiden, Holland.

WOMEN'S INTERNATIONAL DEMOCRATIC FEDERATION (WIDF)

The WIDF has never been as effective as some other front organizations, for it has been under communist control from the start, and no non-communist body of any standing has ever joined it. It was founded in Paris in December 1945 at a communist-convened Congress of Women. The WIDF was expelled by the French government in January 1951 and moved to the Soviet sector in Berlin.

INTERNATIONAL ORGANIZATION OF JOURNALISTS (IOJ)

Founded in June 1946 at a Congress in Copenhagen, the IOJ initially represented nearly all unionized journalists of the world. As usual, the Communists captured the key posts, and by 1950 all non-communist unions had withdrawn. In 1952, the non-communists re-created the International Federation of Journalists (IFJ) which had merged with the IOJ in 1946. The original headquarters were in London; now they are in Prague.

WORLD FEDERATION OF SCIENTIFIC WORKERS (WFSW)

The headquarters are in London, although the Secretary-General works from an office in Paris. The WFSW was founded in 1946 at a conference in London, organized by the British Association of Scientific Workers. Most of the official posts are held by Communists.

INTERNATIONAL ASSOCIATION OF DEMOCRATIC LAWYERS (IADL)

Many non-communist lawyers were among those who attended the inaugural meeting of the Association in October 1946 in Paris. The association was expelled from France in 1950 and set up headquarters in Brussels.

INTERNATIONAL RADIO AND TELEVISION ORGANIZATION (OIRT)

The last of the 1946 crop, the OIRT was founded at a conference in Brussels. It has since transferred its headquarters to Prague. In 1950 the British Broadcasting Corporation set up a rival body, the European Broadcasting Union (EBU) which all leading non-communist organizations have since joined, having deserted the OIRT. In effect, the Organization is now a semi-governmental one, since most of its affiliates are radio and television centres in the communist countries.

INTERNATIONAL FEDERATION OF RESISTANCE MOVEMENTS (FIR)

The FIR incorporates an earlier organization founded in Paris in 1947, the International Federation of Former Political Prisoners of Fascism (FIAPP). The earlier body was founded in Vienna in June 1951. Originally based in Warsaw, it moved back to Vienna—the founding place—in 1952.

WORLD COUNCIL OF PEACE (WCP)

This is the latest name in a string of bodies, the first of which was called the International Liaison Committee of Intellectuals, an offshoot of the World Congress of Intellectuals for Peace, held at Wroclaw, in Poland, in August 1948. Originally based in Paris, the World Council of Peace was expelled in 1951 for fifth column activities, and moved to Prague. The Russians established new headquarters in their occupation zone in Vienna in 1954. But on 2 February 1957, the independent Austrian government banned the SCP and closed its office because it 'interfered in the internal affairs of countries with which Austria has good and friendly relations'. It went on functioning in Vienna however, through an ostensibly new body, the International Institute for Peace.

Index